P9-DGC-244

**An Altitude
SuperGuide**

Canadian
Rockies

An Altitude SuperGuide

Canadian Rockies

Graeme Pole

Altitude Publishing
Banff Alberta Canada

Photo, front cover: Moraine Lake, Banff National Park. Inset photo, front cover: Bill Peyto, ca. 1890.

Photo, overleaf: Peyto Lake and the Mistaya Valley during an August sunset.

First edition 1991
Second, revised edition 1992
Third, revised edition 1993

The topographic maps are based on information taken from the National Topographic System map sheet numbers MCR 221, Jasper National Park © 1985 and MCR 220, Banff National Park © 1985. Her Majesty the Queen in Right of Canada with permission of Energy, Mines and Resources Canada.

Extreme care has been taken to ensure that all information in this book is accurate and up to date, but neither the author nor the publisher can be held legally responsible for any errors that may appear.

Altitude GreenTree Program
Altitude will plant in Western Canada twice as many trees as were used in the manufacturing of this book.

Canadian Cataloguing in Publication Data
Pole, Graeme, 1956–
Canadian Rockies
First ed. has title:
Canadian Rockies SuperGuide
Includes Index
ISBN 1-55153-038-4
1. Rocky Mountains, Canadian (B.C. and Alta.)
– Description and travel – Guide-books.*
2. Natural history – Rocky Mountains,
Canadian (B.C. and Alta.) – Guide-books.*
I. Title.
FC219.P64 1993   917.1104'4
C93-091215-2   F1090.P64 1993

Editor: Elizabeth Wilson

Design: Robert MacDonald, MediaClones Inc.

Made in Western Canada
Printed and bound in Western Canada by Friesen Printers, Altona Manitoba, using Canadian made paper and vegetable-based inks.

This book was published with the assistance of the Department of Communications, Book Industry Development Program.

Altitude Publishing Canada Ltd.

The Canadian Rockies
1408 Railway Ave.
P.O. Box 1410, Canmore, Alberta
Canada TOL OMO

Contents

REFERENCE

TRANSPORTATION

Dual highway...

Road, hard surface, all weather....................

Road, loose surface, all weather...................

Road, loose surface, dry weather..................

Trail..

Route marker, Trans-Canada........................ ⑪ 🍁

Railway, single track...............................

Railway, multiple track............................

Railway, station, stop..............................

Bridge...

Tunnel...

Airfield.. ✈

BOUNDARIES

Provincial...

County or District..................................

National Park..

Provicial Park, Special Area.......................

HYDROGRAPHY

Rapids, Falls, Dam..................................

Intermittent stream, lake..........................

Lake elevation...................................... *1320±*

Marsh or Swamp.....................................

Glacier, Icefield....................................

RELIEF

Contours.. *1000*

Depression contours................................

Spot elevation...................................... •*9058*

Moraine...

OTHER FEATURES

Settlements, 0-500, > 500......................... ○ ●

Built up area.......................................

Building.. ▪

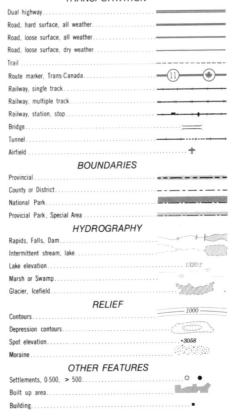

Scale 1: 200 000

4   0   4   8   12   16

kilometres   kilomètres

CONVERSION SCALE FOR ELEVATIONS

Metres 30 20 10 0   50   100   150   200   250   300 Mètres

Feet 100 50 0   100   200   300   400   500   600   700   800   900   1000 Pieds

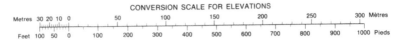

CONTOUR INTERVAL 200 METRES
Elevations in Metres above Mean Sea Level
North American Datum 1927
Transverse Mercator Projection

NATIONAL TOPOGRAPHIC SYSTEM
1:50 000 Scale Map Sheet Coverage

How to Use the SuperGuide

The *Canadian Rockies Super-Guide* is your complete guide to one of the most beautiful mountain environments in the world. It's an informative road guide and reference to the mountain national parks of the Canadian Rockies* designed to be especially useful to first-time visitors. It also contains a wealth of information to enlighten the return visitor, and hundreds of spectacular full-colour photographs. Whether you're planning a trip and looking for the perfect guide, or searching for a book that will serve as a record of your journey through the Rockies, you need look no further than the *SuperGuide*.

In the first section of the book, you'll find a series of overviews of the larger themes in the Canadian Rockies — the layout of the landscape, natural and human history, ecology, conservation, wildlife and recreation. The bulk of the *SuperGuide*'s information follows in the highway guide section. You can use the highway guide as a road guide while you travel. The focus shifts constantly: historical events and personalities, scenery, features of climate and ecology, glaciers, wildlife, recreational opportunities — all of which are described in detail at appropriate locations.

If while reading the highway guide you come across an unfamiliar term or historical personality, please refer to the index for reference to a more detailed description. Each of the highway guide sections contains a map that will help you locate the individual topics along the highway. The legend for the topographic highway maps is presented on page 6 .

The last section of the *Super-Guide* presents handy information in list format — access, weather, accommodation, services, restaurants, shopping, entertainment, tips for safety and enjoyment, useful addresses and phone numbers, and more.

Enjoy the Rockies, and enjoy the *SuperGuide!*

* In the *SuperGuide*, "the Rockies" refers to the area of Banff, Jasper, Yoho and Kootenay National Parks.

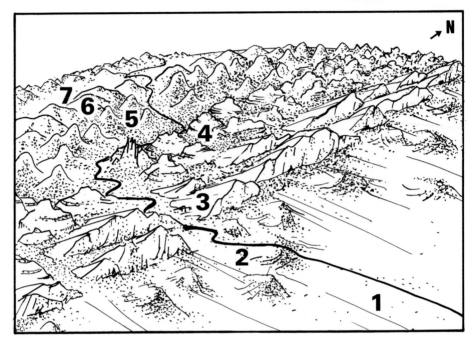

Lay of the Land

This schematic drawing shows an overview of the Canadian Rockies looking from the southeast towards the northwest. 1. the Interior Plains, 2. Foothills, 3. Front Ranges, 4. Eastern Main Ranges, 5. Western Main Ranges, 6. Western Ranges, 7. Rocky Mountain Trench.

Welcome to the Canadian Rockies. These mountains are part of a continuous chain of mountains that forms the backbone of North America. They are different in appearance and origin from the American Rockies, and also from mountains only slightly further west, in British Columbia.

In the *SuperGuide*'s area, which focuses on Canada's four mountain national parks, the grain of the Rockies is oriented southeast to northwest, along the Continental Divide. This height of land separates rivers flowing to the Atlantic Ocean (via Hudson Bay, some 1,700 km away) and to the Arctic Ocean (1,500 km distant) from those flowing to the Pacific Ocean (625 km away).

The Rockies cover a maximum breadth of 120 km. In that short distance are seven distinct topographic units, each with its own unique physical characteristics and climate, and resulting distributions of vegetation and wildlife. As you drive west from Calgary or Edmonton, this is how the Rockies unfold.

The Interior Plains
The cities of Calgary and Edmonton lie on the Interior plains, the

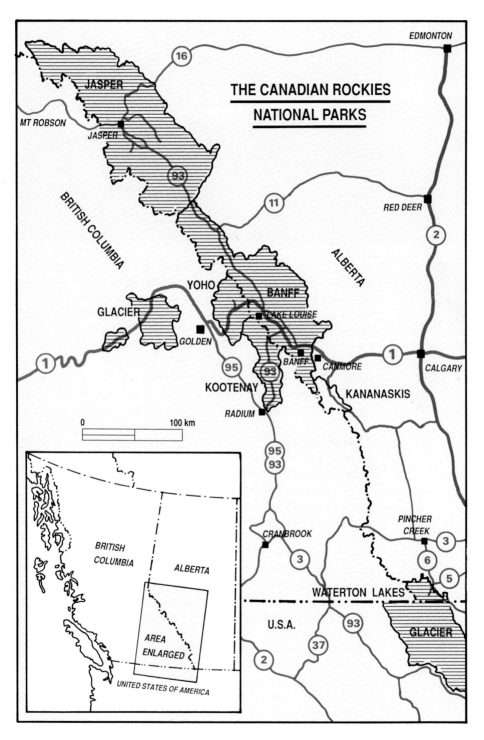

The dramatic transition from rolling foothills to the tilted, grey limestone peaks of the front ranges is revealed driving towards the Rockies from Calgary or Edmonton.

predominantly flat area that covers much of central North America. Typical vegetation on the plains is scrubby woodland and open grassland. Much of the original vegetation has been cleared to allow agriculture. The climate features hot, dry summers and cold, dry winters. Wind and thunderstorms are common.

The Foothills

About 25 km west of Calgary, at Jumpingpound Creek, the Trans-Canada Highway enters the foothills at an elevation of about 1,150 m. If you look at the rock cuts at roadside in this vicinity, you will notice some of the rock layers are tilted vertically. This is the eastern-most effect of the compressive forces of mountain building.

The fertility of the land in this area is in part due to the abundant freshwater flowing from the glaciers and icefields of the Rockies, and to the large amount of soil material eroded from the mountains and deposited here.

River courses in the area are wide and meandering, a product of the relatively flat terrain. The rivers show considerable seasonal variation in volumes of flow, due to their glacial sources. During winter months the climate is frequently moderated by a warm wind called a chinook (shih-NOOK), which blows eastward from the mountain front. Chinooks, in combination with the overall windiness, keep the foothills relatively snow-free.

The Front Ranges

The front ranges make an abrupt and dramatic appearance at Lac des Arcs. Many visitors marvel at the wall-like effect presented by these mountains, the summits of which tower over 1,000 m above the level of the foothills. The lack of any gradual transition is due to the manner in which the Rockies were created, and to the relative resistance of the rock types that comprise the foothills and the front ranges.

During mountain building the sedimentary formations which comprise the Rockies were compressed from west to east, until some broke and slid along thrust faults. The front ranges mark the eastern-most location of such a fault in the Rockies — the McConnell Thrust Fault. Along the plane of this fault, some of the formations that comprise the front ranges slid upwards and eastwards over those which later became the foothills, creating a common and unusual feature of Rockies geology — older rocks over younger ones. In this case, rocks 400 million years apart in age lie next to each other.

This exaggerated difference in height between the front ranges and the foothills is also the product of differential erosion. The limestones of the front ranges are less susceptible to erosion than the shales and sandstones of the foothills, so more of the original height of the foothills has been worn away in the interim. But keep in mind many kilometres of height has been eroded from both the foothills and front ranges in the tens of millions of years since they were created.

The thrust sheets of mountain building have also influenced the overall pattern of front range landscape. The erosion-resistant leading edges of the thrust sheets have become mountain ranges. At the base of these edges, fault valleys have been eroded into the weaker underlying formations. Thus there is a symmetry to the front ranges. Individual ranges are oriented along the southeast/ northwest alignment, and are separated by parallel valleys — like shingles on a roof.

This symmetry is broken by three major river valleys: the Bow, North Saskatchewan and Athabasca. Each of these rivers cuts directly across the grain of the front ranges, to exit onto the plains. It is thought these rivers are as old as the Rockies themselves, and that they initiated their courses before the front ranges were created. As the front ranges piled up during mountain building, the rivers were able to keep pace eroding down. The unusual character of these rivers is exemplified in the drive north and east from Jasper on the Yellowhead Highway, where the Athabasca River is seen to bisect no less than four ranges before reaching the foothills.

The climate in the front ranges is dry, an effect of the rain shadow caused by the higher mountains to the west. The annual temperature range is the greatest of any region in the Rockies. Vegetation is sparse above valley bottoms, and the soils of mountainsides have little ability to retain water. When rain does fall, flash floods often result. Valley bottoms feature the montane meadow ecosite, which provides important range for the larger mammals, especially in winter.

The rock comprising these mountains is typically drab gray in colour. The average elevation

The mountains of the eastern main ranges, such as those in the vicinity of Lake Louise, are characterized by glacier-capped cliffs.

of the front ranges is 2,850 m, and the highest point is the 3,470 metre summit of Mt. Brazeau, south of Maligne Lake in Jasper National Park. As a rule, the front range peaks in Jasper show more severe faulting and folding, and have steeper southwest facing slopes, than those further south in Banff.

The Eastern Main Ranges

The eastern main ranges are the meat and potatoes of the Rockies — the glacier-capped, lake-studded peaks famed world wide. The first prominent examples are visible looking west from Banff townsite. The Trans-Canada Highway enters the eastern main ranges east of Castle Junction, halfway between Banff and Lake Louise.

The eastern main ranges are relatively resistant to erosion. Their sedimentary formations are thick and moved as a single thrust sheet during mountain building. As a result the formations lie for the most part in horizontal layers. The mountains are comprised of some of the hardest rocks in the Rockies: quartzite, limestone and dolomite. Overall, the rocks tend to be more colourful than those of the front ranges.

Most of the mountains of the eastern main ranges rest on compressed rocks at the base of broad downwards folds called synclines, while the major valleys have been eroded into the weaker rocks at the crests of upwards folds called anticlines. The 20 highest summits in the Rockies, all over 3353 m / 11,000 ft, are in the eastern main ranges. The highest of the high is 3,954 m Mt. Robson, which is visible from the Yellowhead Highway in Mt. Robson Provincial Park.

The horizontal orientation of the sedimentary formations, and the frequent alternation of tough limestones and dolomites with weak shales, produces the "layer-cake" shape of the castellated mountain, of which Castle Mountain is the best example. Horn mountains, produced by the erosive effects of cirque glaciers, are also common.

Glaciers and icefields abound in the heavy snowfall areas at high elevations along the Continental Divide, especially on the north and east aspects of mountainsides. The meltwaters of many glaciers empty directly into tarns and glacial lakes, of which there are thousands. The combination of altitude and proximity to ice keeps the air in the eastern main ranges cool. The surface waters of most major lakes, such as Lake Louise, are frozen for upwards of seven months a year.

The rivers of the eastern main ranges have significant erosive power because they carry a large amount of glacial till. River levels fluctuate greatly with the seasonal and daily glacial melt patterns, complicating the establishment of valley-bottom vegetation. High water level for most rivers occurs late May to early June. A secondary high water level occurs in August, at the peak of the glacial melt season.

The eastern main ranges lack the symmetry of the front ranges. The southeast/northwest alignment is present, but the local drainage pattern is irregular — a feature of more extensive glaciation, and the horizontal character of the sedimentary formations. The principal passes on the Continental Divide — Vermilion, Kicking Horse and Yellowhead — cut through the grain of the mountains. It is thought they were scoured by glacial ice sheets nearly two million years ago.

Eastern main range valleys support an abundance of vegetation and wildlife, but growing seasons are short. The mean temperature in valley bottoms is around freezing point. Here, as elsewhere in the Rockies, some mammals hibernate. Mountainsides are covered with subalpine forest, and avalanche paths are a prominent feature on steep slopes.

The Western Main Ranges

A few kilometres west of Field, the Trans-Canada Highway enters the western main ranges. The rock here is older and exhibits more pronounced folding than in the eastern main ranges. The predominant rock type is shale, one of the weakest sedimentary rocks. Consequently these mountains are more easily eroded and have a less angular appearance. There is a relative lack of glaciers and icefields, and typical summit elevations are close to 3,000 m.

The glacially carved peaks of the Van Horne Range, west of Field, typify the more gentle shapes of western main range mountains.

There are significant exceptions to the above statements. The Rockies' largest outcrop of igneous rock (once molten), the Ice River Igneous Complex, occurs in the western main ranges of Yoho and Kootenay National Parks. (It is not visible from the highway.) Several mountain groups also have underlying layers of tough limestone and dolomite of the Ottertail Formation. It is atop this formation that the ninth highest mountain in the Rockies stands, the 3,562 m summit of Mt. Goodsir South. The Ottertail Formation also forms the impressive 900 m high Rockwall in Kootenay National Park, along which many glaciers are found.

The mountain groups and adjacent valleys of the western main ranges are oriented along the southeast/northwest axis, but not in such a striking fashion as in the front ranges. Many western slopes rivers initially cut across this grain as they leave the Continental Divide. Because these rivers do not have as great a distance to travel to reach sea-level, their courses are often much steeper than those of eastern slopes rivers. Many leave the Divide in narrow canyons or gorges, and western slopes valleys have sections that are distinctly V-shaped in character as a result. This can be seen clearly in the upper Kicking Horse Valley, and further west in the Golden Canyon.

The major western valley bottoms lie at lower elevations than those in the eastern main ranges, and receive more precipitation. The moderate climate supports diverse wildlife and vegetation, including several species exotic to the Rockies, such as western red cedar, western hemlock and western yew.

The Western Ranges

The western ranges are a minor topographic unit that occupies the western edge of the Rockies between Golden and Radium Hot Springs. The rock is similar in age, appearance and composition to that of the western main ranges. Whereas the profile of western main range mountains is generally steep on the north and east aspects, and more gently inclined on the southwest, the western ranges are less uniform.

The western ranges were the first mountains created in the Rockies, and their weak shales absorbed a great deal of the forces of compression. Some of the sedimentary formations were tipped upwards and overturned past the vertical, creating a complex landscape. Evidence also indicates the western main ranges escaped significant glaciation. There are no glaciers in these mountains in the present day, and the V-shaped valley is more common here than elsewhere in the Rockies. The western ranges are visible looking west from the Kootenay Parkway, and on the south side of the Trans-Canada Highway between Chancellor Peak campground in Yoho National Park and Golden.

The Rocky Mountain Trench

The last topographic unit is not part of the Rockies proper, but forms the western boundary of the range, dividing it from the older Columbia Mountains. The Rocky Mountain Trench is a broad rift valley that parallels the western slope of the Rockies for hundreds of kilometres. The Trench was created after the Rockies, when formations subsided along the plane of a normal fault. The Trench has since been widened by glacial erosion, and is now home to the Columbia River, the source of which is 45 km south of Radium Hot Springs.

Summers in the Rocky Mountain Trench are warm and dry. Winters are relatively mild. There are almost 100 more frost-free days than in valley bottoms in the eastern main ranges. Some Rocky Mountain locals escape to the Trench when the weather is dreary in Lake Louise, Banff or Field.

Along the Columbia River there are extensive montane wetlands. The dry coniferous forest occupies the lower mountainsides. Elements of the Rocky Mountain Trench climate also prevail at the extreme southwest corner of Kootenay National Park, near Radium Hot Springs.

Mountain Building, Geology and Glaciology

Powerful glaciers from the Freshfield Icefield flow down to the valley below. This wilderness area lies west of Saskatchewan River Crossing in Banff National Park.

The history of the Rockies' creation is written in the rocks. The language of rocks — geology — is unfamiliar to most people. By acquainting yourself with a few concepts and terms of this new language, you will be able to better understand the appearance of the Rockies, and will become aware of the natural forces, both tremendous and subtle, that have created this exceptional landscape.

The creation of the Canadian Rockies involves three stories:
1. How the rocks were made — deposition.
2. How the mountains were built — uplift.
3. How the mountains have been weathered — erosion.

A Visual Glossary
The Basic Mountain Types in the Rockies

There are two common first impressions concerning mountainous areas. One holds the landscape is chaotic, and the other, the opposite, that "all mountains look alike." In the Rockies, the combined effects of mountain building and the processes of erosion have produced some basic mountain shapes that can

Deposition: The creation of sedimentary rock

Unlikely as it may seem, the Canadian Rockies were created from particles of sediment deposited on the floors of ancient seas. One and a half billion years ago, the area which is now the Rockies lay slightly off the western shore of North America, on the sloping edge of the continental plate. Sediments transported by prehistoric rivers collected there, and hardened into sedimentary rock under the weight of accumulated deposits above. The distinctive layers we see on mountainsides today are called sedimentary formations. Each formation records a particular episode during this process of deposition.

The most common sedimentary rocks in the Rockies are limestone, shale, dolomite and quartzite.

Uplift: Mountains created from the floors of ancient seas

How did nearly flat sea bottom become high mountain and deep valley? About 200 million years ago, the continental plate underlying North America reversed its eastward direction of drift. Off the western shore were a series of island and reef-like land masses. It was the collision between the plate and these land masses which supplied the compressive force to initiate mountain building, the process which created the Rockies.

About 120 million years ago, the compression began to deform the western edge of the Rockies. For the next 35 million years, the sedimentary formations were compressed horizontally. Below the earth's surface, the warm rock was pliable, and bowed under the pressure into folds. The stress was so great, some of the folds eventually fractured. Huge sheets of formations broke free, and slid over underlying layers along ramp-like thrust faults, from west to east. Some of these thrust sheets moved 40-60 kilometres. The Rockies piled upwards.

be easily recognized. Familiarity with these shapes will lead to a greater understanding of the process of mountain building, and should help create some order from the apparent chaos.

Synclines and Anticlines

The bow-shaped folds produced during mountain building have greatly influenced erosion in the Rockies. U-shaped folds are called synclines. At the base of a syncline, the rock was compressed, and thus relatively resistant to erosion. On either side of a syncline were usually corresponding arch-shaped folds called anticlines. The rock at the crest of an anticline was stretched, and thus more susceptible to erosion. So synclines frequently remain,

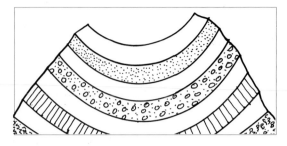

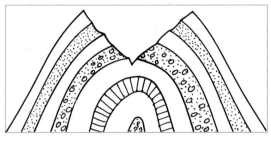

Top: Syncline mountain

Bottom: Anticline mountain

while many anticlines have been eroded away.

Synclines and anticlines may be a few metres across, such as those commonly seen in rock-cuts at roadside, or they may be as wide as valleys and mountain ranges.

Many of the major valleys in the Rockies have been eroded through the weaker anticlines. This is clearest in the Mistaya Valley, looking north from the Peyto Lake overlook. Synclines underlie the axis of many mountain ranges. The Castle Mountain Syncline extends 260 km through Banff and Jasper parks, and its U-shaped fold is prominent in Castle Mountain, Cirrus Mountain and Mt. Kerkeslin.

Mountains that contain both synclines and anticlines are called complex mountains. There are many good examples along the Yellowhead Highway, east of Jasper. Cascade Mountain near Banff is also a complex mountain.

Overthrust Mountain
Typical of the front ranges (Mt. Rundle, Endless Chain Ridge, Sunwapta Peak), overthrust mountains feature a tilted southwest facing slope, and a steep northeast facing cliff. This "writing desk" shape gives a graphic representation of how the thrust sheets slid upwards and over each other from west to east during mountain building. Overthrust mountains frequently contain niche glaciers on their northeast aspects.

Dogtooth Mountain
Found in the front ranges and western main ranges (Mt. Louis,

A Simple Geological Description of the Rockies

They are middle-aged
- 120 million years old
- older than the European Alps, the Himalaya and American Rockies, but younger than the Appalachians

They are sedimentary
- comprised of rock particles deposited on the floors of ancient seas
- these particles subsequently hardened into rock formations

They are layered in appearance
- the different sedimentary formations are readily visible

They are highly eroded
- sedimentary rock is relatively weak
- the past and present effects of moving ice and water on the landscape are quite evident

Mt. Edith, Mt. Birdwood, Cinquefoil Mountain, Spike Peak), the sedimentary formations in dogtooth mountains were thrust nearly vertical during mountain building. Now they stand as relatively resistant spires while the surrounding rock has been eroded away.

Sawtooth Mountain

Another mountain type common to the front ranges (Mt. Ishbel, Sawback Range, Colin Range, Queen Elizabeth Range), sawtooth mountains feature long ridges, which mark the upturned edges of thrust sheets. These ridges are angled perpendicular to the prevailing winds. Precipitation and mechanical weathering have eroded gullies on their southwestern aspects to produce the sawtooth shape. Sawtooth mountains are very photogenic at sunset, or when dusted with snow.

Castellated Mountain

Castellated mountains are the trademark peaks of the Rockies, and are found in the eastern main ranges (Castle Mountain, Pilot Mountain, Mt. Temple, Mt. Saskatchewan, Mt. Amery, Castleguard Mountain). Resistant limestone, dolomite and quartzite formations are separated by weak layers of shale. The resistant formations become cliffs while the weak layers are eroded to become ledges, giving the "layer cake" appearance. All of these formations remained largely horizontal dur-

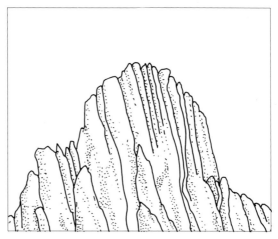

ing mountain building. The sedimentary formations are now visible as bands on the mountainsides. Castellated mountains frequently contain cirque glaciers on their east aspects, and alpine valley glaciers on their north aspects.

Horn Mountain

Most common in the eastern main ranges (Mt. Chephren, The White Pyramid, Mt. Athabasca, Mt. Fryatt, Mt. Assiniboine, Mt. des Poilus, Mt. Carnarvon), horn

Top: Overthrust mountain (Mt. Rundle)

Bottom: Dogtooth mountain (Mt. Louis)

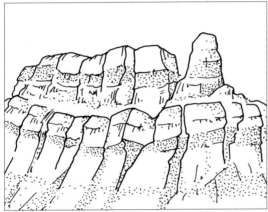

Top: Sawtooth mountain (Sawback Range)

Middle: Castellated mountain (Castle Mountain)

Bottom: Horn mountain (Mt. Assiniboine)

mountains are created when several cirque glaciers erode different sides of a mountain simultaneously. The narrow ridges separating the cirques are called arêtes (a-RETTS), and frequently offer straightforward mountaineering routes to the summit. The Van Horne range, west of Field in the western main ranges, features Mt. King, a classic horn mountain.

Glaciation

Glacial ice forms in areas where more snow accumulates annually than melts — shaded mountainsides or areas of high elevation along the Continental Divide. As fallen snow crystals age, they change shape to grains, and eventually are compacted into ice. It takes an accumulation of 30 m of snow to create glacial ice, and when this ice begins to flow downhill, it becomes known as a glacier (GLAY-seer).

The glaciers we see today, although impressive, are mere remnants of the massive sheets of ice that sculpted the Rockies. A complete discussion of the mechanics of glacial motion, and the ways in which glaciers have eroded the landscape of the Rockies, is presented in the Columbia Icefield section of the *SuperGuide*. The Lake Louise Visitor Centre and the Columbia Icefield Information Centre feature extensive displays on glaciation.

Prominent Glaciers in the Canadian Rockies

Glacier Type and Name	Where Visible	Glacier Type and Name	Where Visible
Icefield		Hector	Icefields Parkway, south from Helen Creek, Bow Lake
Waputik	Hector Lake viewpoint		
Wapta	Hector Lake, Bow Glacier, Peyto Lake viewpoints	Balfour	Hector Lake viewpoint
		Kerkeslin	Mt. Kerkeslin, from Jasper
Mons	Howse River viewpoint		
Wilson	Mt. Wilson viewpoint	Summit	Mt. Robson
Columbia	Parker Ridge, Athabasca Glacier, Sunwapta Flats	Cathedral	Kicking Horse Pass
		Bath	Lake Louise junction
Outlet Valley Glacier		**Niche Glacier**	
Athabasca	Columbia Icefield	Macdonald	Mt. Temple, Lake Louise
Bow	Bow Glacier viewpoint		
Peyto	Bow Summit	Howse Peak,	
Saskatchewan	Parker Ridge	Aries, Stairway	Howse Peak viewpoint
Dome	Icefield Information Centre	Chephren/White	
		Pyramid	Mt. Wilson viewpoint
Stutfield	Stutfield Glacier viewpoint	Epaulette	Mt. Wilson viewpoint
		Kaufmann	Mt. Wilson viewpoint
Yoho	Yoho Valley Road	Sarbach	Mt. Wilson viewpoint
Vulture	Hector Lake Viewpoint	Sunwapta Peak	Icefields Parkway, south from near Endless Chain Ridge
Alpine Valley Glacier			
Crowfoot	Crowfoot Glacier viewpoint	**Cirque Glacier**	
Boundary	Sunwapta Pass	Waputik	
Hilda	Hilda Creek	Escarpment	Hector Lake viewpoint
Stanley	Vermilion Pass	Crowfoot	
Fay	Moraine Lake/Larch Valley	Mountain	Crowfoot Glacier viewpoint
Cavell	Mt. Edith Cavell	Cavell	Mt. Edith Cavell
Victoria	Lake Louise	Mt. Patterson	Mistaya Valley
Aberdeen	Lake Louise	Mt. Jimmy	
Lefroy	Plain of Six Glaciers	Simpson	Bow Pass
Horseshoe	Paradise Valley	Mt. Amery	Graveyard Flats

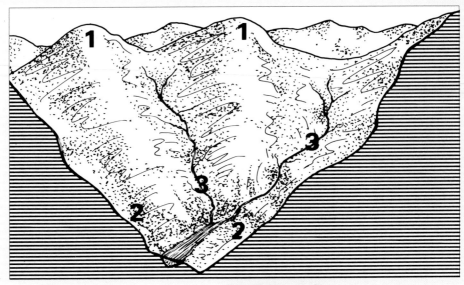

Glaciation and the Canadian Rockies

Ever since the Rockies first started to poke their summits above sea level 120 million years ago, they have been subject to processes of erosion, which break down rock

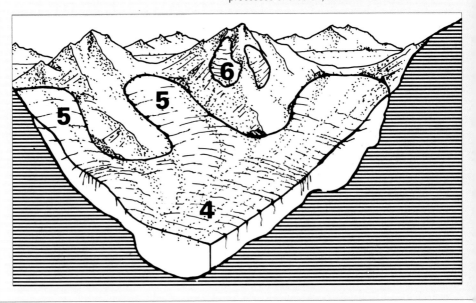

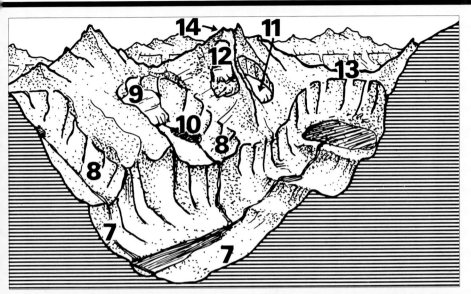

and carry the fragments away. Before the last ice age, (the Wisconsin Glaciation of 75,000-11,000 years ago), the Rockies were rounded and gentle in appearance (1). Ancient streams (3) sculpted the landscape. The hallmark of this water-worn landscape was the V-shaped valley (2).

During the three advances of the Wisconsin Glaciation, ice sheets covered all but the highest Rockies' summits, sending massive glaciers into the surrounding valleys (4). Alpine valley glaciers (5) widened the V-shaped valleys into U-shaped troughs, and niche glaciers (6) formed on upper mountainsides, sharpening the profile of the peaks.

When the ice receded, it left behind the blueprint of the Rockies: broad, U-shaped valleys (7), with tributary valleys hanging above the main valley floors (8). It is at the mouths of these hanging valleys that the Rockies' famous waterfalls and canyons are found. Hanging glaciers (12) and niche glaciers (11) still occupy the shaded north and east aspects of many mountainsides, eroding the horn mountain shape (14). Horn mountains feature triangular faces separated by narrow ridges called arêtes (13). Cirque glaciers (9) nestle in the bowl-shaped cirques they have eroded. Meltwater from these and other glaciers collects in depressions or behind moraine dams, creating tarns (10) - the many glacial lakes for which the Rockies are renowned.

Although glaciation has been the most significant force of erosion in the Rockies, there are many other processes which are constantly turning rock into rubble. Together these are wearing down the Rockies at the rate of about 1 metre every 17,000 years.

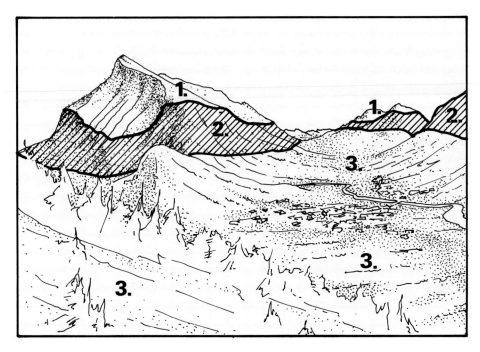

Ecology

This schematic drawing of Mt. Rundle and the Bow Valley shows three ecoregions:
1. Alpine,
2. Subalpine, and
3. Montane.

The simplicity of the concept of ecology — the inter-relationship of all living things — belies the complexity of the many factors linking climate, topography, vegetation and wildlife. Plants and animals in the Rockies occupy specific niches in the environment where their needs are met, and where their characteristics best ensure survival. In turn, they become food for other species, or provide assistance, both subtle and obvious, that helps others to survive. Thus is created the balance from which springs the variety of life in the Rockies.

The fascinating thing about this inter-dependence is that it holds true throughout the ecology of the Rockies, regardless of species or scale. From the tiniest plants on upper mountainsides to the largest, free-roaming mammals, every living thing plays a key role in ensuring this balance is maintained. The elimination or unnatural reduction in the population of a single species upsets the balance, and begins a chain reaction, with effects felt throughout the total ecology.

On the global scale today, we are constantly reminded of such effects. The clear-cutting of tropical rainforests, the disappearance of native prairie grasslands, the damming of wild rivers — each of these actions has tremendous environmental costs affecting the quality of air and water, the availability of habitat and the diversity of species. The beauty of the mountain national parks in the Canadian Rockies is that a century of preservation has spared much of the landscape from the wanton actions of man. Many of the natural relationships are relatively undisturbed. We as visitors have the privilege of viewing the natural order close at hand — an opportunity which has been lost in many areas of the world.

Ecology at Riverside

In a quiet side channel of the Bow River between Banff and Lake Louise is a metre-high mound of sticks and mud. This structure is a lodge, home to a family of beaver. Beavers are aquatic rodents, and require slow moving waters in which to live. In an incredible display of industry, the beaver family has taken advantage of this side channel, and dammed the downstream end with tree trunks, mud and rocks, creating a pond upstream. From their lodge near the centre of the pond, the nocturnal beavers emerge each evening, swimming to shore to fell aspens, birch and poplars to be used in maintaining the lodge and dam. The inner bark, buds and greens of these and other trees and shrubs make up most of the animal's diet.

Trout, washed into the pond during a period of high water in the river, flourish in the nutrient-rich, silt-free waters. Fish-eating birds such as osprey, belted kingfisher and great blue heron take up residence in the trees nearby. A pair of muskrats, who enjoy similar habitat to beaver, have built their own house on the shore of the pond. They will not compete with the beaver for food, preferring instead to eat the lush aquatic vegetation that grows near shore: horsetails, cattails, sedges and rushes A thicket of shrubs, including willows, alder and red osier dogwood, also grows along the bank. Moose, elk and deer browse here in the mornings and evenings.

How Green Are the Parks?

The following figures give very approximate percentages of the area of the four mountain national parks occupied by each ecoregion:

Montane	8%
Lower subalpine	30%
Upper subalpine	20%
Alpine	6%
Glacial ice (mostly alpine elevations)	6%
Bedrock, moraine, river gravel (all elevations)	30%

Species counts of vegetation in Banff and Jasper National Parks indicate:
996 vascular plants (trees, flowers, grasses, etc.)
243 mosses
407 lichens
53 liverworts

Mosquitos use the quiet pond waters for breeding. These insects are eaten by many other species, and their presence attracts dragonflies and a host of birds. Amongst these, and easily recognized by its beautiful song, is the red-winged blackbird, which nests in the cattails and willows at the pond's edge. A pair of Canada geese make the pond their summer home, raising their goslings on the quiet waters.

When the pond freezes, wolf, coyote and lynx will walk across the ice to the lodge, seeking a winter meal. The natural concrete of the lodge is usually adequate defence against this threat. Inside, the beaver does not hibernate — it remains active, venturing beneath the ice to eat from branches cached on the pond bottom the previous autumn.

In creating a safe and favourable habitat for themselves, the beaver family has rendered a great service to many other animals, offering them additional range and sources of food. In time, when the beavers have eaten all their favourite vegetation within safe range of the pond, they will move on. Without the beavers' maintenance efforts, the dam may break and the pond once again become an active river channel. Or the shoreline vegetation may proliferate and spread into the pond, transforming it to marsh. Over a course of many decades, as larger vegetation takes root, this marsh will slowly become a shoreline forest, reclaimed from the river.

Thus the actions of the beaver will have benefited a diverse array of wildlife and vegetation, and produced transitions in the very landscape itself.

Ecoregions

Fortunately, the nature of the mountain environment graphically assists us in understanding its complex ecology. Take a look at any mountainside around Banff or Jasper townsites. You will notice the vegetation is generally dense and varied in the valley bottom, and more sparse as elevation is gained on the mountainside. On the high ridge crests and summits, vegetation is largely absent. Biologists have utilized these natural transitions in dividing the Rockies into three life zones, or ecoregions — the montane, the subalpine and the alpine.

In terms of growing season, the effect of moving from Banff townsite to a high mountainside nearby is the same as travelling to northern Alberta. The increase in elevation produces a harsher climate with a shorter growing season, typical of areas further north. The duration of the growing season in the *SuperGuide*'s area ranges from six months in some of the major valley bottoms to less than two months on the upper mountainsides. The distribution of vegetation and wildlife, and the extent of the ecoregions, are therefore largely governed by elevation and its associated effects.

The Montane Ecoregion

Vegetation typifying the montane ecoregion is found in the major valley bottoms and on sun-exposed slopes of lower mountainsides, especially in the front ranges. Temperatures here are the warmest on average, and the range of extremes is greatest. Average precipitation on the eastern slopes is relatively low, and split roughly equally between summer and winter. Precipitation is slightly higher on the western slopes, and significantly higher in the Mt. Robson area.

The montane is the windiest ecoregion. Sections of the large valley bottoms are oriented parallel to the prevailing southwesterly winds. On the eastern slopes this orientation also allows warm and cold air masses to back up into the Rockies from the plains and foothills. The warm chinook wind — the "snow eater" — is a common winter feature in the front ranges and foothills, and contributes to a relatively sparse snow cover. Easier winter travel in montane valley bottoms, and relative abundance of food, makes this ecoregion important winter range for many animals, especially deer and elk.

Lodgepole pine, white spruce, Douglas fir and the few deciduous trees in the Rockies characterize the forests of the montane. Montane wetlands and montane meadows occupy areas adjacent to the major rivers. The montane is home to more species of vegetation and wildlife than any other ecoregion. But as important as this ecoregion is to wildlife, it comprises very little of the total area of the four mountain parks. Much of the montane has sustained severe impacts from the construction of townsites, railways and roads.

The Subalpine Ecoregion

The subalpine ecoregion occupies mountainsides between the montane and treeline, and also occurs in valley bottoms at high elevations. Treeline is the upper limit of the forest, which in this part of the Rockies is generally 2,200 m on south-facing slopes. Treeline may be considerably lower on north-facing slopes, cliff edges and in proximity to glaciers. Precipitation in the subalpine is heavier than in the montane, and most falls as snow, some of this in summer. Winds are generally light and are influenced by ridges and valleys. In the vicinity of glaciers, pools of cold air called frost hollows are common. These prolong the effects of winter, and stunt the growth of vegetation.

The subalpine is the most extensive ecoregion in the Rockies, and has been subdivided to allow ease of description. In the lower subalpine ecoregion, there is a mixture of cone-bearing, evergreen trees: lodgepole pine, Engelmann spruce, white/ Engelmann spruce hybrids, and scattered subalpine fir. Spruce/ fir forests dominate the upper subalpine ecoregion, thinning towards treeline, where stunted stands of the "wind timber," krummholz, appear. South of Bow Pass, pure stands of Lyall's larch frequently comprise the treeline forest at the limit of the upper subalpine.

The Alpine Ecoregion

The alpine ecoregion occurs above treeline, and is characterized by diminutive and hardy vegetation — wildflowers, mosses, grasses and lichens. Soils are generally rocky. Most of the precipitation in the alpine falls as snow. The mean annual temperature is the lowest of the ecoregions: -4°C is typical just above treeline. The range of temperature extremes is the least. Vegetation patterns are often directly influenced by the manner in which snow accumulates, or is removed, by the actions of ever-present wind.

The Effects of Landscape On Climate

Although elevation is used to roughly assign the limits of the ecoregions, local climates produced by the landscape also influence the distribution of vegetation and wildlife. These local conditions result from topoclimatic factors, which include: mean temperature, type and amount of precipitation, sunshine and shade, soil type, drainage, slope orientation or aspect,

steepness, avalanche activity, proximity to ice, and wind.

These factors interact to produce a myriad of variations on what might "normally" be expected for different locations at any given elevation. The localized ecoregions that result are called ecosites. Over 130 of these have been identified in Banff and Jasper National Parks alone.

Succession
The Process of Change

When we look around the landscape, we tend to think a forest will always remain a forest, a meadow remain a meadow, and a marsh remain a marsh. In the short term this will be true. However, over a period of decades, ecosites proceed through a successional sequence from youth to maturity. The lower subalpine forest best demonstrates this sequence.

A youthful lower subalpine forest is not a forest at all, but a charred mass of burned timber, the product of a forest fire. The lodgepole pine depends on heat from forest fires to melt the resin that seals its cones and allow for effective seeding. This tree regenerates prolifically after a fire. The lodgepole does not tolerate shade, and thrives in the open burn, amidst patches of common fireweed, wildflowers and scattered stands of trembling aspen and balsam poplar — two other trees that grow well on disturbed ground. This open habitat is a good one for wildlife, offering two blessings: access to food in the new growth of the recently burned area, and shelter in the unburned forest nearby.

The lodgepole pine fairs too well. Its dense seeding results in a thick growth of uniform age — a doghair forest. The forest floor becomes shaded, and the undergrowth dies off. The food supply dwindles and the forest loses its appeal to most wildlife. However, since the lodgepole does not grow well in shade, it effectively begins to eliminate itself by overcrowding. Meanwhile, the shade-tolerant species of Engelmann spruce and subalpine fir have slowly been growing beneath the lodgepole canopy. As the lodgepoles thin out, these trees succeed and become the most common. More sunlight reaches the forest floor and the undergrowth becomes more diverse. The forest is at its prime for usefulness to wildlife. The last stage in the cycle of the fire succession forest is the climax forest, when additional generations of spruce and fir trees take seed. Then Nature awaits another forest fire to wipe the slate clean.

Not all the successional cycles in the Rockies are fire-related. Some, such as the montane wetlands and subalpine wet meadow successions, require many hundreds of years, while others, such as the montane grassland succession, may require only a few decades. The absence of major forest fires in the last 50 years has greatly affected the balance of successional habitats in the Rockies, and many areas are now in the climax phase, past their primes as appealing habitat to most wildlife. Following extensive fire history studies, experimental prescribed burns are being introduced to initiate regeneration and vitality to various ecosites in the Rockies.

How Long Will Litter Last?

cigarette butts	1-5 years
aluminum cans and tabs	500 years
glass bottles	1,000 years
plastic bags	10-20 years
plastic coated paper	5 years
plastic film containers	20-30 years
nylon fabric	30-40 years
leather	up to 50 years
wool socks	1-5 years
orange and banana peels	up to 2 years
tin cans	50 years
plastic six-pack holders	100 years
plastic bottles and styrofoam	indefinitely

Wildlife

The Canadian Rockies are renowned for abundant wildlife. This mule deer fawn has the spotted coat it will wear throughout most of its first summer.

Since the first visits of Europeans 200 years ago, the Canadian Rockies have been renowned as an area with abundant wildlife. Today, the opportunity to view wild animals in their natural habitat is a key facet of the mountain national park experience. The visitor to the Canadian Rockies is fortunate that favourite habitat for many of the larger animals occurs at roadside — there's a very high chance of seeing wildlife, especially in early morning and late evening. The history of man's interaction with wildlife in the Rockies chronicles the evolution of changing perceptions on the natural world, and highlights the responsibilities of park managers and visitors in ensuring that representative wildlife populations survive.

The Not-so-happy Hunting Grounds

The days of the fur trade in the 1700's and early 1800's saw very little hunting and trapping in this part of the Rockies. Most of the pelts were taken further west in British Columbia. As the fur traders crossed the Rockies they reported abundant big game. Half a century later, the total animal population, although still far greater than today, was evidently in decline. James Hector of the Palliser Expedition recorded few observations of game during his travels of 1857-60.

With the completion of the Canadian Pacific Railway in 1885, the frontier of the wild west was thrown open to anyone who could pay the fare. By the late 1890's, hunters from Europe and eastern North America were making annual trips to the Rockies. These clients became the mainstay of guiding and outfitting operations such as those established by Tom Wilson and Jim Brewster.

Many of us cringe today when reading accounts of three grizzlies taken in one afternoon, 60 fish hauled from a lake, or pack horses loaded down with more trophy sheep heads than could be carried. However, during the first few years of its existence, Rocky Mountains Park (Banff) had no regulations governing hunting and fishing. Even after regulations were established, enforcement was difficult, and hunters continued this kind of wholesale slaughter both within and beyond the park boundaries.

Some observers soon became concerned about this trend. In 1911 surveyor and mountaineer A. O. Wheeler wrote: "It will readily be seen that to preserve these wild animals in their native habitat will prove of infinitely greater value to the country than to advertise them as spoils of the chase, when they will soon cease to exist."

It wasn't only over-hunting that threatened the natural balance. The Victorian concept of the animal kingdom was markedly different from that of today. Individual animals were categorized as "good" or "bad." The good animals were the game that offered prospects to the hunter, or that could be viewed safely at close range in zoos — deer, elk, bear, moose, bighorn sheep and mountain goats. The bad animals were the predators — cougar, lynx, wolverine, owls, hawks, eagle, coyote and wolf. These last two were particularly persecuted. The concept of balance of predator and prey was still many years away.

Early visitors had a tremendous desire to see animals, but did not want to risk encountering them on their own turf in the wild. To fulfil the visitors' desire, the Parks Branch established zoos at the Buffalo Paddock and the Banff Park Museum.

Three fishermen with a bountiful catch at Lake Minnewanka in the early 1900's. The early outlook on fishing and hunting in the Rockies was one of plunder. Fish this size are rarely caught today, and certainly not in this quantity.

As elsewhere in the world, in western Canada many wildlife habitats have been damaged or destroyed, threatening the animals' chances of survival. The mountain caribou is one of several wildlife species in the Rockies for which the protection offered by national parks may help prevent local extinction.

Decades of Transition

With the passing of the National Parks Act in 1930 came the dawning of an awareness that animals should be protected on their home range rather than in cages. The zoos were disbanded. However, the outlook on certain species remained unchanged. The mandate of the first national park wardens included the eradication of unwanted wildlife. Between 1924 and 1941, over 80 cougars were exterminated in Banff and Jasper parks. Sightings of cougar are rare in these parks today. The wolf was virtually exterminated as part of an anti-rabies program in the 1950's, and it has taken over three decades for this animal to return in numbers to the Rockies.

As a consequence of these predator eradication programs, the populations of some animals went unchecked, and wardens found themselves having to kill off the prey in the same manner as the predator. A mass killing of the burgeoning elk population between 1941-70 was highly unpopular with the public. Not so the earlier eradication of the wolf — an act which directly contributed to the over-population of elk!

During the last two decades, the concept of managing the mountain national parks as an integrated ecosystem has become established. The dire situation now facing many animals outside of the national parks has driven home the realization that any act which tampers with wildlife habitat or population balances affects many species. After decades of manipulating wildlife in the Rockies, park managers today are for the most part leaving matters be, in an attempt to allow natural balances and cycles to return.

There are several exceptions. A stringent policy of forest fire suppression during the last 50 years has resulted in extensive areas of forest becoming over-mature, with a corresponding decline in usefulness to most wildlife. A program of staging prescribed burns in certain areas has been initiated to help regenerate habitat.

Costly, but successful, highway fencing has been installed along the Trans-Canada Highway to help prevent road kills. Additional fencing may be erected along other roads and railways.

A State of Grace

Today, wildlife biologists, park wardens and researchers use the mountain national parks as a living laboratory in which to study wildlife. Some animals are fitted with radio collars, by which they can be tracked and their habits, range and life cycles monitored. Elk, bear, wolf and mountain caribou have recently been studied in this fashion.

Wildlife in the Rockies is currently in a state of grace. Most of these animals are normally fearful of man, but have come to realize the average park visitor poses no threat to their well being. But what may appear to the observer as approachability is in fact nonchalance, and the visitor must not forget these animals are still wild. When pressured or intimidated, their natural instincts will take over. At roadside and in townsites in these very parks, people have paid for this education with their lives.

Amendments to the National Parks Act in 1988 provide stiff penalties for those convicted of hunting in the national parks. Nonetheless, poaching of wildlife, especially elk, deer and big-horn sheep, continues to be a problem. If you suspect suspicious behaviour that may indicate poaching, do not become involved. Record a description of the persons and/or vehicle, and report your information to the nearest park warden or R.C.M.P. officer.

Wildlife Tips

The following guidelines will help protect both you and the wildlife:
1. Do not feed animals. Although it is tempting to offer a crumb to a squirrel or a bird, this practice establishes a dangerous dependency on unnatural food sources. Some of the foods offered are very harmful, especially to animals that hibernate. Animals accustomed to being fed will expect this treatment from all visitors, and will become a nuisance, and possibly a danger.
2. Do not leave food or garbage unattended. Ingesting the packaging on some foods may prove fatal to animals. Bears will frequent campgrounds and townsites if accustomed to easily obtainable food or garbage. Place all garbage in the animal-proof receptacles provided. Store food in the trunk of your vehicle.
3. Do not approach or entice wildlife. Take photographs from a distance. Use a telephoto lens if you have one.
4. Do not interfere with the relationship between a mother and its young.
5. Observe posted speed limits. Reduce speed at night. Pay spe-

cial attention when driving through areas frequented by animals. Do not expect animals to get out of the way of your vehicle. Be prepared to stop instead.

6. Elk, deer, moose, sheep and goats are highly unpredictable during their mating season — September-November. It is best to avoid them completely at these times.

7. Bears are highly unpredictable. If you are fortunate enough to see a bear, remain in your vehicle. Report your sighting to a Park Information Centre.

8. Keep pets restrained on a leash, or confined in a vehicle. Do not take dogs into the backcountry.

Animals in the SuperGuide
RODENTS:
Members of the rodent family are smaller mammals whose characteristic behaviours are gnawing and hyperactivity. They have two prominent incisor teeth on both the upper and lower jaw. Most rodents are active only in daytime, and many hibernate in winter.

● Least chipmunk, page 216
● Golden mantled ground squirrel, page 216
● Columbian ground squirrel, page 216
● Red squirrel, page 216
● Hoary marmot, page 274
● Porcupine, page 138
● Beaver, page 95

RABBIT FAMILY:
Members of the rabbit family are gnawing mammals who have two pairs of incisor teeth on the upper jaw. Only two species are present in the Rockies – the other one is the snowshoe hare.

● Pika, page 148

UNGULATES:
Ungulates have hooves. In the Rockies, two families are represented. Members of the deer family have cloven hooves, and antlers that are branched and shed each year. The bovid family has cloven hooves, and horns that are not branched and never shed.

DEER FAMILY:
● Mule deer, page 102
● White-tailed deer, page 102
● Elk, page 64
● Moose, page 218
● Mountain caribou, page 262

BOVID FAMILY:
● Mountain goat, page 189, 267
● Bighorn sheep, page 92

Wildlife Watch

Poaching — the illegal hunting of protected animals — remains a threat to wildlife in the mountain national parks. The Canadian Parks Service would like to enlist your support in "Wildlife Watch," its anti-poaching campaign. If you observe suspicious activities, involving people, guns and wildlife, report your information immediately to the nearest park warden or R.C.M.P. officer. Include the date, time, location, vehicle licence number, and descriptions of the vehicle and the persons involved. Do not approach the people yourself. Reports of fishing violations, and feeding and harassing of wildlife, will also be appreciated by park wardens. Your identity will not be revealed.

WILD CATS:

There are three members of the cat family in the Rockies (the other two are lynx and bobcat). Wild cats are characteristically carnivorous and usually nocturnal. Their tracks show four toes with claws retracted.

● Cougar, page 298

WILD DOGS:

Members of the dog family are primarily carnivores. The species in the Rockies are mostly nocturnal. Tracks show four toes with claws visible on all feet.

● Wolf, page 117
● Coyote, page 117

BEAR FAMILY:

Bears are the largest carnivores, and have five clawed toes on the front and rear feet.

● Black bear, page 229
● Grizzly bear, page 202

BIRDS:

Approximately 40% of the North American species of birds occur in the Rockies. These can be roughly grouped into four categories: songbirds; waterfowl, raptors (birds of prey) and ground-dwelling birds. The avid birder will find fewer species and numbers of birds than are common in areas of North America that have longer and milder summers. Nonetheless, there are some fine bird-watching locations in the Canadian Rockies. Those in the vicinity of Jasper offer especially good prospects for photography.

Songbirds: Banff and Jasper townsites; Cave and Basin; Bow, Kicking Horse, Miette and Athabasca Valleys

Waterfowl: Vermilion Lakes, Fenland Trail, Cave and Basin, Bow, Mistaya and Kicking Horse Valleys, lakes in the vicinity of Jasper, Athabasca Valley east of Jasper, Miette Valley

Raptors: foothills, Vermilion Pass; Bow, Athabasca, Kootenay and Kicking Horse Valleys, alpine zone, upper and lower subalpine forest

Ground-dwelling birds: upper and lower subalpine forest, Parker Ridge, The Whistlers, glacial and alpine zones

Some of the most interesting birds in the Rockies are profiled in the *SuperGuide*.

RESIDENT SONGBIRDS:

● Common raven, page 248
● Clark's nutcracker, page 134
● Gray jay, page 134
● Black-billed magpie, page 83

RAPTORS:

● Golden eagle, page 96
● Bald eagle, page 96
● Osprey, page 295

GROUND DWELLING BIRDS:

● Ruffed grouse, page 192
● White-tailed ptarmigan, page 238

Conservation

Yellow Orchids, like all mountain wildflowers, eke out a precarious existence in the Rockies. Please take extra care to preserve *all* the wildflowers that you come upon so that everyone may enjoy their beauty.

In recent years the concept of ecology — the inter-relationship of all living things — has been universally embraced. Unfortunately, we have arrived at this perception the hard way — by discovering that, to a large extent, paradise has been lost. In the urbanized areas of the world, natural relationships have been so disrupted that it is difficult for residents to conceptualize, let alone experience, the many facets of nature's balance. Most of us have been living out of touch, and out of step, with the earth beneath our feet.

Canada's national parks are ecological touchstones that provide an opportunity to observe, explore and understand the integral roles that natural processes, wildlife and vegetation play in creating and sustaining nature's balance. The positive and negative effects of man's influence are highlighted. In the national parks we can begin to re-establish our connection to the natural order, to appreciate its workings and learn from our past mistakes. Hopefully we will take some of this awareness with us when we leave, to be applied in the betterment of life in our homes and other places where we travel.

Preservation

Preservation of the mountain national parks would be a relatively simple matter if the only pressures on their integrity came from within. However, added to the scenario of conflicting views on land use inside the parks are the effects of commercial and industrial developments outside their boundaries.

The opportunity to create buffer zones on adjacent lands has already been largely lost, due to provincial policies which give precedence to "multi-use" over genuine protection. Clearcuts and logging roads lead to formerly remote park boundaries. Wildlife habitat, used seasonally by animals that also dwell inside the parks, is threatened. The mountain national parks are shrinking. The arbitrary boundaries set for political and economic reasons in 1930 cannot protect the parks from contemporary pressures.

Even within the parks, transcontinental railways and highways, carrying ever-increasing volumes of non-park related traffic, slice the wilderness into smaller pieces — pieces that may easily succumb if the internal and external pressures continue to mount. The lesson we are painfully learning outside the parks applies within the boundaries too: No arbitrary area or individual species stands alone — in a world of cause and effect, all things interrelate.

An Ever-Green Opportunity

As a visitor to the mountain national parks, you have an opportunity to make contact with a natural landscape, the exceptional quality of which has largely disappeared from many other areas in the world. Even with the many battles pitched over the endless array of development ideas, the Canadian mountain national parks set a wonderful example, and clearly demonstrate the environmental value of preservation. What would these mountains look like if they had been unprotected this past century? Your voice, added to the many others urgently requesting that completion of the Canadian national parks system be given priority in the 1990's, will help generate the necessary political will to achieve that aim.

Your experience of the Canadian Rockies — the fresh water, unpolluted skies, abundant wildlife, and opportunities for recreation and solitude — can inspire you towards incorporating environmentally supportive practices into every aspect of your daily life. The many possibilities available are now common knowledge. Perhaps the greatest environmental challenge facing each of us is to achieve a unity of thought and action that will move us closer to harmony with the natural world and, by effect, with each other.

Highlights of Human History

The First Inhabitants

9000 B.C. The ice sheets of the Wisconsin Glaciation begin to recede, and the glaciers that have filled the valleys of the Rockies retreat to their sources along the Continental Divide. By 6000 B.C. all of the major valleys in the Rockies are ice-free. Native peoples subsequently travel through these valleys on hunting and trading journeys. Some Natives may have stayed in the Rockies year-round.

1700 A.D. The stability of Native life in the Rockies is shattered by an influx of Natives from the east. These people are fleeing the persecution of Europeans, and diseases to which they have no immunity. The Stoney tribe comes to the Rockies as part of this migration.

The Fur Trade

1754 Fur trader Anthony Henday is the first European to see the Rockies.

1799 The North West Company builds Rocky Mountain House. This building, and other "houses" built later, serve as supply depots and trading posts for the fur trade.

1800 Two North West Company traders cross Howse Pass, and establish a fur trade route.

Stoney Indians race their horses across the Morley flats in front of a spectacular Rocky Mountain backdrop.

1807 David Thompson of the North West Company crosses Howse Pass and builds Kootenae House in the Columbia Valley near the present town of Invermere.

1810 Hostile Peigan (PAY-gun) Natives close the Howse Pass route to fur traders.

1811 David Thompson establishes the Athabasca Pass route. Henry House is constructed at Jasper.

1813 Jasper House is constructed at Brûlé (broo-LAY) Lake in the foothills of the Athabasca Valley.

1820's Yellowhead Pass is incorporated into the fur trade route.

1821 The rival Hudson's Bay and North West companies amalgamate.

1827 Botanist David Douglas crosses Athabasca Pass, and assigns exagerrated elevations to Mt. Hooker and Mt. Brown.

1829 Jasper House is moved to near Jasper Lake.

1841 Sir George Simpson crosses the Rockies on his way around the world and makes the first recorded visit by a European to the hot springs at Radium. James Sinclair leads a group of 200 settlers through the Rockies to the Oregon Territory. He takes a dip in the Radium Hot Springs too.

1845-46 Jesuit missionary Father de Smet crosses and recrosses the Rockies. At Jasper House he baptizes 44 people.

1847 Methodist missionary Robert Rundle preaches to Stoney Natives in the Bow Valley.

1850's The western territories of North America have been over-trapped. What furs remain are now shipped from the west coast, rather than packed overland. The fur trade begins to decline.

Exploration

1858 James Carnegie, the Earl of Southesk, travels through the front ranges. In the Pipestone Valley near Lake Louise he shoots a wood bison — this is the last record of this animal roaming free in the Rockies.

1857-60 The Palliser Expedition explores central and western Canada for the British Government. James Hector crosses Vermilion, Kicking Horse, Bow and Howse Passes.

1862 Drawn by the Cariboo gold rush, a group of eastern Canadians known as The Overlanders makes an epic crossing of western Canada by wagon, horse, raft and foot. They use Yellowhead Pass to reach the Cariboo Mountains.

1863 Bungling tourists Milton and Cheadle cross the Rockies via Yellowhead Pass, and live to tell of the ordeal.

1867 Canada is granted independence from Britain under the terms of Confederation.

1870 The Cavell Advance, or Little Ice Age, ends. Most glaciers in the Rockies begin to rapidly recede.

The Canadian Pacific Railway

1871 British Columbia joins Canada and Prime Minister Sir John A. Macdonald promises the

The construction of the Canadian Pacific and the Grand Trunk Pacific railways was instrumental in the founding of Banff, Jasper and Yoho National Parks. In this photograph, a steam shovel clears the grade for the Grand Trunk Pacific in 1911.

new province a railway connection to the rest of the country.

1872 Sir Sandford Fleming, the proposed railway's Engineer-in-Chief, chooses Yellowhead Pass as the route for the railway, and then travels across Canada to examine the route.

1873 Scandal plagues Sir John A. Macdonald's government and its plans for the railway. In November, the government resigns.

1875 Two American hunters make a visit to hot springs on the slopes of Sulphur Mountain near Banff. One of the hunters builds a shack and winters in the area, in hopes of developing a claim to the springs.

1878 Sir John A. Macdonald is returned to power, and the push begins in earnest to organize and complete a Canadian trans-continental railway.

1881 The charter establishing the Canadian Pacific Railway receives royal assent. The Yellowhead Pass route is abandoned. William Cornelius Van Horne, an American, is appointed General Manager of the railway.

1882 Major Rogers, in charge of surveying the route for the railway through the mountains, discovers the pass in the Selkirks now named for him. Tom Wilson discovers Lake Louise and Emerald Lake, and crosses Howse Pass.

1883 The railway tracks reach Calgary. Workers lay 11 km of track in a single day. Later in the summer, the end of steel reaches Lake Louise. Three railway workers stumble onto the hot springs at Banff while prospecting for minerals, and attempt to file a claim. Others get into the act. Dispute over the claims will lead to the establishment of a federal reserve, the forerunner of Banff National Park.

1884 A. P. Coleman, a geology professor from Toronto, makes his first trip to the Rockies, and climbs Castle Mountain. The railway boom town of Silver City flourishes nearby.

Parks, Peaks and Pack trains

1885 After a century of over-hunting, the plains bison is virtually extinct in the wild. Within a period of a week, the last spike of the Canadian Pacific Railway is driven at Craigellachie, B.C. and the Hot Springs Reservation is established at Banff. Surveyor G. M. Dawson discovers coal east of Banff.

1886 The Mt. Stephen Reserve is established, forerunner of Yoho National Park. The Canadian Pacific Railway constructs Mt. Stephen House in Field, and a cabin on the shore of Lake Louise. Development of the Cave and Basin hot springs begins.

1887 Surveyor J. J. McArthur climbs Mt. Stephen near Field. National Park status is bestowed on the reserve at Banff, and it becomes known as Rocky Mountains Park.

1888 The Banff Springs Hotel opens. A. P. Coleman makes the first attempt to find the giant peaks discovered by David Douglas in 1827.

1889 Hunting and fishing regulations are imposed in Rocky Mountains Park. Stoney Natives are brought to Banff to entertain stranded tourists — the first of many Banff Indian Days.

1890 The first chalet is constructed at Lake Louise by the Canadian Pacific Railway. This building burns in 1893, and is immediately replaced by a larger structure.

1892 The area around Lake Lou-

Swiss Guide Peter Sarbach (standing), with mountaineers J. N. Collie (right) and G.P. Baker, at the Banff Springs Hotel, 1897.

ise is added to Rocky Mountains Park.

1893 Pioneer outfitter and guide Tom Wilson sets up shop in Banff. Expatriate American Lewis Swift settles in the Athabasca Valley east of Jasper. While exploring near Lake Louise, Walter Wilcox and Samuel Allen obtain a distant view of Moraine Lake, and make an attempt to climb Mt. Temple.

1894 Wilcox and Allen journey to Lake Louise with other school fellows — the Lake Louise Yale Club — and succeed in ascending Mt. Temple, and exploring more of the surrounding area.

1895 Wilcox makes the first of several trips to Mt. Assiniboine, and explores north towards Bow Pass. Mt. Hector is climbed by members of the Appalachian Mountain Club. Bill Peyto begins guiding with Tom Wilson's company. The forerunner of Waterton Lakes National Park is established.

1896 Wilcox attempts to find Mt. Hooker and Mt. Brown, and helps

Three personalities representing three eras in the history of the Rockies: Tom Wilson (right) — pioneer outfitter and guide; Walter Wilcox — explorer, author and photographer; and Jim Brewster (left) — outfitter and guide, who would successfully make the business transition to the age of automobiles.

pioneer part of the route of the present day Icefields Parkway. Mountaineer P.S. Abbot is killed in an accident on Mt. Lefroy, near Lake Louise.

1897 The first Swiss Guide is brought to Canada and leads a party of nine climbers, who avenge Abbot's death by making the first ascent of Mt. Lefroy. Mt. Victoria is also climbed. One of the party, J. N. Collie, explores further north towards Saskatchewan Crossing. Jean Habel explores the Yoho Valley and "discovers" Takakkaw Falls. Bison are donated to the park at Banff, and the Buffalo Paddock is established.

1898 Collie returns to find the elusive Mt. Hooker and Mt. Brown. He ascends Mt. Athabasca and records the first description

of Columbia Icefield. On returning to England, he puts the myth of Mts. Hooker and Brown to rest.

1899 Outfitter and guide Jimmy Simpson begins work with Tom Wilson's company.

1900 Bill and Jim Brewster begin guiding and outfitting at Banff. Eventually they will corner the guiding market from Wilson. Elk, which have been killed-off by hard winters and over-hunting, are reintroduced to the Rockies.

1901 Edward Whymper, conqueror of the Matterhorn, makes the first of three much heralded visits to the Rockies. Mt. Assiniboine, the "Canadian Matterhorn," is climbed by James Outram. German explorer Jean Habel is the first to visit the north edge of Columbia Icefield.

1902 James Outram climbs Mt. Columbia, second highest peak in the Rockies. Rocky Mountains Park (Banff) is expanded to its maximum size. Canada's second trans-continental railway, the Grand Trunk Pacific, is proposed.

1903 The C.P.R. establishes the town of Bankhead, and begins mining coal from beneath Cascade Mountain. The Banff Park Museum is constructed.

1906 Surveyor and mountaineer A. O. Wheeler founds the Alpine Club of Canada (A.C.C.). The club holds its first annual camp in Yoho Pass.

1907 A. P. Coleman and Reverend George Kinney make the first attempt on the Rockies' highest peak, Mt. Robson. Jasper Forest Park reserve is established. Explorer Mary Schäffer journeys to the headwaters of the Athabasca River.

1908 Coal is discovered on the slopes of Roche Miette in Jasper, and the Pocohontas mine is subsequently developed. Mary Schäffer reaches Maligne Lake.

1909 George Kinney and outfitter Curly Phillips almost reach the summit of Mt. Robson. Kinney claims the first ascent. The Spiral Tunnels are completed. An avalanche destroys many buildings in Field.

Parks and Prosperity

1910 A highway linking Banff and Invermere is proposed. Development of Miette Hot Springs commences.

1911 A. O. Wheeler organizes the joint A.C.C./Smithsonian Institute expedition to Yellowhead

By the 1920's, the automobile had supplanted the pack horse and train as the principal means of transport in the Rockies, and roadside campgrounds were established in the mountain national parks. Some of the present day campgrounds along the Icefields Parkway were formerly highway construction camps.

Pass, Mt. Robson and Maligne Lake. The town of Jasper (then named Fitzhugh) springs up as a divisional point on the Grand Trunk Pacific Railway, which is completed across Yellowhead Pass. J. B. Harkin becomes first commissioner of national parks, a post he will hold for 25 years. Construction of the Banff-Windermere Road commences — it will be 12 years before it is completed.

1913 The first ascent of Mt. Robson is accomplished from an A.C.C. camp. Mt. Robson Provincial Park is established. A third Canadian trans-continental railway, the Canadian Northern, is completed through Yellowhead Pass. The Interprovincial Boundary Survey commences.

1914 Walter Painter's design for the Cave and Basin hot pools is constructed, as is his $2 million tower at the Banff Springs Hotel.

1915 Mt. Edith Cavell is named, and the first ascent accomplished.

1920 British Columbia conveys the lands of Kootenay, Canada's 10th national park. Jimmy Simpson builds Num-ti-Jah Lodge.

1920's With the establishment of the automobile in the mountain parks, the Canadian Pacific Railway begins constructing "auto bungalow camps," at Castle Mountain, Storm Mountain, Radium, the Kootenay Valley, Wapta Lake, Lake O'Hara, Moraine Lake and Emerald Lake.

1921 Pocohontas mine closes.

1922 Jasper Park Lodge opens.

The first dam at Lake Minnewanka is constructed. The town of Bankhead is dismantled. Mt. Assiniboine Provincial Park is established. Abbot Pass Hut is constructed near Lake Louise. The Grand Trunk Pacific and Canadian Northern railways amalgamate as the Canadian National.

1923 The Banff-Windermere Road is completed. The first ascent of North Twin, third highest mountain in the Rockies, is accomplished by J. M. Thorington and party.

1924 The National Geographic Society completes an expedition to Columbia Icefield and Maligne Lake. Most of the Chateau Lake Louise burns. The National Parks Association is founded — Canada's first environmental group.

1925 Mt. Alberta, one of the most difficult mountains in the Rockies, is topped for the first time by a Japanese mountaineering party. The Interprovincial Boundary Survey is completed.

1928 Final construction of the main building at the Banff Springs Hotel is completed.

Preservation and Development

1930 The National Parks Act is passed. The boundaries of the four mountain parks are finalized.

1931 Construction of the Icefields Parkway commences. The project is not completed until 1939.

1936 The Sunshine Ski Area has its humble beginnings.

1937 The Miette Hot Springs are developed.

1940 The Survey Peak burn engulfs much of the forest near Saskatchewan Crossing, forcing closure of the recently opened Icefields Parkway.

1941 A second dam is constructed at Lake Minnewanka. The waters have now been raised a total of 25 metres.

1945 The first ski lift is installed at Sunshine.

1952 Commercial snowmobile rides commence at Columbia Icefield. Jasper Park Lodge burns, and is rebuilt soon after.

1956 The Trans-Canada Highway is completed through Yoho.

1961 Upgrading of the original Icefields Parkway is completed.

1968 A forest fire blazes through Vermilion Pass. Redevelopment of the Aquacourt at Radium Hot Springs is completed. The Whyte Museum of the Canadian Rockies opens.

1970 The Yellowhead Highway officially opens.

1977 The Alberta government establishes Kananaskis Country.

1980 The Sunshine gondola begins winter operation.

1984 Sunshine Village commences operation in the summer season as well.

1985 The national parks celebrate their centennial. The refurbished Cave and Basin opens. H.R.H. The Duke of Edinburgh unveils a monument at Lake Louise, proclaiming the four mountain parks a World Heritage Site. Redevelopment of Lake Louise townsite commences.

1986 Emerald Lake Lodge and Miette Hot Springs are redeveloped.

1988 The Winter Olympic Games are hosted by Calgary. Nakiska at Mt. Allan is site of the alpine skiing events. The nordic skiing events are held in Canmore. The first amendments to the National Parks Act are passed.

1989 The upgraded Bow Valley Parkway is officially opened. The Kicking Horse and North Saskatchewan Rivers are designated Canadian Heritage Rivers. A new visitor centre opens at Field. Redevelopment of Mt. Norquay ski area commences. A new wing is completed at Chateau Lake Louise.

1990 Banff becomes a self-governing community. The Lake Louise Visitor Centre opens. The Athabasca River is designated a Canadian Heritage River. Regular passenger train service through the Rockies is discontinued. The Icefields Parkway celebrates its 50th anniversary. The Lake Louise train station is named a National Historic Railway Building. The Chateau Lake Louise celebrates its 100th anniversary.

Recreation

Hikers relax for a rest on Wilcox Pass overlooking Athabasca Glacier in Jasper National Park.

When the mountain national parks received their new management plans in 1988, "driving for pleasure" was identified as the principal activity of most visitors. This is not surprising. Highways in the Rockies offer close-up views of some of the most spectacular mountain scenery in the world. However, a wide range of other recreational opportunities are available. Your experience of the Rockies will broaden dramatically if you make an effort to walk, paddle or ski away from the highway — even if only for an afternoon. Don't worry if you don't have the necessary equipment with you; it can be rented at a number of locations. Guided raft, horse, bike, fishing, hiking and mountaineering trips are also available.

Camping

The Canadian Parks Service operates 31 roadside campgrounds in the mountain national parks, with a total of 5,003 campsites. Although this seems like a large number, campgrounds frequently fill by early afternoon in mid-summer. At such times you may be directed to "overflow" campgrounds, at which the only facilities provided are pit toilets.

Fees are charged at all roadside campgrounds. The fees vary with the services provided, ranging from $5-$16 per site, per night. Some campgrounds are self-registration. Maximum length of stay is 14 nights. About three quarters of the campgrounds have flush toilets. All sites have picnic tables and access to drinking water. Most campgrounds have cook shelters. Firewood and fireboxes are provided. Please use firewood sparingly and do not remove it from the campgrounds. Also, do not gather wood from the forest floor or riverbeds. There are interpretive theatres at approximately one half of the campgrounds.

Mt. Robson Provincial Park has three roadside campgrounds — Robson Meadows, Robson River and Lucerne—totalling 178 sites. These have water, toilets and firewood, but no hook-ups. A sanistation is provided at Robson Meadows.

Backcountry Camping

Free backcountry camping is allowed at a multitude of campgrounds in the mountain national parks. Most of these are more than six kilometres from the closest road. All overnight trips require a free park use permit, obtainable from Park Information Centres. Some trails have quota systems, and fill early on long weekends, but overcrowding in the Rockies' backcountry is generally not a problem. Less than 2% of park visitors travel more than a kilometre from the roadway! While picking up your permit you can also obtain the latest information on trail conditions and seasonal hazards.

Camp only in designated campgrounds, on the tent sites provided. Practice no-trace camping. Most backcountry campsites are now equipped with bear poles for food storage, but be sure to carry enough rope with you to stow your food out of a bear's reach. Pack out all your garbage. Fires are prohibited in many areas; a lightweight campstove is essential. Groundwater and snowmelt is usually potable. Random camping is allowed only in specific areas, or to mountaineers at the base of some climbing routes. Backcountry travellers may take advantage of the voluntary registration system, which ensures someone will come looking if you are overdue. This permit must be returned at the end of your trip.

There are backcountry campsites in Mt. Assiniboine and Mt. Robson Provincial Parks, and B.C. Parks operates Naiset cabins at Mt. Assiniboine. Fees are charged.

Hiking and Backpacking

The mountain national parks are a hiking and backpacking paradise, with over 3,000 km of trails, spanning the range from short interpretive hikes to wilderness routes nearly 200 km in length.

Walks

Relatively flat,
or short duration

BANFF
Tunnel Mtn Hoodoos
Bankhead
Fenland Trail
Bow Falls
Vermilion Lakes
Johnson L.
Moraine L. rockpile
Moraine L. lakeshore
L. Louise lakeshore
Bow Summit
Stewart Canyon
The Marsh Trail
The Discovery Trail
Mistaya Canyon
Warden L.
KOOTENAY
Marble Canyon
Paint Pots
Redstreak Loop
Sinclair Canyon
Fireweed Trail
YOHO
Emerald L. lakeshore
Hamilton Falls
Centennial Trail
Walk-in-the-Past
Spiral Tunnel
The Great Divide
Deerlodge
JASPER
Athabasca Glacier
Miette Hot Springs
Sunwapta Falls
Athabasca Falls
Buck and Osprey Lakes
Path of the Glacier
Schäffer Viewpoint
Maligne Canyon
Annette Lake
Moose Lake
Mona and Lorraine Lakes
Pocahontas
Lac Beauvert

Half Day Hikes

Longer or more
strenuous

BANFF
Johnston Canyon
Parker Ridge
Bow L./Bow Glacier
Tunnel Mountain
Sundance Canyon
L. Agnes
Little Beehive
Muleshoe
Stony Squaw
Consolation Lakes
KOOTENAY
Stanley Glacier
Juniper Trail
Redstreak
Cobb L.
Dog L.
YOHO
Emerald Basin
Emerald L. lakeshore
Sherbrooke L.
Paget Lookout
Ross L.
Leanchoil Hoodoos
Waptas Falls
JASPER
Maligne Canyon;5th Bridge
Cavell Meadows
Whistler summit
Valley of the Five Lakes
Wabasso L.
Buck and Osprey Lakes
Old Fort Point
Stanley Falls
Geraldine Lookout

Full Day Hikes

Long and strenous

BANFF
Ink Pots
C-Level Cirque
Hillsdale Slide
Bourgeau L.
Plain of Six Glaciers
Paradise Valley
Boulder Pass
Boom L.
Sunset Lookout
Glacier L.
Sarbach Lookout
KOOTENAY
Floe L.
Kindersley Pass
YOHO
Hamilton L.
Wapta Highline
Iceline
Twin Falls
Yoho Glacier
Mt. Hunter
JASPER
Devona Lookout
Sulphur Skyline
The Palisade
Maligne Canyon: 6th Bridge
The Whistlers
Wilcox Pass
Opal Hills
Bald Hills
Geraldine Lakes
ROBSON
Kinney L.

Many of these hikes are described
in detail in the Altitude
SuperGuide *Walks and Easy
Hikes in the Canadian Rockies*

and for the adventurous, track-less high passes beckon to seldom travelled side valleys, offering many opportunities for exploration.

Backpackers require a free park use permit — available at Park Information Centres — and must be familiar with the do's and don'ts of no-trace camping, and travelling in bear country. Snow lingers in the high country year-round. Lightweight, durable and waterproof equipment is essential, as is a campstove. Fires are prohibited in many areas. In general, camping is allowed only in designated campgrounds.

The most popular backpacking areas are:

Banff: Skoki/Baker/Pipestone Valleys; Egypt Lake.
Jasper: Skyline Trail; Nigel, Jonas and Poboktan Valleys; Tonquin Valley; Fryatt Valley.
Yoho: Yoho/Little Yoho Valleys.
Kootenay: The Rockwall.
Mt. Robson: Berg Lake.
Mt. Assiniboine: all trails leading to Magog Lake.

For the casual hiker, the chart on page 48 summarizes the opportunities. Many of the shorter walks feature self-guided, interpretive displays. Carry binoculars for observing birds and animals, and always be prepared for changing weather.

In addition to the scheduled interpretive hikes offered by the individual parks, several private companies specialize in offering guided hikes.

Boating and Rafting

Non-motorized boats are allowed on most lakes and rivers in the mountain national parks. Power boats may be launched only on Lake Minnewanka, Upper and Middle Waterton Lakes, and Pyramid Lake. Boats with electric motors and no on-board generator may be launched on any lake where non-motorized boats are permitted. Power boating is allowed on Yellowhead and Moose lakes in Mt. Robson Provincial Park.

Canoe and boat rentals are available at many of the popular lakes: Louise, Moraine, Emerald, O'Hara, Patricia, Pyramid, Cameron, Upper and Middle Waterton, and Maligne. Commercial boat tours operate on Lake Minnewanka and Maligne Lake. Several companies offer rafting trips on the Athabasca, Maligne, Bow, Kootenay and Kicking Horse Rivers. Day and overnight excursions are available.

Canoeists and kayakers will find a variety of calm and white-water on the major rivers in the Rockies. There are usually two high water levels — one in late spring, and another at the peak of the glacial melt season in early August. River guides have been compiled and may be consulted at Park Information Centres.

The lakes of the mountain national parks are not recommended for boardsailing. Waters are cold and winds are sporadic. Some lakes are closed to this activity. Consult a Park Information Centre for details.

Horses in the mountains — an enduring image of the Canadian west.

Trail Riding

Horseback has been a traditional means of access and travel in the Rockies for over a century. Horse use results in the rapid degeneration of trail surfaces, and in recent years the mixture of horse and foot traffic on some trails has led to complaints from the hiking faction. Nonetheless, commercial outfitters offer day rides and pack trips at several locations in the Rockies. To alleviate conflicts, these concessions operate on specific trails, and horse/hiker separations have been instigated in some areas where trails are shared.

Hour long, half day, day long and multi-day rides may be booked at the Banff Springs Hotel, Chateau Lake Louise, Emerald Lake and Jasper Park Lodge. Sleigh rides are offered at several locations in winter.

Public horse use is allowed on some trails. Obtain details and a grazing permit from a Park Information Centre.

Fishing

A century ago, many lakes and rivers in the Rockies contained abundant populations of fish. However, the glacially fed waters are cold and low in nutrients, and over-fishing has reduced both the quantity of fish and the average size of individual specimens. To compensate, some lakes have been stocked. This practice satisfies anglers, but the introduction of non-native species threatens various natural balances, including the viability of some native fish populations.

Various species of trout and char comprise most of the catch in the Rockies. The most popular roadside lakes for fishing are Minnewanka, Emerald, Wapta, Bow, Patricia, Pyramid and Maligne. Consult a Park Information Centre to determine open seasons for the waters you would like to fish, catch limits, and other restrictions which may apply. A national park fishing licence is required. Provincial fishing licences are required in the provincial parks.

A successful day of fishing is not necessarily measured by the size of the catch. Fishing offers the chance to relax amidst spectacular surroundings, with the opportunity for viewing birds and other wildlife. In acknowledgement of the dwindling fish populations in most lakes, many anglers now use barbless hooks, and practice catch and release.

Bicycling

Bicycle touring in the Rockies has become a very popular summer activity in recent years. Two short tours in particular are renowned world-wide as classics: The Golden Triangle, and the Icefields Parkway.

The Golden Triangle utilizes the Trans-Canada Highway, B.C. Highway 95 and the Kootenay Parkway to make a circuit that crosses the Continental Divide twice. The triangle requires three days and has some good hills. It can be ridden clockwise or counter-clockwise, beginning at Banff, Castle Junction, Lake Louise, Golden or Radium.

Wide shoulders, spectacular scenery and frequent campgrounds and hostels combine to make the Icefields Parkway one of the best cycle touring roads in the world. Three to five days suffices for a one-way trip and some sightseeing. The hills are steeper, but shorter, if biked north to south. Arranging transportation at either end of the route will necessitate two vehicles, or bus travel. If you have the time, you can simplify logistics by biking the Parkway both ways! The annual Jasper/Banff relay race takes place along the Icefields Parkway in early June.

The town and environs of Banff are particularly rewarding when explored on bicycle. Enjoyable day rides can be made along the Bow Valley Parkway towards Lake Louise. Kananaskis Country also offers the combination of first-rate bicycling and scenery. Most bike shops are happy to assist visitors planning a cycling trip in the Rockies.

Mountain Biking

In the mid-1980's, the all-terrain bike, or "mountain bike," began to appear on trails in the Rockies. Mountain biking has since come into its own as a pursuit, and fishermen and mountaineers often employ bikes for quick access and exit on backcountry trips. After some cautious years monitoring the effects of mountain bikes on trails and mountain environments, the Canadian Parks Service has designated certain trails as open to bikes. These include many of the old fireroads. Most "no biking" trails are now clearly posted, but check with a Park Information Centre to ensure the permissibility of biking before you go on your trip. Similar restrictions apply in the provincial parks. When mountain biking, please stay on the trails, and be particularly alert for hikers, wildlife, fallen trees, washouts, and other hazards. Carry a repair kit, extra clothing and food. Wearing a helmet is a good idea, too.

Mountaineering

Climbing mountains was the original recreational pursuit in the Rockies, and it continues to be popular today. The variety of terrain and scope of routes varies from walk-ups to demanding north faces in remote settings — the Rockies have it all. The benchmark elevation in the Rockies is 3048 m / 10,000 ft. There are some 700 peaks that exceed this elevation.

Because of their sedimentary origin, most of the rock in the Rockies is crumbly — not a desired characteristic for mountaineering. As a result, the tendency in the Rockies is to climb routes which incorporate glaciers, snow and ice. Mountaineering in the vicinity of Lake Louise and Columbia Icefield focuses on these routes. Other high mountains that lure many climbers are Mt. Robson, Mt. Edith Cavell and Mt. Assiniboine.

With improvements in clothing and equipment, winter mountaineering is becoming more popular. Many mountains lend themselves to ski ascents and descents — particularly those on the Wapta, Waputik and Columbia Icefields. The Alpine Club of Canada administers an icefield hut system that can be utilized in multi-day ski mountaineering tours. In winter, the abundance of frozen waterfalls also makes the Rockies an international mecca for the pursuit of waterfall ice climbing.

Rock climbing on steep cliffs is popular on Yamnuska Mountain, Cascade Mountain, Mt. Rundle and in the vicinity of Lake Louise and Canmore. (Rock climbers are not intent on reaching a summit, but in scaling difficulties encountered following a particular line to the top of a cliff). Guidebooks to these areas are available. Check at Mountain Magic or Monod Sports in Banff for the latest news concerning the local crags.

What about the walk-ups? There are a number of mountains that have rough trails leading to the summit. Most of these mountain tops can be reached by anyone who is reasonably fit and prepared. Ask at a Park Information Centre for suggestions suited to your experience and ability. The voluntary safety registration system is available, free of charge, to all climbers and mountaineers.

Professional mountain guides are available in Banff, Lake Louise, Field, Canmore, Jasper and Golden. These men and women can be hired by anyone determined to add the thrill of one of the Rockies' high alpine summits to their vacation memories.

Golf

Golfing can be a pleasant way to enjoy fresh air and great scenery. The Banff Springs Golf Course is rated as one of the 10 most scenic links in the world. There are other public courses at Jasper Park Lodge, Kananaskis Village, and outside the parks in Canmore, Golden, Wintergreen, Radium and Fairmont. Contact the individual courses for details regarding tee times and green fees. As a plus, the elevation in the Rockies will add some distance to your drive.

Downhill Skiing

Four downhill ski areas in the mountain national parks and two in Kananaskis Country offer a variety of terrain and scenery to slopes enthusiasts. The oldest ski area is Sunshine Village, nestled on the Continental Divide west of Banff. The Village is reached by gondola, from which 12 lifts provide access to 61 marked runs. Sunshine's terrain is 20% novice, 60% intermediate and 20% expert, and is open longer than any other ski hill in Canada — early November to the May long weekend, on average. On-hill accommodation is available.

Mt. Norquay's steep mountainside has been used for ski jumping competitions and World Cup events. Norquay's reputation as an expert's hill has changed with the addition of new intermediate runs cleared during 1989. Night skiing is available three nights a week. Norquay hosts the first leg of the Banff Mountain Madness relay race, during the annual winter carnival in late January.

The Lake Louise Ski Area is the largest in the Rockies, with three day lodges and 11 lifts, servicing over 40 marked runs on three mountainsides. Many runs feature snowmaking. Additional terrain is being added.

Free shuttle service is available from most Banff hotels to these ski areas. Special ski packages are sold, combining lift tickets, instruction, accommodation and local transportation. For in-

On the way to the top, a skier rides the chairlift to the upper ski runs on Mt. Norquay.

formation contact:
Ski Banff/Lake Louise
P.O. Box 1085
Banff, Alberta T0L 0C0
403-762-4561

The 30 marked runs at Marmot Basin in Jasper are serviced by six lifts. Terrain is divided equally between novice, intermediate and expert. Local hotels participate in ski packages, and transportation to Marmot is available from Jasper. Contact:
Marmot Basin
P.O. Box 1570
Jasper, Alberta T0E 1E0
403-852-3816

Nakiska at Mt. Allan in Kananaskis Country was the site of alpine skiing events during the 1988 Winter Olympic Games. Six lifts give access to over 20 runs. Seventy per cent of the terrain is

Hikers in the Canadian Rockies need to be prepared for more than just steep climbs!

intermediate. Lodging and services are available nearby at Kananaskis Village. Contact:

Nakiska

P.O. Box 1988

Kananaskis Village, Alberta

T0L 2H0

Further south in Kananaskis Country is Fortress Mountain. Seven lifts service terrain that is 20% novice, 50% intermediate and 30% expert. Contact:

Fortress Mountain

P.O. Box 720, Station E.

Calgary, Alberta T3C 3M1

All of these ski areas offer lessons, equipment rentals, sales and repairs. Rentals are also available at many locations in Banff, Lake Louise and Jasper, including some of the major hotels.

Cross-country Skiing

Cross-country skiing was the fastest growing sport in Canada during the 1980's. The mountain national parks feature an abundance of trails that offer the visitor a refreshing way to experience winter.

Most cross-country ski routes in the Rockies travel the major valley bottoms. In several areas, loop systems that are regularly groomed have been developed. These include: Johnson Lake, Banff Springs golf course, Sundance Canyon, Lake Louise, Pipestone and Whitehorn, in Banff; and the Pyramid bench and Maligne Lake loops in Jasper. Most skiers will find enough skiing to fill a day at any one of these areas.

Backcountry hikers are silhouetted against a stunning mountain backdrop in this photograph taken near Lake O'Hara.

Many of the summer hiking trails also serve as cross-country trails, but most involve travel in avalanche terrain. Skiing these trails should not be attempted by unprepared parties and, even then, not without due regard for conditions. The latest avalanche information is available by phoning 762-3000 in Banff, or by visiting any Park Information Centre or Warden Office.

Instruction in cross-country skiing may be obtained by contacting any of the downhill ski areas. Equipment can be rented at many locations in Banff, Lake Louise and Jasper, and at Emerald Lake. Dogs are not allowed on cross country ski trails in Banff. This may soon be the case in other parks.

Other Activities

The frozen surfaces of most roadside lakes provide excellent prospects for skating in the early winter. In some years, the lakes freeze before the first significant snowfall, becoming huge sheets of skateable ice. This happened at Lake Louise in 1987 and 1988. The Chateau Lake Louise maintains rinks on the lake until warm spring temperatures impair the quality of the ice. The Vermilion Lakes are also popular for early winter skating. Public indoor skating is available at arenas in Banff and Jasper.

In the national parks, vehicles must stay on designated roads. Use of dirt bikes, all-terrain vehicles and snowmobiles is not permitted.

The sports desks at many of the larger hotels provide contacts for seasonal activities not mentioned above. These include dog sledding and hay rides. Park Information Centres can also inform you of special seasonal and historic interpretive events, which might involve a walk around town, along a trail, or even up a mountainside.

Kananaskis to Banff

The Three Sisters lie southeast of the town of Canmore. they are locally recognized as Canmore's signature mountains.

The Trans-Canada, Canada's principal east/west road, is the longest paved highway in the world. The section that runs through the Rockies is certainly among the most spectacular scenic drives anywhere.

Design and construction of the Rocky Mountain section of the Trans-Canada highway commenced in the mid-1950's. The road was completed through Rogers Pass in the Selkirks in 1962. Although upgrading is taking place, and proposals to extend the twinned section are being considered, the Trans-Canada is behind in its ability to handle the present-day volume of traffic, and can get very crowded.

As a result, it is not a particularly safe road. A great deal of the traffic is commercial, and these drivers are intent on getting through the Rockies as quickly as possible. The remainder travels at a more leisurely pace, conducive to sightseeing. This is a dangerous mix. Visitors are advised to make safe driving a priority on the Trans-Canada. If something catches your eye, or if you want to check the *SuperGuide* for information, stop safely on the shoulder or in a nearby pull-out.

JOINS PAGE 69

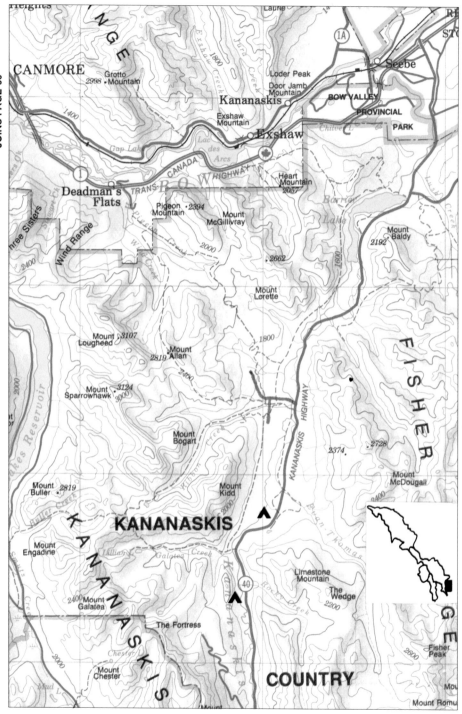

JOINS PAGE 58

JOINS PAGE 57

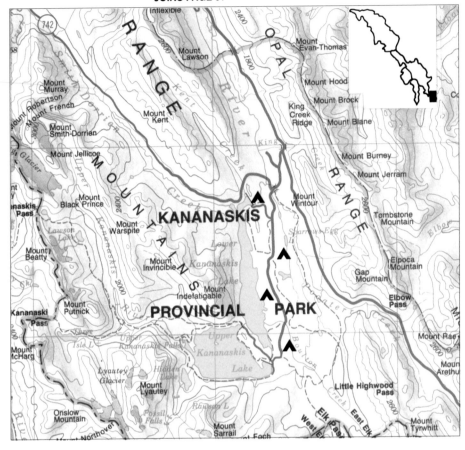

Despite this caution, the drive through the Rockies from Calgary to Golden has many spectacular highlights: the open vistas of the plains and foothills; the dramatic transition at the mountain front; the picturesque Bow Valley; glacier-capped peaks near Lake Louise; Kicking Horse Pass; and the Golden Canyon. All this tremendous scenery is subject to the ever-changing patterns of mountain light and shade — a constant delight to the eye. A more varied and visually rewarding drive of such short distance would be difficult to find in Canada, or anywhere else in the world.

Chinook Country

The mountain front is typically a windy place. The Bow Valley funnels winds into the foothills through the break known as The Gap. This area is also frequented by a peculiar, warm, winter wind, the existence of which is related more to larger weather systems than local topography.

The chinook (shih-NOOK) wind, "the snow eater," can raise local temperatures as much as

40°C in a few hours. It results when warm air from a Pacific storm system breaks into the cold air of an arctic, high pressure mass situated over the foothills and plains. The storm system sheds its moisture west of the Continental Divide, and its dry air is heated as it sweeps rapidly to the ground on the eastern slopes.

In a typical winter there will be 10-20 chinook days in this area. (Jasper averages 12 chinook days a year, and Waterton close to 30.) The effects of chinooks which last several days will be felt as far east as Medicine Hat in southeastern Alberta. During a chinook, the weather along the Divide is usually very unsettled.

In areas frequented by chinooks, Lodgepole pine trees are subjected to a condition called red-belt. The warm winds dry out the pine needles when the sap is flowing too slowly to replenish them. The foliage subsequently turns brown.

The combined effect of local windiness and chinooks keeps snow accumulation at the mountain front low. Elk and deer find food sources more readily here in winter. It is unfortunate this favourable range land was removed from the national park in 1930, as there is now very little in Banff.

Kananaskis Country

Kananaskis Country is a 4,000 sq km parcel of provincial land that lies to the south of the Trans-Canada Highway between Morley and Canmore. Unlike the national parks, where resource extraction and most motorized rec-

Steeply tilted limestone peaks, and valley bottoms covered in montane forest and grassland, typify the front ranges of the Rockies along the Trans-Canada Highway, and in Kananaskis Country. This photograph is of King Canyon in Kananaskis Country.

reational pursuits are excluded, Kananaskis Country is a "multi-use" area, incorporating three provincial parks, natural areas, forest reserves, grazing lands, mining and petroleum lease-holds, a resort, and recreational developments.

Provincial funds from the Alberta Heritage Savings Trust have been lavished on the Kananaskis, and the outdoors enthusiast, camper and sightseer will find a wide range of opportunities, and well-equipped support facilities. There are over 3,000 auto-accessible campsites in some 20 campgrounds. Reservations can be made at many of these. The backcountry features more than 30 campgrounds for the backpacker and trail rider.

Most of the Kananaskis one sees from roadside lies in the front ranges, and in the montane eco-region. Large mammals you may see here include elk, mule deer, black bear, grizzly bear and bighorn sheep. It was on the montane grasslands in this area that some of the province's first cattle ranches were established.

The Trans-Canada Highway passes directly through Bow Valley Provincial Park, and the park Information Centre can be reached easily from the Highway 1X exit for Exshaw. Displays give an overview of the local environment and the processes that shaped the Rockies, and half a dozen short walking trails are oriented to various interpretive themes. Picnic and camping facilities are available.

The most popular destination in Kananaskis is the 500 sq km Peter Lougheed Provincial Park, centred on the Kananaskis Lakes. The park Visitor Centre is 56 km south from the Trans-Canada Highway on Highway 40. With its varied and accessible terrain, the park is a veritable playground for hikers, mountaineers, cyclists, mountain bikers, trail-riders, skiers, boaters, campers and fishermen. Several facilities for the handicapped and disabled have been developed. Complete services are available, and there are a variety of roadside and backcountry campgrounds.

En route to Peter Lougheed Park, Highway 40 passes Kananaskis Village, a year-round resort featuring three hotels, tennis courts, two world-class 18 hole golf courses and a recreational vehicle park. In winter, downhill skiers have two facilities to choose from: nearby Nakiska at Mount Allan, the site of alpine skiing events during the 1988 Winter Olympic Games, and Fortress Mountain Ski Area.

Also in K-Country is the Canmore Nordic Centre. This facility was the site of the nordic skiing events during the 1988 Winter Olympics, and features 56 km of cross country ski trails. In summer the trails are used for hiking, mountain biking and interpretive walks.

Continuing south from the Nordic Centre, the Smith-Dorrien/Spray Road leads through

Whiteman's Pass to Spray Lakes Reservoir. This area was formerly within Banff National Park, but was removed to allow the hydro-electric development seen from the road. Followed further south, the Smith-Dorrien/Spray Road provides an alternate summer approach to Peter Lougheed Provincial Park.

The name Kananaskis was first applied to features in this area by Captain John Palliser of the Palliser Expedition. Kananaskis was a Native commemorated in local legend. Two meanings given for the name are "man with tomahawk in head," and "meeting of the waters." The Kananaskis River is a principal tributary of the Bow River, and the two rivers merge near Bow Valley Provincial Park.

More complete information on opportunities in Kananaskis Country is available from the Bow Valley Provincial Park headquarters, or by writing to the address provided in the Contacts section.

Lac des Arcs

When William Cornelius Van Horne, general manager of the Canadian Pacific Railway, first saw Lac des Arcs in 1883, he was favourably impressed with the scene. He immediately suggested the area be set aside for a park reserve, and promised to "build a fine house on that island in the lake." The Department of the Interior complied, and surveyed the area so the C.P.R. might proceed with development of a resort.

Next time Van Horne passed the lake, he was more familiar with the merits of Banff as a potential C.P.R. resort. A typical mountain front windstorm was blowing at Lac des Arcs. The setting had lost its appeal, and the issue was never raised again. It's just as well — a "fine house" the size of the Banff Springs Hotel would never have fit on the tiny island! Those in the know thereafter jokingly referred to the lake as "Van Horne's park."

Lac des Arcs was eventually protected in Banff National Park, when the park reached its maxi-

Alberta's mountain playground, Kananaskis Country, offers the outdoors enthusiast a wide range of recreational opportunities. Golf, downhill and cross-country skiing, camping, trail-riding, fishing, hiking and mountaineering are a few of the possibilities.

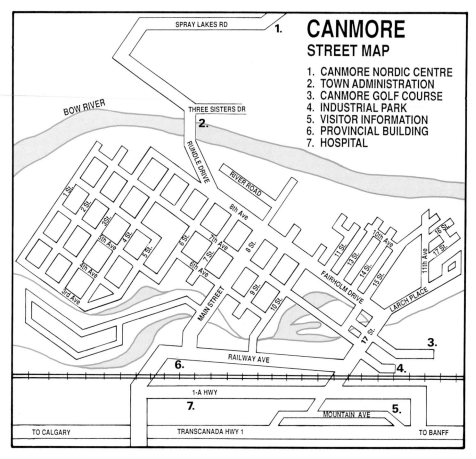

CANMORE
STREET MAP

1. CANMORE NORDIC CENTRE
2. TOWN ADMINISTRATION
3. CANMORE GOLF COURSE
4. INDUSTRIAL PARK
5. VISITOR INFORMATION
6. PROVINCIAL BUILDING
7. HOSPITAL

mum size in 1902. However in 1930, concessions were made to the interests of resource extraction which had begun in 1905, and to proposed hydro-electric development, and the Bow Valley east of Canmore was removed from the area of the park. Quarrying of limestone, cement operations, and milling of magnesite continue near Lac des Arcs today.

Lac des Arcs is French for "lake of the bows." Natives found wood suitable for bow making along the banks of the Bow River.

Canmore

As with many towns in the Canadian Rockies, the origins of the town of Canmore are tied to the construction of the Canadian Pacific Railway, which reached here in 1883. But unlike some other railway towns, which quickly came and went, outcrops of coal in the base of Mt. Rundle immediately guaranteed Canmore a future. The coal was mined to fire the railway's locomotives, and the town's population reached 450 in 1888.

The discovery of oil in the Turner Valley in 1914 largely sealed the fate of Canmore's industry. Most of the mines closed by 1922, but operations at one seam continued until 1979. Since then Canmore has successfully completed the transition from industrial town to residential community and visitor centre.

In 1979 the city of Calgary succeeded in its bid to host the 1988 Olympic Winter Games. Canmore was chosen as the site for the nordic events, and the Canmore Nordic Centre was constructed. The Games were highly successful, and the facilities are now open for public use, year-round — skiing in the winter, and hiking and biking in the summer. The town also sports an 18-hole golf course.

Considering its proximity to mountains, Canmore has a relatively moderate and dry climate. The town is in a rain shadow, and winter chinook winds frequent this part of the Bow Valley, raising temperatures and keeping snow cover to a minimum.

The town of Canmore is on the Trans-Canada Highway in the front ranges, adjacent to Banff National Park. It was the site of the nordic skiing events during the 1988 Winter Olympic Games.

Motor Vehicle Permits

All vehicles stopping in a national park require a motor vehicle permit, obtainable for a fee at the park gate ahead. One day, four day and annual permits are available. Affix the permit to a window on the driver's side of the vehicle.

Canadian seniors obtain their permit free of charge. Commercial and non-stop traffic does not require a permit. Vehicles travelling the Icefields Parkway require a permit, whether they're stopping or not.

The elk is the most numerous large mammal in the Rockies. Motorists will commonly observe these members of the deer family at roadside, especially in spring and autumn.

Elk

The montane ecoregion of the Bow Valley in Banff National Park is ideal habitat for members of the deer family, especially elk. Half again as large as an adult deer, a bull elk stands 1.5 m tall at the shoulder. The coat is light brown, darker on the neck and legs, with a shaggy fringe on the underside of the neck. The Native name for elk is wapiti (WAH-pih-tee), which means "white rump," and the tawny or white rump patch, with short tail of matching colour, help identify the animal.

The elk prefers to eat grasses and tender vegetation. It will occasionally peel the bark from trees, an act which results in a characteristic black scarring of the lower tree trunk. Like other members of the deer family, elk ruminate: while resting they chew cud — food regurgitated from their multi-chambered stomachs.

Female elk (cows) spend most of the year in the valley bottoms with the offspring and immature males, sometimes forming herds of 50 or more animals. One or two calves are born in late May or early June. Mature bulls venture to higher elevations in late spring, where they spend the summer alone or in small groups before returning to the valleys in late August or early September.

The antlers of the male begin to grow in April. It is true the number of "points" on each side of the antlers gives a rough indication of the animal's age. Six points, the usual maximum, indicates an animal older than four years. Such an antler rack may reach 1.5 m in length, and 1.8 m in width. The antlers fall off in February or March. The antlers play a major part in the annual courtship, the rut, which begins in late summer. The idea is for each mature bull to see how large a harem of breeding-age females he can attract, and the locking of antlers is sometimes used to settle the dispute. Elk in rut are very unpredictable, so please keep your distance. These animals are familiar winter residents of Banff, Jasper and Field townsites, and townsfolk have learned to tolerate their presence with humour, which can be difficult given that, in their quest for food, elk do much damage to gardens.

In recent years Canmore has become something of a "bedroom community" for Calgary, and for those wishing to escape the rents of Banff. The present population is over 5,000. Visitor services and accommodation are available, and Canmore is central to a wide range of recreational opportunities.

Banff National Park
Canada's First National Park

The first national park in Canada, and the third created in the world (after Yellowstone, U.S. and Royal, Australia), had its humble beginnings in a dispute over hot springs discovered at what is now known as the Cave and Basin. These springs were well known to Natives, and had been visited by two American hunters in 1875, one of whom wintered in a shack built nearby. But it was the re-discovery of the springs, on November 8, 1883, which set the national park ball rolling.

Three railway workers stumbled onto the springs while prospecting on a day off from construction of the Canadian Pacific Railway, which had then entered the mountains. Their subsequent inept handling of the discovery literally got the trio into hot water, as many claims and counterclaims were made to "ownership" of the springs. There was no plumbing in the wild west, and hot water was as valuable as gold. Everyone wanted a piece of the action.

The Canadian government was forced to convene a hearing and settle the dispute. The outcome: most parties claiming an interest in the springs were compensated for expenditures made in "improvements," and the springs and a surrounding area of 26 sq km was set aside as a federal reserve — the forerunner of Banff National Park.

In 1886, George Stewart, the surveyor appointed to identify the boundaries of the Banff Hot Springs Reservation, recommended additional area warranted consideration as a national

Banff, Canada's first national park, was created in 1885. Today the park protects 6641 sq km, and is part of the four mountain parks block. These parks were designated a World Heritage Site in 1984.

Where Have All the Antlers Gone?

With all the antlers dropping off every year, why aren't we tripping over them every time we go for a walk? You will occasionally find a dropped antler in the woods, but many discarded antlers are eaten by rodents who crave the minerals in the bony material. The remainder quickly decompose. Antler collecting is not permitted in the national parks.

Left: In 1847, Methodist missionary Robert Rundle became one of the first Europeans to travel in the Bow Valley. He preached to Stoney Natives near Banff. The park's most famous mountain is now named for him.

Right: Mt. Rundle and the Bow Valley, seen from the overlook on the Mt. Norquay Road.

park. His comments were quickly heeded, and in June 1887, Rocky Mountains Park was established. Stewart served as its first superintendent for eleven years.

Regulations governing the protection of forests and wildlife followed by 1889. The area around Lake Louise was designated as a forest park reserve in 1892, and incorporated into Rocky Mountains Park in 1902 when the park area reached its maximum size.

The forerunners of Yoho and Glacier national parks were created in 1886, Waterton Lakes in 1895, and Jasper in 1907. Kootenay National Park was established in 1920. Today, Banff protects 6,641 sq km, and is part of the contiguous area of the four mountain parks, which includes 20,160 sq km. Over three million people visit Banff National Park each year.

Mt. Rundle
(2949 m/9676 ft)
The impressive cliffs of Mt. Rundle parallel the Trans-Canada High-

way for some 20 km from Canmore to Banff townsite, presenting one of the longest mountain walls visible from any roadway in the Rockies. These cliffs are nearly a mile (1.6 km) high at their highest point. They are comprised of sedimentary formations of the Palliser/Banff/Rundle sequence, which also forms many of the other massive cliffs in the front ranges.

The mountain is named for Robert T. Rundle, Methodist missionary to the Natives of the Bow Valley in 1847. Mt. Rundle was first climbed by pioneer surveyor J.J. McArthur in 1888. The highest point is the third summit south from Banff. Rundle's cliffs are popular with rock climbers in summer and waterfall ice climbers in winter.

Where's the River?
As you drive past the Cascade hydro-electric plant, the high banks on either side give the impression the Trans-Canada Highway is following a river

course. But if you look for the river, you won't find it.

It is likely the Bow River once flowed here, but moraines deposited at the end of the Wisconsin Glaciation blocked the river's course. Eventually a new course was eroded through the gap between Tunnel Mountain and Mt. Rundle, leaving this river bed abandoned. Many incomplete, pillar-like hoodoo formations have been eroded into the old river banks.

Tunnel Mountain

Tunnel Mountain was known to Natives as Sleeping Buffalo Mountain, because of its skyline profile when viewed from the east. It seems the original Canadian Pacific Railway survey of this part of the Bow Valley must have been cursory at best, for in 1882 the surveyor indicated a 275 metre long tunnel should be cut through the mountain. A follow-up investigation found ample room for the railway in the Bow Valley north of Tunnel Mountain, but the name has stuck.

Tunnel Mountain is actually an extension of Mt. Rundle. Glacial ice and the Bow River have eroded the channel that now separates the two. As is the case with many rounded summits in the Rockies, Tunnel Mountain was completely covered by glacial ice during the Wisconsin Glaciation.

Banff — Siding 29

Several of the key political and financial players in the construction of the Canadian Pacific Railway were Scottish. They left a legacy of Scottish names along the length of the railway in Alberta and British Columbia.

Banffshire, a picturesque Scottish county now named Grampian, was the birthplace of Sir George Stephen, the railway's first president. At a meeting in Montreal convened to discuss the railway's building of a resort hotel in the new Banff Hot Springs Reservation, the C.P.R. land commissioner, knowing the name would be a sentimental favourite to Stephen and C.P.R. stockholder Donald Smith (also from Banffshire), suggested the name "Banff." However, the decision for naming the resort really rested with the railway's manager, William Cornelius Van Horne, who was also present. Van Horne liked the name too, and so Siding 29, as it had been known until then, became Banff.

The original siding was located in the vicinity of the Buffalo Paddock. The first Banff railway station was constructed in 1887 near the present location, and Siding 29 was removed ten years later.

Variations on pronunciation of the word "Banff" are endless and comic: Ba-NIFF ... BARNFF ... BAN-fuh-fuh. According to Webster's, the correct pronunciation is BAMPFH.

Banff Townsite

The Cave and Basin
Birthplace of Banff

Sunset on Mt. Rundle and the Vermilion Lakes near the town of Banff is one of the classic views in the Canadian Rockies.

In 1875, two American hunters located the Cave and Basin hot springs, using information provided by Stoney Natives. A cabin was built nearby, and the two wintered in the area, trapping furs. One of the hunters intended to develop a claim on the springs, but lacked the means to hire a surveyor, The springs faded into obscurity.

In November 1883, three men employed in the construction of the Canadian Pacific Railway came to the vicinity of Banff on a day off, with the intention of prospecting for minerals on the slopes of Sulphur Mountain. As they approached the mountain they stumbled onto the springs now known as the Basin. Further investigation revealed the entrance to the Cave.

On a subsequent trip Frank McCabe and brothers William and Thomas McCardell used a limbed tree as a ladder, and climbed down into the Cave for a dip. In those days there was no plumbing in the wild west; a hot bath was a rarity. The prospectors had found liquid gold. They

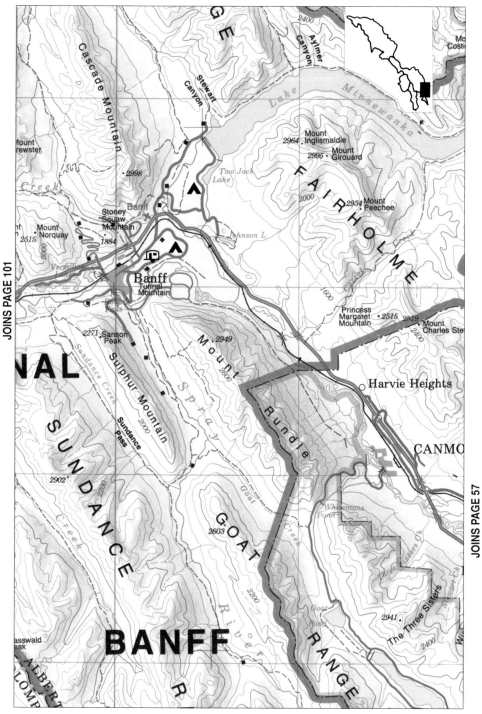

JOINS PAGE 101

JOINS PAGE 57

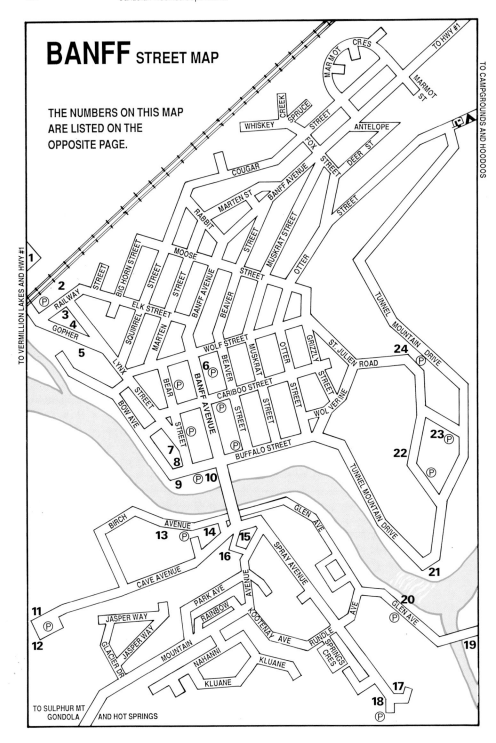

BANFF STREET MAP

THE NUMBERS ON THIS MAP
ARE LISTED ON THE
OPPOSITE PAGE.

built a crude fence around the springs, and a rough shack to establish their claim. Other explorations in the area located the Middle Springs and the Upper Hot Springs.

The trio's designs on the springs were confounded by their own bungling and by government red tape. The land around Banff was not surveyed, and the Ministry of Mines did not recognize hot water as a mineral on which a claim could be established — Catch-22. The whereabouts of the springs soon became local knowledge. The scent of dollars was as strong as that of sulphur emanating from the water, and attracted many others who attempted to file their own claims. To thoroughly confuse the issue, McCabe conspired to sell the trio's interest without consultation — to a federal Member of Parliament, no less!

Unknown to the prospectors, railway magnates Sandford Fleming and William Cornelius Van Horne were about this time suggesting a federal reserve be established in the vicinity of Banff — with the Canadian Pacific Railway to receive preferential treatment in matters relating to its development. The Canadian government realized the importance in having the railway pay its own way, and saw the opportunity a developed hot springs presented. Prime Minister Sir John A. Macdonald quipped: "these springs will recuperate the patient and recoup the treasury."

The Minister of Mines was instructed to draw up the necessary wording, and the 26 sq km Banff Hot Springs Reservation was established on November 28, 1885. The claimants would be dealt with later. It was neither the first nor the last time the C.P.R. would have its way in matters connected with the mountain national parks.

The Hot Springs inquiry convened in 1886. The outstanding claims were settled for the total of a few thousand dollars. The government had acquired the hot springs for a song, the C.P.R. had its hold on the area and Canada had the forerunner of Banff — its first national park.

Hot and Cold Running Water

Since Roman times, healing properties have been attributed to the waters of hot springs. While the validity of this is questioned by some, there is no question the presence of hot springs in the Rockies, close to settlement and transportation routes, was crucial to the initial popularity of the mountains with the gentry of the late Victorian era. For all the clear, cold, running streams in these mountains, a few hot springs received more praise in the early days.

The heated water that emerges at a hot spring was all originally surface water that filtered down through cracks and joints in the underlying rock. Rock within the earth's crust is hotter than on the

The following numbers refer to the map on the opposite page: 1. The Banff Recreation Centre and Ice Rink, 2. Train Station, 3. Police (RCMP), 4. Bus Terminal, 5. Mineral Springs Hospital, 6. Banff Park Information Centre, 7. Whyte Museum and Gallery, 8. Public Library, 9. Central Park, 10. Banff Park Museum, 11. Trail to Sundance Canyon, 12. Cave and Basin Pool and Interpretive Centre, 13. Recreation Grounds, 14. Luxton Museum, 15. Banff Park Administrative Building, 16. Cascade Rock Gardens, 17. Banff Springs Hotel, 18. Banff Springs Conference Centre, 19. Banff Springs Golf Course, 20. Bow Falls, 21. Banff Springs Lookout, 22. Banff Centre for the Arts, 23. Eric Harvey Theatre, 24. Tunnel Mountain Trail

Early swimmers enjoy the hot waters of the Basin, now part of the Cave and Basin exhibit.

surface. The temperature increases approximately 1°C for every 33 m descent into the earth until, 2.5 km below the surface, the temperature is hot enough to boil water. Any groundwater that manages to filter down this far is heated and pressurized, and naturally percolates back to the surface along other crack systems.

With the eight hot springs at Banff, the return to the surface is conveniently achieved along the Sulphur Mountain Thrust Fault.

During the round trip, the water dissolves and absorbs mineral content from the surrounding rock. As a result some of the hot springs are slightly radioactive — formerly a desired healing property. The "rotten egg" smell is partly due to sulphur in the water, but more due to the fact that algae in the water metabolizes the sulphur, and gives off hydrogen sulphide as a by-product. The minerals and algae combine to give the waters their unique colours.

Mineral deposits of crumbly tufa (TOO-fah) mark active and inactive outlets of hot springs. Tufa is sponge-like in appearance,

Developed Hot Springs in the Mountain National Parks

Name	Temperature °C (Average)
Upper Hot Springs, Banff	47.3
Cave, Banff	32.8
Basin, Banff	34.5
Radium Hot Springs	47.7
Miette Hot Springs	53.9

and is mostly comprised of calcite — crystallized deposits of calcium. The tufa deposits in the vicinity of the Cave and Basin are seven metres thick.

If the groundwater does not filter to a significant depth, or if it becomes mixed with cold water on its return to the surface, the discharge from a spring will not be hot. Such springs are called mineral springs. The Paint Pots in Kootenay and The Ink Pots in Banff are examples. There are also many cold water springs in the Rockies.

Developing the Feature Attraction

Developments at the Cave and Basin began the year after the reserve was established. In 1887, bathhouses were installed, and a tunnel was blasted to reach the Cave. Whether seeking miracle cures, soaking tired joints, or just enjoying the high life, bathers paid ten cents a swim.

In an event that foreshadowed things to come, part of the adjacent cliff fractured and collapsed into the swimming pool. Cold water was discovered seeping into the area. To protect the park's feature attraction, George Stewart, the first park superintendent, decided to encase the pools with concrete.

During a visit in 1911, J. B. Harkin, the first national parks commissioner, was impressed by the popularity of the hot springs. He also noticed that facilities at the Cave and Basin could not handle the demands of heavy visitation. The following year,

The Cave and Basin has been one of Banff's premier attractions since the park was founded. The initial structures were replaced in 1914 with a facility designed by Walter Painter. In 1985, the Canadian Parks Service reconstructed this building as part of the National Parks Centennial. Over one million people now visit the site annually.

architect Walter Painter, who designed renovations at the Banff Springs Hotel and Chateau Lake Louise, was hired to design a new swimming facility. Constructed between 1912 and 1914 at a cost of $200,000, the new Cave and Basin featured the largest swimming pool in Canada at the time. In its architecture and finishing, the structure was hailed as a masterpiece for its aesthetic combination of function and form.

Minerals in the hot spring water contributed to the eventual demise of the original Cave and Basin. When crumbly deposits of tufa beneath the pool settled, the walls cracked, and the building became unsafe. Public health regulations demanded chlorination of the hot pools, and it was found the chlorine combined with minerals in the water to produce an unhealthy sediment. Looking every bit its age, the Cave and Basin was closed in 1976.

Amidst proposals to turn the site into a commemorative garden in time for the national parks centennial in 1985, the "Save the Cave and Basin Swimming Pools Committee" was formed locally to garner public support for a restoration project. Over 21,000 people signed a petition, supplying impetus for the grant of funding and, instead of building a

A Touch of the Tropics

The eight hot springs in the vicinity of Banff have a combined outflow of over 3,800 litres/minute. Most of this hot water eventually drains into the montane wetlands west of Banff townsite, where it has a moderating effect on the local environment.

Calypso orchid

Wild orchids commonly occur in the Rockies in damp locations such as this, but not normally with such abundance. Six species bloom here in spring. The hot springs water raises the temperature of the wetlands enough that they remain largely ice-free. Migratory bird species, including ducks, Canada geese and killdeer, sometimes take advantage of this, and save themselves the flight south or west by becoming year-round residents.

There are minnows and sticklebacks that are native to these warm waters, but in the past aquarium buffs tampered with Nature's balance, installing their own favourites to see if they would survive. Mosquitofish were also introduced as part of an official government attempt to cut down on mosquitos in the Banff area. Some of these introduced species have fared too well, and competition with the two native fish species threatens them with extinction. One of these fish, the Banff Longnose dace, occurs nowhere else on earth. The non-poisonous wandering garter snake, a rarity in Banff, may also be seen here.

garden, the Canadian Parks Service spent $12 million rebuilding the Cave and Basin as a replica of Painter's 1912 design. A facsimile of the original 1886 bathhouse was also constructed, complete with rental bathing suits of that era. The Cave and Basin Centennial Centre was officially opened by the Duke of Edinburgh during a royal visit in 1985. Over one million people now visit the site annually.

Several walking trails depart from Cave and Basin. The Discovery Trail leads to the upper entry of the Cave, and details the story of its discovery. Displays along the Marsh Trail describe how the hot spring water affects the local ecology. Another trail leads to Sundance Canyon.

Dr. Brett's Sanitarium

Dr. R. G. Brett, a medical supervisor for the Canadian Pacific Railway, knew a good thing when he saw one. Hot springs, a new railway, a new park, and the Victorian fascination with "healing waters" meant potential for big business. Soon Brett was installed as doctor to the park as well, and opened a private spa/hospital at Banff.

Brett's Sanitarium was one of two hotels hastily constructed in Banff in 1886. It could accommodate 50 guests and 40 of the doctor's patients. Hot spring water, advertised to cure every ill, was piped 2,400 m from the Upper Hot Springs, to a variety of baths.

For the privilege of using the water, Brett paid the government $15 per tub, per year. For the benefit of soaking, clients paid substantially more — $2 a day — and not all in Banff were happy with developments: "The Sanitorium, which being under skilled medical supervision, enjoys a practical monopoly of those visiting the springs in search of health." Despite the complaints, many clients testified to the healing powers both of the waters and Dr. Brett's treatments.

Also in 1886, Brett constructed the Grandview Villa at the Upper Hot Springs. By its own advertisement, the Villa doubled as massage parlour and billiard hall. "Ice cold temperance drinks" were sold. When the Villa burned in 1901, the government didn't renew the lease, and took over subsequent development of the Upper Hot Springs itself.

As with many frontier businessmen, Brett diversified, operating a transportation service, a

Dr. R.G. Brett operated a number of facilities in Banff in the late 1800's and early 1900's. The most famous of these, Brett's Sanitarium, was a combination spa and hospital, in which hot spring water was used to cure ailments. This building stood on the site now occupied by the park administration building.

Top: The Upper Hot Springs are one of eight hot springs in the vicinity of Banff townsite. The waters are significantly warmer than at Cave and Basin.

Bottom: When the Banff Springs Hotel opened in 1888, it was the largest hotel in the world. Room rates started at $3.50 per day.

drug store, and an opera house, selling bottled "Banff Lithia Water" and becoming involved in politics. He served 13 years as a member of the provincial Legislative Assembly, and later was Lieutenant Governor of Alberta. Mt. Brett, in the Massive Range west of Banff, commemorates him.

The Sanitarium, subsequently named the Bretton Hall Hotel, burned in 1933. The site has been occupied by the Banff National Park administration building since 1936. The building's colourful and well-tended garden makes a picturesque foreground for the view along Banff Avenue to Cascade Mountain.

Upper Hot Springs

"I threw away the crutches I had used for four years, after I had been here ten days." During Banff's early days, many such testimonials were uttered as to the healing powers of the hot spring water. Handrails on the stairway to Dr. Brett's Grandview Villa were reinforced with crutches no longer needed by patients — although it was reported that upon arrival, the doctor issued all patients with crutches, whether they required them or not!

In 1901, the government cancelled Dr. Brett's lease and began development of a public facility at the Upper Hot Springs. The present structure was completed in 1935. Fifty years later, the operation of this facility was considered for privatization. In an announcement that recalled the roots of Canada's national park system, the Minister of the Environment stated the hot spring water belonged to all Canadians, and should not be given over to private interests.

Banff Springs Hotel

The Canadian Pacific Railway was completed through the Rockies in 1884. While the essential objectives in building a trans-continental railway were to bind the

young country together, and to make accessible new lands for settlement, it was apparent it would be some years before commerce in western Canada would reach a level to allow the railway to become a paying proposition.

The huge debt incurred in constructing the railway demanded a more immediate cash flow. With an eye on the splendid scenery of the Rockies, and with the presence of hot springs and national parks thrown in, C.P.R. Vice President and General Manager William Cornelius Van Horne had the answer: "Since we can't export the scenery, we'll have to import the tourists."

The C.P.R.'s chain of mountain hotels was initiated in 1886 with the construction of railside structures such as Mt. Stephen House in Field. For Banff, Van Horne envisioned more of a resort, and chose a site at the confluence of the Bow and Spray Rivers. Famed architect Bruce Price was commissioned to design the building, which would eventually cost a quarter of a million dollars, and construction of the C.P.R.'s first "chateau-style" hotel began.

In the summer of 1887, Van Horne visited the construction site and was shocked to see the building improperly oriented, by a factor of 180°! The kitchen overlooked the rivers, and the guest rooms faced the forest. He hastily sketched additions to correct the matter. Amidst much national interest, the 250-room hotel, complete with sulphur water

The view from the Banff Springs Hotel features the Bow River and the gap between Mt. Rundle and Tunnel Mountain. The Fairholme range can be seen in the distance.

Today the Banff Springs Hotel can accommodate 1,100 guests in its 578 rooms.

piped 2,100 m from the Upper Hot Springs, opened June 1, 1888. It was the largest hotel in the world at the time. Room rates started at $3.50 a day.

The Banff Springs Hotel was opulent in appearance, if initially lacking in ability to deliver matching service. Its immediate effect was to turn the tiny community of Banff into a destination resort for the gentry of the late Victorian era. Over 5,000 visitors arrived in the year after the hotel opened. The capacity of the building was increased to 500 in 1903. In 1904, almost 10,000 guests registered, and many were turned away to sleep in railway cars at the train station. The season was lengthened as needed to accommodate business.

Plans were drawn in 1911 to completely overhaul the building, but initially only one major expansion was undertaken — the $2 million Painter Tower, designed and constructed by C.P.R. architect Walter Painter and completed in 1914. "Rundle rock" from a quarry along the Spray River was used to face the addition. As one visitor commented: "The building is high. There is only one thing higher in the attractive concern, which is the price of liquor."

Between 1925 and 1928, the remainder of the expansion and reconstruction took place, yielding the building we see today. It has been described as having "corridors for the invalid, turrets for the astronomer, and balconies for the lovers." In the midst of this construction, the original wooden north wing burned to the ground.

The C.P.R. lavished a great deal of money on furnishing the pride of its hotel fleet. Talented craftsmen worked with the finest materials. Windows were imported from Europe, and stone from Manitoba. The furniture and ornaments were painstakingly detailed to match period pieces. For a short while when it was first completed the new Banff Springs Hotel itself eclipsed the scenery as the principal drawing card in the Rockies.

Over the past century, the Banff Springs has housed many noted guests — movie stars, royalty, diplomats, and heads of state

Norman Luxton

In a community whose history is noted for its colourful, larger-than-life figures, one Banff resident assumes prominence — Norman Luxton. The son of a Winnipeg newspaper editor, Luxton was a man of adventure. He arrived in Banff at the turn of the century after several of his newspaper ventures in Vancouver had failed, and after he had taken part in paddling a Native dugout war canoe partway across the Pacific Ocean.

Luxton immediately resurrected the local newspaper, *The Crag and Canyon*, which he published until 1951. Using its presses he also wrote and published guidebooks to Banff and vicinity. In 1906 Luxton was instrumental in Canada's purchase of a threatened bison herd from Montana, which he helped transport to Wainwright, Alberta. Descendants of these animals can be viewed today at Elk Island National Park.

Luxton changed the way Banff viewed itself as a resort when he constructed the King Edward Hotel. Up until that time, Banff was a seasonal town, with facilities open during summer only. At the hotel's opening, Luxton announced the King Edward would operate year-round and never close. To illustrate the point he threw the front door keys into the bush. The annual Banff Winter Carnival was soon organized by Luxton to help generate winter business.

It was for Luxton's relationships with Stoney Natives from Morley and Nordegg that he will be most remembered. For 47 years he was involved in the organization of the Banff Indian Days, and for his forthright dealings and sincere interest in Native culture, he earned the trust and respect of the Stoneys. He married a Native from Morley, and was always quick to assist on the reservation when needed.

In 1952 Luxton announced he would be opening a Native museum in Banff at his Trading Post on the Bow River. Later, with the backing of Calgary's Glenbow-Alberta Institute, Luxton moved his record of 60 years' involvement with the Stoneys into an adjacent building. The Luxton Museum of the Plains Indian still operates today. Luxton died in 1962 at the age of 86. Stoneys in full Native dress attended his funeral.

52. CORKSCREW DRIVE, BANFF

Top: At Bow Falls the Bow River is eroding downwards into a joint between the underlying rock formations. The falls are reached in a short walk from the Bow River Bridge, or the Banff Springs Hotel.

Bottom: Corkscrew Drive was a feature of Tunnel Moutain drive in the 1920's.

The golf course at the Banff Springs Hotel is considered one of the 10 most scenic in the world. The original course was completed using prisoner-of-war labour during the First World War. The course was completely redesigned by Stanley Thompson in 1927, to a length of 6,729 yards, and par 71.

Bow Falls

A visit to nearby Bow Falls is a popular walking excursion from the Banff Springs Hotel. The Bow River takes its name from a Native Cree word for "bow," in reference to the fact that wood suitable for making hunting bows was found along its banks. The headwaters of the river is the Wapta Icefield above Bow Lake, 90 km to the north.

Tunnel Mountain Drive

If you think traffic in Banff is bad today, consider the situation facing horse and buggy on the original Tunnel Mountain Drive! A series of tight switchbacks climbed the steepest section of the road, giving rise to the name Corkscrew Drive. With the advent of motor vehicles in the park in 1915, the switchbacks were removed.

Tunnel Mountain Drive is Banff's back road, and it's particularly suited to cyclists. This road is closed to vehicles in winter.

an array of colourful events connected with the hotel has been recorded. For instance, Banff's air strip was built in the 1930's, when jazz musician Benny Goodman wished to visit the hotel — by plane!

Today, the Banff Springs Hotel is no longer operated by the railway, but by Canadian Pacific Hotels. It can accommodate 1,100 guests in 578 rooms. The staff are are housed nearby in residences constructed in 1988.

Top: Constructed in 1959, the Sulphur Mountain Gondola provides fast access to a mountain top environment, with a panoramic overview of Banff and the Bow Valley.

Left: The opportunity to observe and appreciate wildlife is central to the mountain national park experience.

Sulphur Mountain Gondola

The eight minute gondola ride to the crest of Sulphur Mountain whisks you to an elevation of 2,285 metres, and is the easiest way to a mountain top near Banff. The gondola was built in 1959. Since then over nine million visitors have stepped aboard. The pano-

Members of the famous red-coated Royal Canadian Mounted Police march in the July 1 Canada Day Parade on Banff Avenue.

ramic view from the gondola's upper terminal includes Banff townsite, the Bow Valley, Lake Minnewanka and the surrounding mountain ranges, and is highly recommended.

Sulphur Mountain is a favour-ite haunt of bighorn sheep. You may be surprised and alarmed at how tolerant these particular animals have become of humans. They are accustomed to being fed, and now expect similar treatment from all visitors. Please refrain from this harmful practice.

Norman Sanson, for whom the north peak of Sulphur Mountain is named, frequented this ridgetop for over 30 years earlier this century, without the benefit of a gondola. In his capacity as curator and meteorologist for the Banff Park Museum, Sanson was required to make trips every other week to the observatory, to record weather data. Evidently he liked the job, or the exercise, or the view, for he doubled the required frequency of ascents of the mountain, eventually logging

Banff's Big City Problem

Banff is crowded in the summer, and parking is at a premium. To help alleviate traffic and parking problems, you might consider leaving your vehicle where allowed, and walking to reach various points of interest in the townsite. But please note, time limits on parking were enacted in 1990, and are being enforced.

Large recreational vehicles and trailers are not permitted in the townsite, and should be parked at the designated trailer drop-off sites near the industrial compound and at the train station.

over 1,000 trips. The last of these was in 1945, to make observations of a solar eclipse. The Vista Trail leads to the now abandoned observatory.

The Banff Park Museum
The University of the Hills

The Victorian gentry visiting Banff around the turn of the century had a tremendous fascination with the animals of the "wild west." Although many of these visitors would never stray too far from the carriage roads and bridle paths, they still needed close contact with game animals to complete their mountain experience.

The government of Canada obliged, and in 1895 created a museum that displayed stuffed examples of the wildlife of western Canada. In 1903 the present museum building was constructed, at the then considerable cost of $10,000. Reflecting the contemporary "railway style" of architecture, the museum was finished inside with Douglas fir, and designed to allow natural lighting.

This building, which still houses the Banff Park Museum, was restored in 1985 as part of the National Parks Centennial. It has been designated a National Historic Site, and is the oldest natural history museum in western Canada.

From 1904 to 1937, the grounds between the building and the Bow River were occupied by a zoo and aviary. Eventually, over 60 species were represented. Not all were native to the Rockies — one of the most popular was a polar bear! Attitudes gradually changed, and it became evident that protection of animals in the wild was more consistent with the aims of the National Park Act than having them caged and on display. The zoo was closed in 1937, and the animals were shipped to other institutions.

While many of the exhibits in

Black-billed Magpie

The black-billed magpie is one of the most easily recognized birds in the Rockies. Its black hood and bill contrast with the white chest and white wing flashes. The wings and long tail are highlighted with green.

This vocal member of the crow family is a common, year-round resident of townsites. You'll often see magpies on sidewalks and around garbage cans — anywhere there is a chance for an easy meal. They have a shameless appetite and eat almost anything, including young from other birds' nests. Their own nests are large, garish collections of sticks. Look for them in trees along the Bow River in Banff townsite.

Cascade mountain remains largely the same, but times have changed the look of Banff Avenue in the past century. Self-government for the town will see a spate of construction, as business and residential development expands to fill newly zoned areas.

the museum reflect the "trophy head" mentality that prevailed in the early 1900's, some demonstrate a perception decades ahead of its time — the portrayal of animals as integral parts of an ecosystem.

The Campus in the Clouds

The Banff Centre for the Arts had modest beginnings as a summer theatre school in 1933. The first campus on Tunnel Mountain was constructed in 1947. This facility was affiliated with the University of Calgary until 1978. To the performing artist, The Centre provides resources and instruction for advanced artistic development amidst inspirational surroundings. Artists of many disciplines attend; some live in resi-

dence on campus. The benefits to the public are frequent recitals, concerts, readings, displays and performances.

The Banff Festival of the Arts is held during the summer, and a centre for management stages several annual events, including the Banff Television Festival and the Banff Festival of Mountain Films. These attract international entries and attention.

The Centre's Eric Harvie and Margaret Greenham theatres are the venues for film, theatre, ballet, dance and concerts. The Walter Phillips Gallery presents art exhibits of an international calibre. Check the Centre's schedule for entertainment opportunities.

Whyte Museum of the Canadian Rockies

Artists Peter and Catharine Whyte had already made tremendous personal contributions to the artistic heritage of the Rockies when they decided to preserve the writings, artwork and memorabilia of other Rocky Mountain artists and pioneers. In the mid-1950's they established the Whyte Foundation, and began collecting materials. In 1968 this collection became available to the public, when the Whyte Museum of the Canadian Rockies opened. Housed in the museum is the Archives of the Canadian Rockies—the largest existing collection of artistic and historical materials related to these mountains, with some 4,000 volumes. Also included are manuscript collections, oral history tapes of many pioneers, explorers and outfitters, and extensive photographic collections. Featured are those of Byron Harmon and the Vaux family. The museum also houses the

Leslie Taylor
First Mayor of Banff, 1990

I'm an army brat – I went to 11 different schools in 13 grades, in four countries. But that's very good preparation for being the mayor of Banff, actually. I first came here as a ballet student at The Banff Centre for the Arts in 1968, and then I came back in the late '70s to work for the Canadian Parks Service here, as a park naturalist and planner, after I'd done a degree in fisheries and wildlife biology. Then in 1981 I came here permanently to work on the Cave and Basin Centennial Project, the reconstruction of the hot springs.
***

The decision to run for mayor took about eight months to make. There were all kinds of components to it. A lot of people were urging me to run, and saying 'we need you to do this job.' I was excited by the potential of the job, and I've been concerned for a long time about the difficulty of managing a town like Banff, with its constraints, and its very special ambience which is so fragile, and could easily be destroyed. So, I believed that the challenge was an exciting one. On the down side, my husband and I knew what it meant in terms of loss of privacy and in work load. Eventually, and it was very much a joint decision, we decided that I should run. And largely thanks to the work of about 40 volunteers, we won.
***

My platform was one of trying to reach some sort of a balance between quality of life for the residents and a good visitor experience for our visitors. It would probably be easier if you only focussed on one or the other. It's the balance between the two that is so difficult to find. But I think that's what my mandate is.

Whyte Foundation also has in its care two heritage homes and four log cabins, built and formerly occupied by Banff area pioneers. Tours are available.

The Whyte Museum makes a particularly good rainy day diversion in Banff. It is open daily in the summer, and operates with reduced hours in the winter. The upper level gallery and archives are wheelchair accessible.

Cascade Mountain
2998 m/9836 ft

2,075 volume Alpine Club of Canada library.

Three exhibit areas in the building feature displays of contemporary and historic art, and the largest gallery is also frequently the venue for lectures, films, readings and concerts. The

The mountain that forms the northern backdrop for the town of Banff was named by James Hector in 1858, as a translation from the Stoney name Minnehappa — "mountain where the water falls." Coal seams occur in the lower flanks of the mountain,

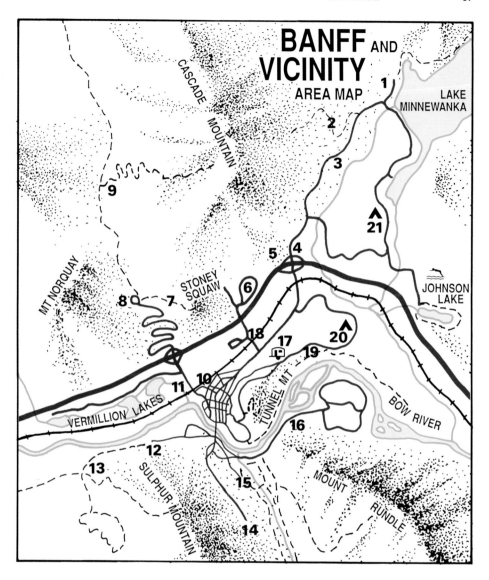

BANFF AND **VICINITY**
AREA MAP

Legend

1. Lake Minnewanka Boat tours
2. "C" Level Cirque trail
3. Bankhead exhibit
4. Cascade Pits picnic site
5. Banff airstrip
6. Buffalo Paddock
7. Stoney Squaw Mountain trail
8. Norquay ski area
9. Cascade Amphitheatre trail
10. Banff townsite
11. Fenland trail
12. Cave and Basin
13. Sundance Canyon trail
14. Sulphur Mountain Gondola
15. Banff Springs Hotel and Spray River trail
16. Banff Springs Golf Course
17. Tunnel Mountain campsite (R.V.)
18. Banff Industrial Compound and trailer dumping station
19. Hoodoo viewpoint
20. Tunnel Mt. campsite (tent)
21. Two Jack campsite

and the mining of these gave rise to the town of Bankhead in 1903.

Cascade Mountain was first climbed in 1887, by a party that included outfitter Tom Wilson. Although the mountain has a formidable appearance, an easy, if long, mountaineering route lies along the left skyline. The frozen waterfall is popular with ice climbers.

Banff Train Station

Banff's original train station, Siding 29, was located in the vicinity of the present day Buffalo Paddock. As the principal destination for those getting off a train in Banff was the hot springs and the Banff Springs Hotel, it soon became evident to the Canadian Pacific Railway that a station closer to these attractions was required.

When William Corenlius Van Horne, the railway's general man-

David Morrison
President, Brewster Transportation and Tourism

I'm originally from the Maritimes, and I began working with Brewster's as a driver. One of the things I've tried to do is to help reshape the focus of the company back to landscape experience, authenticity and accuracy. Back, in fact, to the company's original goals, which were quite consistent with the national park values. I saw that visitors were getting more sophisticated, and that at the same time there was a renewed interest in landscape. In order to satisfy visitors' expectations, we aimed to give the highest possible quality interpretation and the best quality of equipment.

***

It's interesting, with Brewster's you have what was once a very small local company, started by the two Brewster brothers back in the late 1800s, that now, as a result of the new recognition of the importance of unspoiled natural landscapes, finds itself in a geographical position that is a focus of global tourism interest. And as a result of that this small company has really become global in nature.

***

It's absolutely essential to our survival that the parks be maintained in excellent natural condition. The national parks are the main attraction for visitors who want to use our services. And we have distinguished ourselves from our competitors by becoming absolute experts in our efforts to understand the park and communicate and interpret the park values and park experiences. Now, parks get heavy use — the only way their quality is going to be retained is if that use is minimum in its impact. And that's one of the things that we can do as a company. Because we keep to the highways. We concentrate people in a single vehicle. And we try very, very hard to celebrate those park values.

From Buckskin to Buses

The history of exploration of the Rockies in the late 19th and early 20th centuries is essentially one of travel by packhorse, over trails new and old. To the outfitters and guides fell the responsibility of equipping a party of city folk for weeks or months of travel in the wilds, suggesting and clearing the route, and dealing with the various disasters that could befall greenhorns on horseback in an unforgiving environment. The colourful characters attracted to the profession of outfitting and guiding left behind more than a legacy of tall tales. In one case, a transportation and tour business with packhorse origins at the turn of the century still thrives today.

Outfitting was a tough market to break into, but two young brothers from Banff, Bill and Jim Brewster, gained a foothold in 1902. That year, the C.P.R. sent them to a sportsman's show in New York City to drum up business for the Rockies and, by agreement, for themselves. They were successful on both counts, and soon had the finances to begin outfitting large parties.

The company came under the control of Jim Brewster in 1909, and the various interests were divided into two operations: Brewster Trading, and Brewster Livery (or transportation). In 1912, a 60-room hotel was purchased. Renamed the Mt. Royal Hotel, this attractive building eventually gave Brewster the opportunity to market complete vacation packages in the Rockies.

In 1915, regulations governing automobiles in the national parks were relaxed, and Jim became owner of the first automobile in Banff National Park. Impressed with its potential, he committed to the massive and expensive enterprise of turning a horse-oriented carriage and outfitting business into a motor-oriented tour company. The Brewster Transport Company, forerunner of today's Brewster Transportation, came into existence.

In 1913 it was said of Jim Brewster that he had "done more to put the town on the map ... than all the other residents combined." Through his many enterprises and interests, Brewster continued to be a spokesman and emissary for tourism in Banff and the Canadian Rockies until his death in 1947.

Family ownership of Brewster Transportation ended in 1965, with purchase by Greyhound Canada. The company still operates under the name Brewster, and today utilizes a fleet of buses and Snocoaches to provide transportation and sightseeing tours to Rocky Mountain visitors.

The Tunnel Mountain Hoodoos have been sculpted by water from deposits of glacial rubble. Capstones formerly protected these pillars, allowing them to become free-standing, while the surrounding material weathered away.

ager, visited Banff in 1887 to inspect the construction of the Banff Springs Hotel, he twice demonstrated his renowned reputation as a man of action. First, when he saw the hotel was incorrectly oriented by a factor of 180°, he sketched plans for a rotunda to salvage the view. Next, when asked about plans for the new railway station, he grabbed a piece of paper, fired off another quick sketch and said: "Lots of good logs there. Cut them, peel them, and build your station."

The log structure was subsequently expanded and saw service until 1910, when the present stone and stucco structure replaced it. This newer building is commonly referred to as the "most famous railway station in Canada."

The federal government suspended transcontinental passenger service through Banff in early 1990. A privatized, tourist-oriented service, which operates during the summer only, began operations the same year.

Tunnel Mountain Hoodoos

Surface water and rainfall running down riverbanks of glacial till have eroded narrow, vertical furrows, creating the distinctive, pillared shapes of the Tunnel Mountain Hoodoos. At one time the hoodoos were probably all covered in capstones which protected the material directly beneath, while the adjacent unprotected material weathered away.

Natives thought the hoodoos were giants turned to stone, who

slept by day and terrorized travellers by night. Another legend tells how the hoodoos are teepees that house "bad gods." Other hoodoos in this area are found at the east exit for Canmore. Incomplete formations are at roadside east of the Cascade hydro-electric plant. Hoodoos with huge boulder caps occur at the east end of Lake Minnewanka.

Bankhead

In 1885, surveyor George Dawson reported the existence of high grade coal known as semi-anthracite, outcropping in the mountains east of Canmore and Banff. The Canadian Anthracite Company was first to begin mining this coal in 1886, and entered into a supply agreement with the recently completed Canadian Pa-

cific Railway, the tracks of which passed conveniently nearby. Not wishing to depend on an outside supplier, the railway acquired the rights to other claims in the area, and in 1903 created a subsidiary company to mine coal to fire its locomotives.

The C.P.R. selected narrow seams in the base of Cascade Mountain for its mining operations. Rather than digging mine shafts down into the mountain as is common, reaching the seams necessitated burrowing upwards on a slight angle. The coal was then knocked down into mining cars, which gravity assisted in returning to the mine portal. Three points of entry at different levels gave access to the seams, and 55 km of mining tunnels were excavated. Production peaked in

A mining town called Bankhead flourished at the base of Cascade Mountain between 1903 and 1922. When coal mining operations folded, all of the buildings were destroyed or removed. Many are now in Banff and Canmore. Today the visitor can explore the abandoned townsite on a self-guiding interpretive trail.

1911, with 300 men employed below ground and 180 above, and 250,000 tonnes of coal mined.

A boom town developed near the mine. Named Bankhead, after yet another Scottish town, it had every convenience of the day, including a hotel, skating rink, tennis courts, library, and an electricity plant sufficient to supply power to Banff townsite as well. At the height of the mining operations, over 1,000 people, mostly immigrants, lived at the

Bighorn Sheep

The bighorn sheep, symbol of Banff National Park, is frequently seen in the Rockies. Visitors often confuse bighorns with mountain goats: just remember that sheep are brown and goats are white.

The bighorn ram is about one metre tall at the shoulder and, when mature, sports a set of thick, brown horns that spiral. The horns are not shed, and it is possible to determine the age of rams by counting the prominent sections of a horn — one for each year. The bighorn's grayish-brown winter coat is shed in June, temporarily giving it a shabby appearance. In summer, the coat is a light or medium brown, with matching brown on the short tail and a tawny rump patch. The female (ewe) is considerably smaller than the ram, and grows thin brown horns that curve backwards.

Bighorns live in flocks of up to 50 animals. A hierarchy is established amongst the mature rams. At any time during the year, rams will pair off and duel, rearing up on their hind legs and charging head first in an impressive and noisy spectacle. After the tremendous impact (rams can weigh to 125 kg), they hold still to allow inspection of each other's horns. The ram with the less impressive set will usually defer, but if the horns are of similar size the two may duel to the point of exhaustion. Rams are protected from serious injury in these battles by the mass of the horns, and by special armour bones within the skull.

The dominant male leads the rams away from the ewes and young lambs in summer, moving to favourite grazing territory. In autumn, the flock regroups in the valleys for the rut, and the dominant male must defend his position again in order to collect a harem of breeding-age ewes. While the position of the dominant male in the flock changes frequently, the dominant female, who dictates the summer movements of the ewes and lambs, may endure many years. A single lamb is born in late spring.

In common with the mountain goat, bighorn sheep will often descend to mineral licks at roadside. They are generally quite tolerant of people, sometimes too much so — the sheep at Tangle Falls and Lake Minnewanka are becoming more and more bold with each passing year, and have even been observed at automotive mineral licks ... eating the rust off parked vehicles!

Road kills are a major drain on the population of bighorn sheep — please reduce your speed, and be prepared to stop.

base of Cascade Mountain.

A sad aspect of life at Bankhead was that of the 60 or so Chinese labourers. These men had the dirtiest of jobs — sorting the different coal pieces by hand. They lived apart from the Europeans in an area known as Chinatown. Rhubarb that they planted in their gardens still grows at Bankhead today.

Labour unrest and failing economics put an end to the mining in 1922, and soon thereafter every building in the town was removed or demolished. Many were transported intact to Banff, Canmore and Calgary. The miners either took up a new way of life locally, or moved on to other coal mining areas in western North America.

Today, the visitor can enjoy an interpretive walk through the ruins of Bankhead. Hikers can follow the C-Level Cirque trail onto the flanks of Cascade Mountain, passing the highest mine entrance en route. New mining claims have not been allowed in the mountain national parks since the passing of the National Parks Act in 1930, and the last mining operation ceased in Yoho in 1952.

Lake Minnewanka

Lake Minnewanka — the largest body of water in Banff National Park — is a reservoir. The outlet of the original lake was first dammed in 1912. With the loss of the hydro-electric plant at Bankhead in 1922, a new facility was installed to supply power for Banff. In 1941, yet another dam was constructed, to greatly in-

Lake Minnewanka is an artificial reservoir, and the largest body of water in Banff National Park. Several dams have been constructed at the lake's outlet to facilitate hydro-electric development. These dams have lengthened the lake by eight kilometres, and raised the water level by 25 m. The town of Minnewanka Landing, which formerly stood on the lakeshore, now lies submerged.

The Wood bison (buffalo) was formerly an endangered species, but largely due to the success of breeding at Banff and a few other sites, it has been removed from the endangered list.

crease the output of the Cascade hydro-electric plant.

One translation for the Native name "Minnewanka" gives "Lake of the Water Spirit." Apparently the spirit is not benign, for the more common translation is "Devil's Lake." A Native legend tells of a creature — half fish, half human — that can move the lake waters at will. Apparently such creatures formerly lived in other lakes in the Rockies, too. According to Natives, many were killed by lightning.

Boating and fishing have been popular on Lake Minnewanka since the 1880's. A 15 kg lake trout was caught here in 1987. The motor launches *Daughter of the Peaks* and *The Aylmer* once plied the waters from the resort village of Minnewanka Landing. The vil-

lage, complete with warden station, was submerged when the resevoir was created, and scuba divers often explore the ruins. Today a commercial boat tour operates on the lake. Minnewanka is the only lake on which gas-powered motor boats may be launched in Banff National Park.

Other highlights in the vicinity include the presence of fossils in many of the rock outcrops, a short walk to Stewart Canyon (suitable for families), a plaque commemorating the Palliser Expedition and a particularly bold flock of bighorn sheep.

Buffalo Paddock

The bison is North America's largest land mammal. ("Buffalo" is more correctly applied to certain wild cattle of Africa and Asia.)

As the water level rises upstream from the dam, a pond is created. The pond must be deep enough not to freeze in winter. The beaver selects an elevation on the pond bottom on which to build a large, dome-shaped house — the lodge. The industry required to create and maintain the dam, pond and lodge is a family effort. The beaver remains in its lodge all winter, feeding from a food supply cached underwater.

The beaver is chiefly nocturnal, thus compensating for its vulnerability while on land. In the water, when alarmed, the beaver smacks its tail on the surface as a warning, then dives. If the lodge is nearby, it heads home. Otherwise it can remain submerged for 15 minutes.

Beavers mate for life and breed annually. The kits are born in mid-spring and stay with the parents until the beginning of their third year, so there may be three generations of beavers living in a single lodge. When the young adults move out, they travel as much as several hundred kilometres to find a suitable location for their own pond.

In creating a pond, the beaver does a great service to other animals. Moose, deer and elk, which also require wetland vegetation, are provided additional range. Populations of fish inhabit the waters, and fish-eating birds such as the osprey and great blue heron take up residence. But for the beaver, there comes a point of diminishing return for its incredible industry. The pond eventually begins to fill with sedges and, as its nearby food supply diminishes, the beaver is forced to relocate.

The Fenland Trail and Vermilion Lakes are two of the best places in the Rockies to view beaver.

Beaver

The beaver, Canada's national animal, whose likeness appears on the nickel coin, is the largest rodent in the Canadian Rockies. Remarkable swimmers, beavers possess a large, flat tail that functions as a rudder, a source of propulsion, and as a prop to balance when gnawing at tree trunks.

The beaver prefers to eat the inner bark of deciduous trees — especially trembling aspen. Shrubs, saplings, and aquatic plants are also prominent in its diet. At home in the water, the beaver creates wetlands to ensure it can safely travel to and from its favourite sources of food. It builds a dam on a slow-moving waterway using trees, branches, rocks and mud. Trees are felled with the incisors, towed by mouth, and put into place with agile hands. Beavers are known to fell trees 1.7 metres in diameter, but prefer those 20-25 centimetres.

There are two subspecies, Wood and Plains. The Wood bison was native to this area. The last record of a Wood bison in the wild in the Rockies was 1858, when one was killed in the Pipestone Valley near Lake Louise.

Respected and utilized by Natives for millenia, the bison was subjected to wholesale slaughter by both Natives and Whites when firearms, horses and farming were introduced onto its range. The animal was depleted through hunting from an estimated population of 30-60 million to virtual extinction in the wild in just over a century.

The animals in the Banff Buffalo Paddock are Wood bison, transplanted in 1981 from free-ranging herds in Wood Buffalo National Park. From 1897 until that time, the Banff paddock had contained non-native Plains bison descended from animals donated to the park in 1897-98. The longest-lived of these animals, named "Sir Donald" after its donor, was considered to be one of the last existing range-born bison when it died at the age of 38. To the buffalo was added a collection of elk, moose, deer, mountain goats, bighorn sheep, coyote, cougar, fox and even yaks. For a while this 320 hectare mountain menagerie was a popular attraction. Today, only bison are kept here.

The Wood bison was formerly an endangered species, but largely due to the success of breeding at Banff and a few other

Eagles

Along with the bear, the eagle is a familiar symbol of wild places in North America. The Canadian Rockies are summer home to two species: the bald eagle, which is found along lakes and rivers in the valley bottoms, and the golden eagle, which is occasionally seen soaring above meadows in the subalpine and alpine ecoregions.

Eagles are the largest commonly observed birds in the Rockies, with wingspans on the order of two metres. The adult bald eagle has a light brown body, with a white head, white on the tail, and a gold beak. The golden eagle is brown, with a golden head and yellow talons. Fish, rodents, hares and carrion comprise the diets of both birds. The bald eagle builds a large nest, in the top of a dead

Bald Eagle

tree. The golden eagle nests on cliff ledges. Both species mate for life, and usually migrate in winter. In recent years, bald eagles have nested at Vermilion Lakes.

sites, it is now classified as threatened. Offspring from the Banff herd are periodically transfered to other paddocks in Canada and the U.S.

The bison is potentially a dangerous animal. Visitors are not allowed into the Buffalo Paddock on foot or bicycle.

Vermilion Lakes

The extensive montane wetlands immediately west of Banff are likely the remainder of a large lake that once occupied this part of the Bow Valley. Moraines deposited at the end of the Wisconsin Glaciation, 11,000 years ago, blocked the course of the Bow River, causing the lake to form. Its waters eventually found an outlet between Tunnel Mountain and Mt. Rundle near the present site of Bow Falls. Today the lakes are sustained by annual floods from the Bow River.

There are three principal Vermilion Lakes, reached from the Vermilion Lakes Drive, which parallels the Trans-Canada Highway for four kilometres. Photographers will recognize the lakes as setting for the postcard view of Mt. Rundle.

In order to preserve boating and fishing opportunities, the water level of the First Vermilion Lake was formerly controlled by a man-made dam. Since the controversial removal of the dam, the lake level has dropped and the basin has begun to fill with aquatic vegetation — the first stage in succession from montane wetland to floodplain forest. In a few hundred years, the Vermilion

The Vermilion Lakes provide the setting for the postcard view of Mt. Rundle, Banff's most famous mountain. The shallow lakes are excellent habitat for beaver and many migratory birds.

Lakes may look like the forest along the nearby Fenland Trail. Water levels of the second and third lakes are controlled naturally by beaver dams. Maximum lake depth is about five metres.

Osprey and bald eagles nest in the vicinity of the First Vermilion Lake, while beaver and muskrat can be seen at the second lake. The Third Vermilion Lake, near road's end, is partially fed by the warm waters of a hot spring. The moderating effect of these waters keeps part of this lake ice-free, and provides winter habitat for some birds which might normally migrate. The area is one of the best in Banff for bird-watching.

The Vermilion Lakes are also a good place to see coyote and elk, especially in winter. Moose are less common here now, but the trimmed shrubs and willows indicate the vegetation is a popular food source for other members of the deer family. The wetlands contrast with the slopes of Mt. Norquay, on the opposite side of the Trans-Canada, where a herd of bighorn sheep frequents the dry coniferous forest.

E.J. (Ted) Hart
Director, Whyte Museum of the Canadian Rockies

I came to Banff in 1972 as the Archivist of the Peter Whyte Foundation, which was then known as the Archives of the Canadian Rockies. The job was arranged for me by my thesis advisor at the University of Alberta in Edmonton in conjunction with Maryalice Stewart who was the Director of the Archives at that time. The previous year I had just finished my M.A. in Western Canadian History.
***

When I first arrived I had to learn the profession of an archivist. I was responsible for organizing and describing the manuscript collections in the Archives, so that researchers could have access to them. During that time I also became involved with organizing and describing the historic photographic collections, including the first important large collection we had received, that of Byron Harmon. Soon after, I began actively collecting and meeting with old timers who had important collections reflecting the history of the Canadian Rockies.
***

I am now the Director of what the Peter Whyte Foundation evolved into, the Whyte Museum of the Canadian Rockies, which is the premier cultural institution in Canada dealing with mountain material through its Archives, Art Gallery, Heritage Collection and Education departments. We have expanded during the past number of years to become an international centre for "the celebration of the relationship between culture and mountains".

The Fenland Trail

From the brochure *Fenland, Self-Guiding Trail*, which is distributed by Banff National Park to visitors to the trail:

It's just minutes away from Banff, and an eternity away in mood, yet here perhaps more than anywhere else in the park, man and wildlife co-exist. For 11,000 years people have come to this spot. For most of that time they have been native hunters stalking elk and gathering plants. A century ago the silence was broken by the axes and hammers of the Canadian Pacific Railway's surveyors and construction crews. Today, visitors stroll or jog along the trail, enjoying this patch of wilderness.

The Fenland is unbeatable as a short, accessible walk near Banff — it's a level, 1.5 km loop — and it offers good birdwatching and wildlife-spotting opportunities, too. The trail runs through an isolated wetland in a valley of forests that has been protected from development. The nutrient-rich waters, sedges, rushes and grasses of the fen provide the many animals and birds that live there with food and cover.

Be sure to pick up a copy of the Fenland brochure as you begin your walk — it's numbered to correspond with numbered posts along the trail, and contains lots of interesting information. And please note the sensible request on the back cover: "Keep this brochure as a souvenir of your visit if you wish. Otherwise, please return it to the box at the trailhead. This helps reduce our costs."

The Fenland Trail provides a close-up view of the floodplain forest and montane wetlands in the vicinity of the First Vermilion Lake, with the opportunity of seeing beaver, elk, deer and songbirds.

The Bow Valley Parkway

The jagged ridges of the Sawback Range parallel the east side of the Bow Valley Parkway between Banff and Castle Junction.

You have two routes to choose from between Banff and Lake Louise: the Trans-Canada Highway, and the Bow Valley Parkway. The latter offers a less hectic, more scenic alternative, with greater chances for viewing wildlife: bighorn sheep, deer, elk, wolf, coyote and black bear. Recent improvements to the road make it ideal for cyclists and motorists alike. With stops at the many interpretive displays and Johnston Canyon, you might want to allow a half day for this drive. Services are available at Johnston Canyon and at Castle Mountain Village. The Bow Valley Parkway was completed in 1920 as the original road between Banff and Lake Louise.

The speed limit is 60 km/h. The most recent improvements to the road, which included the divided sections, were completed in 1988, and the new road was officially dedicated the following year.

The First Visitors

The recorded human history of the Rockies spans less than 200 years, but for thousands of years

JOINS PAGE 111

JOINS PAGE 181

JOINS PAGE 69

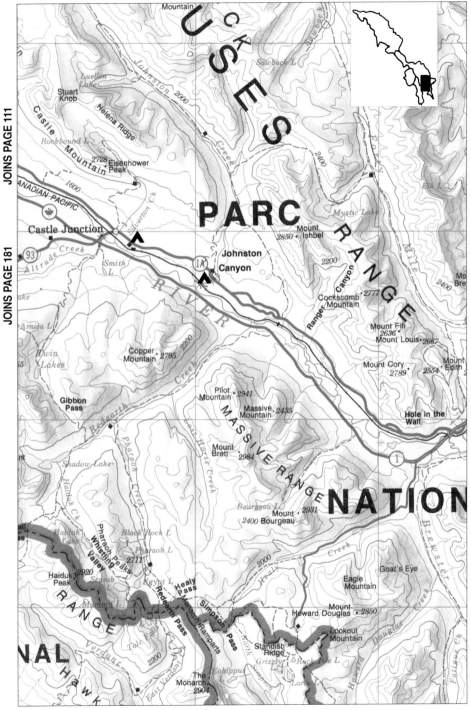

preceding, Native peoples travelled and lived here. More than 240 Native campsites have been discovered in Banff and Jasper National Parks. Some of the best-studied of these are adjacent to the Bow Valley Parkway. Artifacts from the various sites include arrowheads, animal bones and iron-stained mud called ochre. Examples of rock art exist at some locations in the Rockies.

The Bow Valley in the vicinity of Banff was probably first visited

Deer

The two species of deer in the Rockies are similar in size and appearance. Both have reddish-brown coats in summer, changing to gray in winter. The coats of the young are spotted. Adult males (bucks) stand about one metre tall at the shoulder. The more common mule deer has larger ears and eyes, and a narrow white tail with a black tip. The tail of the white-tailed deer is wider, matching the colour of the coat on top, and completely white underneath. Both have whitish rump patches.

The antlers of mule deer bucks are equally branched, while those of the white-tailed branch upwards from a forward reaching, main beam. White-taileds and mule deer are occasionally known to crossbreed in the Rockies, producing the muletail; it has the ears and eyes characteristic of the mule deer, and the tail and antlers of the white-tailed.

When alarmed the white-tailed raises its tail and gallops away with the tail switching from side to side. The mule deer flees in hops and bounds. Both species initially bolt a short distance when surprised, often exhaling loudly through the nostrils. From a safe vantage they will turn around to study their pursuer.

Because they lack upper incisors, deer tear vegetation away from the ground or from branches, rather than cropping it the way a horse does. Wolf, coyote, cougar, wolverine, lynx and grizzly bear are the predators of deer. Healthy animals are not often caught, but the young, and adults weakened by worms, parasites, or lack of food, are frequently taken. Deaths due to road kills and collisions with trains account for three quarters of recorded mule deer mortalities in Banff and Jasper National Parks. Please drive carefully.

Top: Mule deer
Bottom: White-tailed deer

The trembling aspen, a common deciduous tree at montane elevations in the Rockies, frequently grows at the mouth of mountainside streams. This view is at Muleshoe.

soon after the ice of the Wisconsin Glaciation began to recede, 11,000 years ago. The Natives were hunter/gatherers, but not strictly nomadic; it appears 10% of the sites were occupied year-round. The Natives lived in small family groups, and movements were largely dictated by the presence and absence of game.

It is likely the Bow Valley was also a travel route, used when Natives from the plains traded with those from the interior of B.C. Ochre from the Paint Pots in Kootenay National Park was probably an important trading commodity.

Locally, the Natives with whom European explorers made contact were of the Stoney tribe (also known as Assiniboine). Originally

Hole-in-the-Wall is a shallow cave high on Mt. Cory. In the background of this Byron Harmon photograph, the meandering nature of the Bow River is clearly visible in the vicinity of Muleshoe.

from central Canada, the Stoneys arrived in the Rockies in the early 1700's, displaced from their home territory by other tribes, who in turn were fleeing the presence of Europeans. Beginning a century and a half later, the Stoneys offered their knowledge of the mountains to Sir George Simpson, James Hector, A.P. Coleman, Tom Wilson, Mary Schäffer and many other explorers.

After the arrival of Europeans, and the disappearance of the Plains bison, Native peoples used the area of the mountain national parks as hunting grounds for a few decades, until the establishment of reserves. Descendants of the Stoneys now live on one of these reserves near Morley.

The archaeological sites in the Bow Valley have suffered heavily from visitation, and are designated special preservation areas. They may not be visited without permission from the park superintendent.

Backswamp and Muleshoe

This reach of the Bow River is very gentle in gradient, dropping only 13 centimetres in each kilometre. Across the Bow River from Backswamp viewpoint, Brewster Creek enters the main valley, forcing the river to the near side.

Upstream, a lake formerly existed, dammed by debris deposited by the creek. This lake has now been filled with the vegetation of swampy wetlands — the first stage in succession from shallow pond to floodplain forest. The Backswamp is underlaid

with peat to a depth of nine metres. Peat is decomposed vegetable matter that is partially carbonized — in other words, on its way to becoming coal.

The wetland at Muleshoe was created by a different process. Bends in a river are known as meanders. As a river erodes more deeply into a valley bottom, it occasionally abandons some meanders for a more direct course, leaving behind crescent-shaped pools called ox-bow lakes. At Muleshoe, the bed of the Canadian Pacific Railway was built between the river and the ox-bow, sealing the ox-bow's fate. Instead of filling with sediment washed into its basin from the river at high water, the stagnant Muleshoe is now filling with vegetation.

James Hector of the Palliser Expedition named Castle Mountain while travelling in the Bow Valley in 1858. It is easy to see how the name was inspired.

Tree-in-the-road

The Bow Valley Parkway divides at several places, offering eastbound and westbound travellers slightly different views of the valley. In one place it divides for but a few metres, to by-pass a large tree that formerly stood here.

There are two stories connected with this tree. One tells how it was a favourite of the park superintendent when the road was built, and was saved from destruction at his request. The other relates how when crews were clearing the right-of-way for the road, a particularly intimidating foreman took a nap under the tree. The workers did not want to invoke his wrath by waking him, so the tree, a white spruce, was spared. It blew down in a violent thunderstorm in 1984.

The walkway in Johnson Canyon gives an interesting perspective on the erosive powers of flowing water.

Hole-in-the-Wall

Some 600 m above the valley floor on Mt. Cory is Hole-in-the-Wall. The hole is a solution cave, dissolved from the limestone bedrock by meltwaters of the ancestral Bow Glacier when it filled this valley. Although its massive entrance hints at great things, Hole-in-the-Wall is only 30 m deep. There are many other solution caves nearby, particularly on Mt. Norquay.

The predominant tree at this viewpoint is trembling aspen, a hardy species that fairs well in gravels, especially those at the base of mountainside streams. You will notice the bark of these tress is scarred to a uniform height; elk and mule deer eat the tree bark and underlying layer in winter, producing the scarring. On windy days it is apparent why this type of aspen is named "trembling." Native peoples called it "noisy leaf."

The vegetation in montane wetlands is a favourite with moose, and the small lakes and stagnating ponds become home to beaver, muskrat, osprey and waterfowl.

The Muleshoe hiking trail climbs the hillside to a viewpoint overlooking this part of the Bow Valley. Bighorn sheep frequent these slopes, as does the wood tick, a parasite that looks like a

Paintbrush

Paintbrush is one of the most abundant wildflowers in the Rockies. It is usually red, red-orange or crimson at roadside. Purple, yellow and cream-coloured varieties are found at higher elevations. The bloom is long-lasting. Paintbrush is a semi-parasitic plant that often attaches its roots to those of nearby trees. Varieties of paintbrush occur throughout western North America.

reddish-brown, flattened spider. Apart from aggressive bears, stampeding bison, summer traffic, and elk and moose in rut, the wood tick is the only threat to visitors in the Rockies. The danger: it attaches to the skin and can transmit Rocky Mountain spotted fever, the complications of which can be fatal to humans. Hikers should check themselves carefully for this tiny mite in late spring and early summer.

Hillsdale Slide

The hilly terrain at this point on the Bow Valley Parkway is the product of a massive landslide that occurred 8,000 years ago. When the ice of the Wisconsin Glaciation filled the Bow Valley, it undercut the surrounding mountain walls. After the ice receded, some of the mountainsides collapsed. The Hillsdale Slide is one of the largest measured landslides in the Rockies.

Johnston Canyon

Although not quite as grand in scale as the Maligne Canyon in Jasper, Johnston Canyon, by virtue of the walkway constructed within it, is one of the best places in the Rockies to appreciate a limestone canyon.

Johnston Creek formerly flowed east of here, but was diverted into its present course by the Hillsdale Slide. Johnston Canyon has been eroded by the creek into cracks in the predominantly limestone bedrock. At its deepest point, the canyon is 30 m deep,

Silver City was a mining and railway boom town that flourished near Castle Mountain in the 1880's. At the time, it was larger than Calgary. The silver for which the town was named turned out to be the stuff of dreams, not reality, and the town was soon abandoned.

while in places it is less than six metres wide. Seven waterfalls mark the locations of relatively resistant outcrops of rock. The "lower falls" are 15 m high, and slightly more than a kilometre from the trailhead. What is special about the hike to these falls is the ingenious walkway, which takes you not along the lip of the canyon, but into its depths. The "upper falls" are 30 m high, and 1.6 km further.

American dipper and black swift are two interesting birds that may be seen on this hike.

A group of seven mineral springs known as the Ink Pots is six kilometres from the trailhead. Rain and meltwater that has filtered into cracks in the surrounding rock returns to the surface at the Ink Pots. Air carried in the water disturbs sediments in the spring basins. These sediments reflect certain wavelengths of light, giving the Ink Pots their blue-green colours. Two of the Ink Pots are rich with clay, and therefore milky in appearance. The bases of all contain a deposit of quicksand.

Silver City

Silver City was a railway boom town, with the rumoured existence of nearby silver thrown in to heighten the rush. But the only ore nearby was low-grade copper and lead on the slopes of Copper Mountain. The town came and went in the space of two years, but at its peak in 1884 Silver City was more populous than Calgary, and two thousand people lived on these meadows.

A few people had profited from the boom of Silver City, but in the bust many settlers and prospectors moved on — curiously, to the town of Golden, another boom town where the rumoured gold was just as non-existent as Silver City's silver. The only one to stay was Joe Smith, Silver City's third resident. Park wardens turned a

Doghair Forest

Most trees in this part of the Bow Valley are lodgepole pine. The lodgepole requires the heat of a forest fire to crack open its resin-sealed cones, to allow for effective seeding. Much of the Bow Valley burned in the decades immediately following the construction of the Canadian Pacific Railway, so dense stands of lodgepole pine, known as doghair forest, are common. Lodgepoles eventually give way to a more balanced mixture of spruce, pine and fir. For more information on the role of fire in the ecology of the Rockies, please refer to the Vermilion Pass burn entry, and the Ecology overview.

blind eye as he hunted and trapped in the area until his health failed in 1937.

Storm Mountain Viewpoint

The Wisconsin Glaciation was an ice age that started 75,000 years ago and ended 11,000 years ago. Within that broad period there were three distinct glacial advances and retreats in the Rockies. The first two reached beyond Canmore. The last advance stopped here, 11,000 years ago. Looking across the Bow Valley from this viewpoint, the many irregular elevations you see in the forest are piles of rubble left behind by the retreating ice.

Storm Mountain is the southern bastion of Vermilion Pass on the Continental Divide, and its name is indicative of the weather that frequently travels from west to east through the pass. The mountain was first ascended in 1889 by a surveying party that included outfitter Tom Wilson.

Morant's Curve

This viewpoint offers a spectacular panorama of the Wenkchemna Peaks, Mt. Temple and other summits of the Bow Range in the vicinity of Lake Louise. Mt. Temple is 3543 m/11,626 ft high — the third highest mountain in Banff National Park — and was first climbed in 1894.

Nicholas Morant, a photographer for the C.P.R., popularized this view on postcard, and it has since been known as Morant's Curve. In the foreground is the Bow River and the Canadian Pacific Railway

Banff to Lake Louise

Sunshine Meadows
An Alpine Garden

Sunshine is one of two places in the Rockies where the visitor is granted easy access, via gondola, to the land above treeline — the alpine ecoregion. But in contrast to the stark summit of The Whistlers at Jasper, the lush, vegetated Sunshine Meadows are a delight to the eye.

Spanning a 14 km arc along the Continental Divide on the crest of the Rockies, Sunshine is referred to by some as the largest alpine meadow system in the world. In truth these meadows

are something of an oddity in the Rockies, occupying as they do such a large region in what is usually the domain of glacial ice and rock. This fact makes the meadows even more remarkable.

The Sunshine Meadows are at an average elevation of 2225 m/ 7300 ft. Frost occurs many nights of the year and snow patches linger well into July. The vegetation here has adapted to a growing season of less than two months. Most of these plants are very low in stature, with small flowers and leaves. The less surface area a plant offers to the moisture-robbing effects of cold, wind and

Storm clearing, Mt. Baker, Wapta Icefield, Banff National Park.

JOINS PAGE 199

JOINS PAGE 151

JOINS PAGE 101

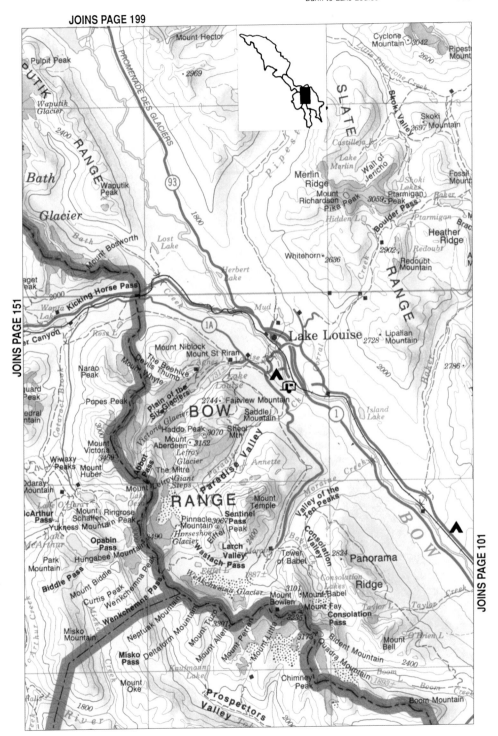

Sunshine Meadows is an extensive alpine meadow system on the Continental Divide. The vegetation here struggles against the rigours of the alpine climate, blooming in July and August. A gondola provides summer visitors with rapid access to hiking trails. In winter, the gondola transports skiers to the lifts operated by Sunshine Ski Area.

harsh sunlight at this altitude, the more moisture and nutrients it retains for its own growth. The observant eye will recognize miniature versions of many plants common at lower elevations. In a colourful celebration of Nature's aptitude for ensuring the survival of species, this multitude of wildflowers blooms mid-summer.

The view south from some of the slopes above Sunshine Village includes the "Matterhorn of the Rockies," Mt. Assiniboine (a-SINNI-boyne). Hikers and climbers bound for this mountain sometimes use the Citadel Pass trail, departing from Sunshine.

Mountain Heather

The minuscule evergreen, mountain heather, is the indicator species of the alpine ecoregion. Along with alpine willow and snow willow, heather often forms dense mats in moist areas above treeline. This combination of vegetation is extensive at Sunshine Meadows, comprising an area known to botanists as a heath tundra. There are three species of heather — pink, white and yellow — all with bell-shaped, nodding flowers. Heather is a member of the family of plants which includes blueberries.

Sunshine Ski Area

The Sunshine Ski Area had its beginnings in a humble cabin built by the Canadian Pacific Railway in 1928 for its summer trail riding vacations. Between 1929 and 1932, several skiing parties from Banff journeyed into the area, and were delighted with the skiing conditions they found. Jim Brewster, president of Brewster Transportation, was one of these skiers. In 1934 he leased the cabin from the C.P.R. for winter use, buying it outright in 1936 — for $300! Brewster hired mountain guides in the winter to teach skiing, and the popularity of the area grew rapidly.

The first permanent ski lift was installed in 1945. At that time skiers reached the village via a hair-raising bus ride from the Bourgeau parking lot. The gondola, completed in 1980 at a cost of $12 million, greatly improved access to the ski hill. The gondola climbs 450 m / 1500 ft in its 4.3 km ride to the village. There are 10 ski lifts and over 60 marked runs within the ski area boundary. Cross-country skiing and ski touring off-trail are also popular. Sunshine Village is comprised of a hotel, which was constructed in 1965, and various dining facilities. The much-renovated original cabin is still in use.

In 1984, Sunshine Village opened for the summer season, and traffic on the meadows increased dramatically. In 1989, 32,000 visitors used the gondola. In consideration of the fragile na-

Skiing began at Sunshine in the 1930's. Mt. Assiniboine is the high mountain in the background on the right.

Mt. Assiniboine is the sixth highest mountain in the Canadian Rockies.

ture of Sunshine Meadows, summer visitors are asked to keep to the maintained trails, and to leave the beautiful wildflowers for others to enjoy.

Mt. Assiniboine
3618 m / 11,870 ft

The summit of the highest mountain in this part of the Rockies, Mt. Assiniboine, is visible from

Sunshine Meadows. The mountain was named by surveyor G.M. Dawson in 1884, for the Native Assiniboine tribe. The name means "those who cook by placing hot rocks in water." Locally, the Assiniboine are called Stoney.

The quest to become the first to ascend Mt. Assiniboine drew many expeditions in the 1890's, including several organized by American explorer Walter Wilcox. The first ascent was made in 1901 by James Outram and guides. Outram trooped directly to Assiniboine from a series of first ascents in Yoho, in a remarkable summer of mountaineering.

Mt. Assiniboine Provincial Park lies entirely within British Columbia, and was created in 1922. In 1973 the park was expanded to its present area of 38,600 hectares. Roughly triangular in shape, the park occupies the angle created by the boundaries of Banff and Kootenay parks, thereby adding its protected area to the block of the four mountain national parks. Apart from Mt. Assiniboine, the park's chief attractions are glacially fed lakes, abundant wildlife, and extensive alpine meadows.

There is no motor vehicle access to the park, but six backpacking approaches can be made. Alternately, restricted helicopter access is available from Canmore. Mt. Assiniboine Lodge has operated in the park since the 1920's.

Remembered for Their Contributions

Two mountains above the Sunshine access road commemorate two key figures in the history of Banff National Park, one an explorer and the other an administrator.

Mt. Bourgeau (boor-ZJOWE) on the north side of the road was named in 1858 by James Hector of the Palliser Expedition for the Swiss-born expedition botanist Eugene Bourgeau. In the course of the four year expedition, Bourgeau collected 460 species and 60,000 specimens. Apparently Bourgeau was not a capable horseman, and spent most of his time in the Rockies camped in

Helicopters

The helicopters you may see buzzing through the air around Banff are not transporting hikers and skiers to the mountain tops nearby. These machines are being used by park staff in wildlife surveys, search and rescue operations, and to transport materials to remote work sites.

Heli-skiing and heli-hiking are not allowed in the national parks. Access to remote areas of the parks is therefore only possible by foot, ski, boat,* bike or horseback. While this precludes access to many areas by the casual visitor, it assures wildlife will not be subjected to the stress induced by helicopter traffic. Outside of the National Parks, this machine is being used more and more extensively for industry, access and recreation.

*Gas-powered motor boats are permitted only on Pyramid Lake in Jasper, Upper and Middle Waterton Lakes, and Lake Minnewanka in Banff.

the Bow Valley, while Hector and the others explored the passes on horseback.

Mt. Howard Douglas, to the south of the road, was named for the second Superintendent of Rocky Mountains Park (Banff), and later Dominion Commissioner of Parks. Howard Douglas enthusiastically supported enlargment of the park in 1898, realizing that with the forthcoming establishment of the province of Alberta, land for an expanded national park would soon be very difficult to obtain. Chiefly through his recommendations, the park's area was increased in 1902 from 413 sq km to 7,000 sq km. But, this was too much too soon, and the fledgling forestry branch of the Department of Interior was un-

Rust, Blights, Bugs and Parasites

The trees of the Rockies are relatively healthy, with few large-scale, destructive infestations of bugs. Pine and fir beetles, gall aphids, spruce sawfly and twig moth occur, but so far to a minor extent. As the treed areas of the Rockies become over-mature due to the absence of forest fires, these and other afflictions may become more prevalent, as Nature seeks ways to thin the forests.

Reddish needles on pine trees may indicate the presence of the mountain pine beetle. The trunks of aging lodgepoles are used as egg depositories by this beetle, usually with fatal results to the tree. Red belt — drying out of tree branches during winter chinooks — will also produce rust-coloured pine needles.

Various other rusts and needle casts occur in spruce and pines, but the most common affliction visible on lodgepoles is the parasitic pine dwarf mistletoe. The roots of this plant attach to a pine trunk or branch, and the mistletoe blooms into a dense mass of branches, commonly called witches broom. Many people mistakenly assume that these clusters are the nests of birds or squirrels. A fungus in spruce and fir trees sometimes produces a similar growth. These brooms appear to have little effect on the health of mature trees.

Tree lichens are extensive on coniferous trees in the Rockies. Most common are the pale green *Usnea*, and black *Bryoria* — commonly called hair lichens. The bright green wolf lichen is quite often found on standing dead trees, especially Lyall's larch. Some tree lichens are an important source of food for caribou.

Witches broom

Coyote and Wolf

The coyote (KEYE-oat, or keye-OAT-ee) and the wolf, the two most common wild dogs in the Rockies, are at first glance similar in appearance. The coyote is smaller, slighter and fox-like in profile. The coat is gray on top, brown on the sides and pale underneath. When running, the coyote carries its bushy, white-tipped tail low, between its legs. Frequently seen alone or in pairs, coyotes occasionally band together to hunt larger game.

The coat of the wolf shows much more variation in colour. Brown is common, but black and white animals occur in the Rockies. The eyes are yellow and the profile is much more stocky and blunt. The tail is carried straight out when running. Wolves usually travel in packs of up to a dozen or so. The "lone wolf" accounts for about 10% of the population.

The wolf is one of the most infrequently seen large mammals in the Rockies. Travelling in family packs, wolves range over territories of several hundred square kilometres. The movements of the pack often coincide with those of the herds of deer, elk, and caribou which make up a big part of the wolf's strictly carnivorous diet.

The coyote pack is less structured socially than that of the wolf, although coyotes share the custom of hunting big game from a pack, especially in winter. These hunts are generally not as successful as the wolf's, but the coyote is crafty and uses teamwork to advantage in taking smaller animals. The coyote is a true scavenger, and has a scrappy personality to match. Much of its diet is made up of the carrion left at kills made by other animals. Road kills are a major strain on wolf and coyote populations.

In recent years there have been instances in the Rockies of both provoked and unprovoked attacks of humans by coyotes. As with all wildlife, it is recommended a safe distance be kept from this unpredictable animal.

The coyote (top) and the wolf best demonstrate the change in outlook towards wildlife in the mountain national parks. As recently as the 1950's, many of the larger predators, including these animals, were poisoned, with the aim of eradication. It is now understood that the balance of predator and prey must be struck naturally. Today, populations of gray wolf and coyote have recovered, and these animals frequent many of the valleys in the Rockies.

able to administer the larger area.

From then until 1930, the area of what is now Banff National Park went through a series of reductions to accommodate provincial demands for access to resources. By advocating expansion of Banff National Park at a time when it was still possible, Howard Douglas ensured a significant area would remain protected, and unknowingly guaranteed the future existence of the four mountain parks block.

Castle Mountain
2766 m/9128 ft

Of all the names bestowed in the Rockies, Castle Mountain is one of the most appropriate. James Hector of the Palliser Expedition named the mountain in 1858. In 1946, it was decided the name should be changed to Mt. Eisenhower, to honour Dwight D. Eisenhower, commander of Allied forces in Europe and later U.S. President. The story goes that Eisenhower was supposed to attend the official ceremony at this spot, but failed to show up when he was detained by a golf match elsewhere. Locals took a sarcastic view of the name change, and thereafter the grassy terrace on the south end of the mountain became known as "Eisenhower's green."

In 1979 the name Castle Mountain was re-applied to the main mountain, with Mt. Eisenhower being reserved for the southernmost tower.

The Castle

Mountains of the eastern main ranges are markedly different in appearance from those of the front ranges, and nowhere is this more obvious than in comparing Castle Mountain and Mt. Ishbel (to your right) from this viewpoint. In contrast to the front ranges, where the sedimentary formations are tilted and folded, those that make up the eastern main ranges are very thick, and lie for the most part in horizontal layers. As these layers erode, they produce a mountain shape that is frequently turreted, pinnacled, and fortress-like in appearance — the castellated mountain. Front range mountains are typically drab gray in colour, like Mt. Ishbel, while pinks, buffs, yellows and browns are more common in the rocks of eastern main range mountains.

Although an impressive mountain, Castle is far from being one of the high peaks of the Rockies. It is likely that several thousand mountains are higher. The highest of Castle's many summits is not the tower, but the one furthest north. A.P. Coleman made the first ascent of the mountain in 1884, and the tower was first climbed in 1926. The cliffs of Castle continue to be popular with rock climbers today.

Mt. Hector
3394 m/11,135 ft

Between Castle and Lake Louise junctions, westbound travellers obtain several fine views of Mt. Hector, with the Bow River in the foreground. Mt. Hector is one of 53 mountains in the Rockies that exceed 3353 m/11,000 ft. It is named for James Hector of the Palliser Expedition, and was first climbed in 1895. An alpine valley glacier is concealed from view on its north slopes.

Castle Mountain, one of the best known peaks in the Rockies, is a classic example of a castellated mountain. The sheer limestone and dolomite cliffs, separated by broad shale ledges, are typical of mountains in the eastern main ranges.

Lake Louise and Moraine Lake

By the summer of 1882, the survey line of the Canadian Pacific Railway had been staked as far as Kicking Horse Pass. Outfitter Tom Wilson was packing supplies for the survey crew. While camped with some Stoney Natives at the confluence of the Bow and Pipestone Rivers, Wilson heard the sound of avalanches booming through the valley. He asked the Natives about the source of the sound, and was told it came from "snow mountain above the lake of little fishes." The following day Wilson and his Native guide journeyed to the lake to investigate.

Mt. Victoria provides the backdrop for Lake Louise, one of the best known scenes in the Rockies

Although Wilson would later ramble at great length about how he never before gazed upon such a "matchless scene," his initial impression of Lake Louise, recorded at the time, was rather perfunctory — it was just another pretty lake in the mountains. (Walter Wilcox a subsequent explorer, called it "a muskeg filled with mosquitos and stumps.") Wilson named it Emerald Lake. Two years later the name was changed to honour Princess Louise Caroline Alberta, the daughter of Queen Victoria and wife of the Governor General of Canada. The province is also named for her.

Lake Louise is 2.4 km in length, just over half a kilometre wide and 90 m deep. The elevation at the lake is 1,731 m—slightly more than a mile above sea level, and 200 m above the floor of the Bow Valley. In the chilling presence of the glaciers, the water temperature reaches a maximum of 4°C in August, and the lake's surface is frozen from November until June. It's no wonder the fishes are little!

The First Overnight Guest

In 1884, A.P. Coleman, a geology professor from the University of Toronto, became the first tourist to arrive at Lake Louise, then known as Laggan. That he travelled by construction train was bad enough, but his first experience with accommodation in the area marked an inauspicious beginning for a destination that would eventually owe its contin-

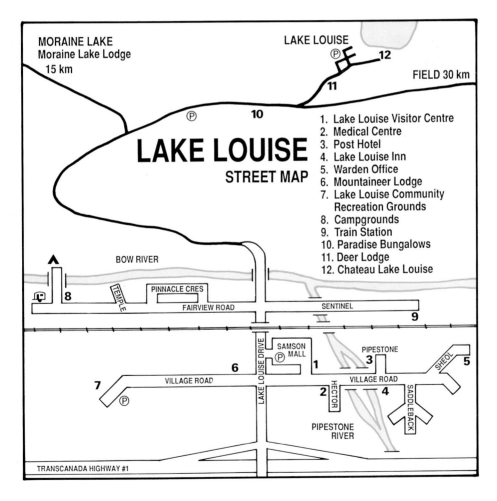

MORAINE LAKE
Moraine Lake Lodge
15 km

LAKE LOUISE

12

FIELD 30 km

11

10

LAKE LOUISE
STREET MAP

1. Lake Louise Visitor Centre
2. Medical Centre
3. Post Hotel
4. Lake Louise Inn
5. Warden Office
6. Mountaineer Lodge
7. Lake Louise Community Recreation Grounds
8. Campgrounds
9. Train Station
10. Paradise Bungalows
11. Deer Lodge
12. Chateau Lake Louise

BOW RIVER

8

PINNACLE CRES

TEMPLE

FAIRVIEW ROAD

SENTINEL

9

SAMSON MALL

1

PIPESTONE

3

5

LAKE LOUISE DRIVE

6

VILLAGE ROAD

7

2

HECTOR

VILLAGE ROAD

4

SHEOL

SADDLEBACK

PIPESTONE RIVER

TRANSCANADA HIGHWAY #1

ued existence solely to tourism, not railway building.

"When darkness fell I paid for my bed in advance, according to the cautious practice of the hostelry, and retired to the grey blankets of bunk No. 2, second tier, in the common guest chamber, trying to shut out sights and sounds from the barroom by turning my back. An hour or two later another man scrambled into the bunk, somewhat the worse for whisky, and tucked himself into the blankets beside me. It appeared that my half-dollar paid for only half the bed."

Undeterred, Coleman made other arrangements for the following evening. He returned to the Rockies frequently over the next 45 years, and accomplished much important exploration.

As a stay at the lake was the principal reason for getting off the train at this spot, the name Lake

Tom Wilson

"I knew you'd be back. You'll never leave these mountains again as long as you live. They've got you now." It was 1882. Major A.B. Rogers, surveyor of the line through the mountains for the Canadian Pacific Railway, was addressing Tom Wilson, an outfitter with whom he had worked the previous year. Rogers was right. The future of the twenty-two year old Wilson, and the exploration of the Rockies, were to be inextricably bound for the next 25 years.

Wilson had an uncanny ability for being in the right place at the right time during the heyday of exploration in the Rockies. Several firsts are credited to him, any one of which would have assured some degree of fame: one of the earliest crossings of Kicking Horse Pass, a solitary crossing of Howse Pass, and the discoveries of Lake Louise and Emerald Lake. Wilson also claimed many other discoveries, some disputed: the finding of ore on Mt. Stephen, the discovery of Marble Canyon and the first journey to the Yoho Valley. His knack for being in the limelight is best underscored in the most famous Canadian photograph, "The Last Spike." In the background you can see Wilson in Stetson hat, eyes fixed on the camera at the historic moment the C.P.R. was completed.

Wilson began his outfitting business in 1885, leading hunting clients into the Rockies. His knowledge of the mountains, gained during his surveying days, served him well. Mountaineers soon began to seek his services so they might have a better chance of reaching summits during their journeys of exploration. Tom quickly became the premier outfitter and guide at Banff, and most of the early guides had their start with his company.

Larger than life, with memories to match, Tom Wilson died in Banff in 1933, after outliving many of his contemporaries. His name is commemorated in Mt. Wilson, near Saskatchewan River Crossing.

Louise replaced Laggan in 1913, to prevent confusion among the increasing number of visitors.

Chateau Lake Louise

As with the Banff Springs Hotel, the Chateau Lake Louise has undergone many changes in architectural style over the years. (Chateau, pronounced "sha-TOE," is a French word meaning "mansion.")

The first building at the lake was a log cabin built in 1886 by C.P.R. worker Dave White. This cabin was replaced in 1890 by another log structure — the original "chalet." When explorers Samuel Allen and Walter Wilcox arrived for the summer season in 1893, they were told to bring a tent. The chalet had burned to the ground. It was succeeded by a split-level, wooden structure which housed 12 guests. Two timbered wings were added to this structure in 1900, and the building was a bizarre, yet attractive, combination of Tudor and Victorian styles, with a capacity of 200 guests. A hydro-electric generator was built nearby on Louise Creek, bringing modern comforts to the remote setting.

Named for its architect, Walter Painter, the 94-room Painter Wing, including the Victoria dining room, was completed in 1913. This addition boosted the building's capacity to 400 guests. While the Canadian Pacific Railway marketed the Banff Springs Hotel as the all-round resort in the lap of luxury, the Chateau was more

Top: The original building on the shore of Lake Louise was a rough log cabin built in 1886. Visitors to the lake were few, and arrived on horseback or foot.

Bottom: The C.P.R. began earnest development of its hotel at Lake Louise in the early 1900's, culminating with the addition of the Painter Wing in 1913. With a capacity of 400 guests, the Chateau became a major destination in the Rockies, second only to the Banff Springs Hotel.

rustic, and was oriented to those with an active interest in the outdoors. The sales pitch worked, and the Chateau experienced the same boom in popularity that had befallen its sister hotel in Banff.

The alternately dusty and muddy carriage road from Lake Louise station was a constant source of complaints. The situation was rectified when tracks were laid for a narrow-guage tramway in 1912. This mini-train with internal combustion engines operated until 1930, making as many as 30 round-trips to the Chateau a day. Today the abandoned tram grade is a popular walking and ski trail.

The older, wooden wings of the Chateau burned to the ground on July 3, 1924. By the following summer, a new concrete wing had been constructed, and the Chateau was open for business again. In appearance the hotel changed little for the next 60 years. The Tom Wilson restaurant was added in 1983, and the exterior was resurfaced in 1984-85.

Above: Commencing in 1986, a complete re-development of the Chateau was undertaken. The new Glacier Wing was constructed, along with a new parkade, entrance lobby and retail area. This expansion boosted the Chateau's capacity to 1000 guests.

Left: guests at the Chateau Lake Louise can enjoy accommodation with a world fmous view.

Oppostie: Lake Louise.

The most common flower growing on the Chateau grounds is the Icelandic poppy, native to Siberia. The seeds of this flower have spread, and it is now found throughout the Lake Louise area.

Some of the 650 summer staff are accommodated in five residence buildings on the hill behind the Chateau. Visitors are encouraged to browse through the public areas of the building, and take refreshment in the various lounges and restaurants. The Chateau celebrated its 100th anniversary in 1990.

School Days

The surveyors of the Dominion Topographic Survey had been routinely topping summits as part of their work for five years, but recreational mountaineering in the Rockies commenced in earnest in 1891, the year Samuel Allen first arrived. Allen's mother, a member of Philadelphia's aristocracy, had been with the Vaux family and Mary Schäffer on a visit to Lake Louise in 1889. It was the custom of the Vauxes to give presentations detailing their summer outings when they arrived back in Philadelphia, and so Allen, a Yale student, was introduced to the Rockies.

Commencing in 1986, after much consultation with the Canadian Parks Service, a $50 million redevelopment was undertaken. The 150-room Glacier Wing was constructed, and a 400 vehicle concrete parkade was added, along with a new entrance, lobby and retail area. The last phase of this development will see the addition of a convention facility.

The poppies that grow on the Chateau grounds are not native species. The many-coloured, smaller variety is the Icelandic poppy, native to Siberia. The larger, reddish-orange variety is the Oriental poppy.

The present capacity of the hotel is 1000 guests in 515 rooms. The Chateau has been open year-round since the winter of 1983.

Allen made ascents of Mt. Burgess at Field and Devil's Thumb near Lake Louise in 1891. After climbing the Matterhorn in 1892, he returned to the Rockies in 1893 with a school mate from Yale, Walter Wilcox. Their exuberance for tackling the "unconquered difficulties" of mountaineering near Lake Louise was matched only by their relative ignorance of the dangers involved. The pair made two attempts to climb Mt. Victoria and

one attempt on Mt. Temple. Given their scant mountaineering experience and primitive equipment, their lack of success was not surprising.

The following summer Allen and Wilcox returned again, teaming up with three other students — The Yale Lake Louise Club. None of the newcomers had experience in mountaineering. They survived the summer's exploits — although just barely. Three of the party made first ascents of Mts. Temple and Aberdeen and, amongst other travels, the first visits to Paradise Valley and The Valley of the Ten peaks were recorded.

Between Kicking Horse Pass and Moraine Lake, Allen and Wilcox bestowed many names that summer. Most of those chosen by Allen were purported to be Stoney names he had learned from the Natives who helped pack supplies to their camps. Frequently, Allen and Wilcox each chose a different name for the same features, and a competitive element entered into the relationship between Allen and Wilcox.

This culminated when both explorers published maps and accounts of their travels. Wilcox's large volume, "Camping in the Canadian Rockies," eventually went through many best-selling editions, which also chronicled his attempts on Mt. Assiniboine, and his quest to the headwaters of the Athabasca River. His map of the Lake Louise area was remarkably accurate in comparison to Allen's privately published chart, and was relied on by others for over a decade. Wilcox also published his "Guide to the Lake Louise District," which, in the eyes of the public, made him the authority on the area.

The mountain that Allen named "Shappee" — peak six of the Wenkchemna Peaks — is today known as Mt. Allen. Mt. Wilcox and Wilcox Pass opposite Columbia Icefield commemorate Walter Wilcox. The youthful spirit

Left: The members of the Yale Lake Louise Club spent an exciting summer at Lake Louise in 1894. Although relatively inexperienced in mountaineering, they accomplished first ascents of Mt. Temple and Mt. Aberdeen, while exploring and naming many features of the surrounding area.

Right: Samuel Allen on the south side of Opabin Pass in 1894. Opabin is a Stoney Native word that means "rocky." Allen applied many Native names to features in the area. Some of these names are still in use today.

Top: The ascent of Mt. Lefroy (3423 m/ 11,230 ft) was attempted by members of the Appalachian Mountain Club in 1896. Near the summit, P.S. Abbot fell to his death. This led to the introduction of guides from Switzerland, in an attempt to improve safety on climbs in the Rockies.

Bottom: Dapper in attire, with trademark rope and alpenstock always at hand, the Swiss Guides led thousands of mountaineering ascents in the Rockies. Since the 1950's, most mountaineers have preferred to climb without guides.

in which these adventurers passed their summer vacations carries into the present. Today the Rockies are as much a mountaineer's playground as they were 100 years ago.

The Swiss Guides

In August 1896, pioneer mountaineers Charles Fay, P.S. Abbot and members of the Appalachian Mountain Club from New England made an attempt on the as-yet-unclimbed Mt. Lefroy. It was a tragic and pivotal day in the history of mountaineering and tourism in the Rockies. Near the summit of the mountain, Abbot unroped from the others to explore a gully, slipped, and fell 500 metres to his death. It was the first fatality in North American mountaineering.

Many in the Club questioned

the purpose of mountaineering after this shocking event. But in the style of the day, it was decided to avenge Abbot's death. In 1897 Fay and British mountaineer H.B. Dixon organized a group of the world's foremost mountaineers to make an attempt on the mountain that Abbot had died on.

To increase the chance of success, Dixon brought along Peter Sarbach, a Swiss mountain guide with whom he had climbed in Europe. Without incident, Sarbach led nine climbers, including Fay and Scottish mountaineer J.N. Collie, to the summit, a year to the day after Abbot's death. Shortly thereafter, Sarbach guided Fay, Collie and another climber to the summit of Mt. Victoria. Attention then turned for the first time to Mt. Balfour and the peaks north of Lake Louise.

Two things were clear to the Canadian Pacific Railway: Lake Louise was supplanting Banff as the departure point for mountaineering explorations, and the presence of mountain guides made the mountaineering safer, and likely more successful. Successful clients were happy clients who would return. In 1899 the C.P.R. imported Swiss Guides of its own, and mountaineering in the Rockies became big business.

Members of the Feuz family (FOITS) were among the most celebrated of the Swiss Guides. Father Edward, sons Edward Jr., Ernest and Walter, and their cousin Gottfried made a tremendous contribution to mountain-

eering in Canada. Between them they led 130 first ascents in the Rockies and Selkirk Mountains. Most prolific was Edward Feuz Jr., who accounted for 78 of these ascents between 1903 and his retirement in 1944.

Of course, when not exploring new ground, the guides were routinely trooping experienced mountaineers and novices alike up and down the slopes of the most desired summits — Mts. Lefroy, Temple, Victoria, Stephen and Sir Donald — for the fee of $5.00/day. As a tribute to the guides' skills, in all the mountaineering outings undertaken during a period spanning five decades not a single client was seriously injured.

The five summits of Mt. Lyell (lie-ELL) west of Saskatchewan River Crossing were named in honour of five of the Swiss Guides in 1972. Most of the other guides

A lasting tribute to the hard work and skill of the Swiss Guides was the construction of Abbot Pass Hut in 1921. This stone shelter sits atop Abbot Pass between Mts. Lefroy and Victoria, at an elevation of 2,940 m. The construction materials were packed on horseback along the Victoria Glacier to a point where a large crevasse made the route impassable. Human brawn took over at that point, and the two tonnes of supplies were carried or winched the rest of the way to the pass. The hut was the highest habitable building in Canada for 60 years, until the Neil Colgan Hut was constructed above Moraine Lake.

Top: Mt. Victoria is one of the most popular mountaineering peaks in the Rockies. The "regular" route on the mountain is to follow the ridge crest from Abbot Pass on the viewer's left.

Right: In places, the southeast ridge of Mt. Victoria is less than a metre wide.

Mt. Victoria
3464 m / 11,365 ft

More than one million people stroll in front of the Chateau Lake Louise each year, and they take over one million photographs of the lake. While most photographers are no doubt attempting to capture the incredible beauty of the lake, the backdrop — Mt. Victoria — is an inseparable element of the scene's symmetry. As a result, Mt. Victoria is probably the most photographed peak in the Rockies.

Mt. Victoria is also one of the most frequently climbed mountains in the range. The initial attempts on the north peak were made from the Upper Victoria Glacier by Samuel Allen and Walter Wilcox in 1893. Given their lack of climbing experience, it is

had prominent mountains named for them earlier in the century. Edward Feuz Jr., the last of the original Swiss Guides, died at Golden in 1981, at the age of 96.

not surprising that they failed. Today the easiest route to the centre summit is to follow the sinuous and spectacular southeast ridge (viewer's left) from Abbot Pass, as did the first ascent party of 1897.

Unlike many mountains, whose popularity fades after the first ascent, Mt. Victoria has continued to be a focus for mountaineering efforts. Early in this century, it was the mark of a suc-cessful alpine vacation to have climbed the mountain. Mt. Victoria North, the right hand peak, is only slightly lower than "centre peak." It was first ascended in 1900 by a party that included James Outram, who also made many other first ascents in the Rockies. The first complete traverse of the mountain, along the skyline ridge from north to south, was accomplished in 1909. The imposing northeast face (facing the Cha-

Georgia Engelhard

Georgia Engelhard first visited Chateau Lake Louise as a 20-year-old in 1926. Swiss Guide Edward Feuz Jr. led her to the summit of Pinnacle Mountain near Moraine Lake. Edward was impressed with her stamina, skill and zest for climbing. His impression had merit. Georgia Engelhard had found her element, and in a few years would establish herself as a first-class alpinist almost without peer. One of the other Swiss Guides commented: "When she goes uphill she goes like a rocket. What she needs is a mountain goat, not a guide."

In the summer of 1929 Georgia climbed nine mountains in nine days, including Hungabee Mountain — one of the most difficult in the region. In 1931 she made 38 ascents, including eight of Mt. Victoria. In 1933 she and Edward Feuz Jr. made the first traverse of Mt. Victoria from south to north (left to right). They took only six hours to travel from Abbot Pass Hut to the teahouse at the Plain of Six Glaciers.

In 1935, Engelhard met O. E. Cromwell in the Swiss Alps. They became inseparable, climbing in Europe and Canada without guides. Eventually they married. Between them they accomplished 86 first ascents in the Rockies and Selkirks, and Edward Feuz Jr. said of Georgia that she had been to the summits of more mountains in her 25 years climbing than he had in his 50 as a guide.

The couple retired to Switzerland, close to the Feuz family's home. Georgia Engelhard died in 1985, and Cromwell followed her a few months later.

teau) was first climbed in 1922. In 1968 this route was followed to the summit in winter by a group of local mountaineers.

Although a relatively easy peak by contemporary standards when good weather and conditions prevail, an ascent of Mt. Victoria is not without its hazards. Avalanches on the approach are principal amongst these, but the "walk" along the summit ridge seems to allow for a lowering of the guard in a situation where a mis-placed step cannot be allowed. In places the icy ridge is less than a metre wide. In 1954, seven Mexican climbers perished in a fall on the mountain's northeast face. A memorial plaque was later taken to the summit, a grim reminder to mountaineers of the risks in their pursuit.

The Plain of Six Glaciers

Most of the "snow" on Mt. Victoria's steep flanks is actually glacial ice. The long ridge of the mountain is oriented exactly perpendicular to the prevailing southwesterly winds. Snow is readily deposited on the lee side of the mountain, facing the lake, and because of the cooling effects of elevation on temperature, most of this snow is eventually transformed into ice.

While a trip to the summit of Mt. Victoria is in the domain of

George Schwarz
Owner of the Post Hotel, Lake Louise

I was born in Switzerland, grew up there, and I came here as a ski instructor in 1972. I worked for one season, then got involved in a restaurant, which I ended up buying. It's now called Ticino's, but at the time it was Felice's. I ran it for five years on my own — cooking, waiting on tables, everything. Then in 1978 my brother André and I bought the Post Hotel in Lake Louise.
***
We renovated the place little by little, as much as we could afford, and got a good name for the restaurant. We had some

excellent chefs and good staff, good food. We always laughed about having the nice rooms to go with it. Finally in 1986 we started construction on a $7 million new hotel, and we opened in July of 1987 with a 95 room hotel, with swimming pool, with jacuzzi bathtubs and fireplaces in the rooms.
***
I enjoy being in the mountains, and once I've finished work here, it's so close to go skiing, to go golfing, to go for a run or something like that, and so beautiful. And I love waking up in the morning and looking out and seeing the mountains. This is home.

mountaineers, the popular hike to the Plain of Six Glaciers is recommended for those who have the better part of a day to invest in obtaining a close-up view of this glaciated landscape. The hike is a continuation of the lakeshore trail, and initially passes directly beneath hundred metre cliffs that are a favourite spot for rock climbing. In winter, seeping water freezes on part of this cliff, creating Louise Falls, a waterfall ice climbing destination of moderate difficulty.

The Victoria Glacier was first studied by amateur scientists and photographers of the Vaux family of Philadelphia in the 1890's. In those times, the glacier extended farther down the valley than it does now. It is estimated the ice

The Plain of Six Glaciers is the rubble-covered area immediately in front of the lower Victoria Glacier, where six glaciers are visible. A popular hiking trail leads from Lake Louise to the plain and a nearby tea-house.

has receded 1,220 metres in the last 160 years. Old terminal moraines mark the former extent of the ice, and a prominent trimline shows where the advancing ice came into contact with living forest.

The Plain of Six Glaciers tea house was built by the Canadian Pacific Railway in 1925, and operates during the summer months, serving lunches and refresh-ments. It is nestled in the upper subalpine forest, just out of harm's way beside a large avalanche path. The area offers excellent prospects for observing mountain goats. Pika and hoary marmot also live in the boulders nearby.

Capable hikers, prepared for chill winds and changeable weather, may continue another 3/4 kilometre beyond the tea-

Gray Jay and Clark's Nutcracker

The two most common birds on the Chateau grounds are the similar-looking gray jay and Clark's nutcracker, members of the crow family. While the chipmunks and ground

squirrels have been eyeing your picnic lunch or ice cream cone from ground level, these two birds have undoubtedly taken an interest from the air. Initially endearing in their complete lack of fear of humans, the fascination with these ever-present scavengers will likely wear off when they depart on the wing with part of your lunch.

The gray jay is the smaller of the two, with grayish-white plumage, a light-coloured face, dark neck and a blunt beak. Immatures are dark gray. The Clark's nutcracker is more chunky in build, with gray plumage and black and white wings. Its long beak is designed for extracting the seeds from pine cones.

The Clark's is the noisier of the two birds, with its guttural, crow-like sounds. The gray jay, a quieter neighbour, makes cooing noises most of the time. Both birds stash food to tide them over the colder months, although the Clark's nutcracker heads a short distance out of the mountains for most of the winter season.

Although it is tempting to feed these birds, please refrain from doing so.

Top: Gray jay
Bottom: Clark's nutcracker

house, to a vantage overlooking the lower glacier and the approach to the Death Trap and Abbot Pass Hut. Here you are literally in the heart of a glacial landscape. Beneath the viewpoint are the fissured crevasses and surface moraine of the lower glacier. Above, 500 metre high cliffs glisten with ice and drip melt water. Always there is the unnerving sound of falling rock, as the glacial ice wears down the mountains. Witnessed from here, avalanches from the headwall of the upper glacier are a memorable (and loud!) event. Travel beyond this point is for experienced mountaineers only.

If you are late in your return from the Plain of Six Glaciers, you may witness the wanderings of beaver that live at the far end of Lake Louise. They often walk along the trail nibbling the willows, oblivious to tourists.

Lake Agnes
The Lakes in the Clouds

When Tom Wilson first visited Lake Louise in 1882, his Native guide told him of two other lakes high on a neighbouring mountainside. One of these was named "the goat's looking glass." According to legend, mountain goats combed their beards while gazing at their reflections in the still

All Aboard!

Having twice staked his political fortunes on his "National Dream" — the construction of a railway from ocean to ocean — Prime Minister Sir John A. Macdonald was now inspecting the completed project first hand. Perhaps weary from the years of political battles and desperate financial dealings which

Lady Agnes Macdonald

made the railway a possibility, Macdonald retired to his private car for much of the trip, where he indulged in the bottled strength upon which he had become reliant. His wife, Lady Agnes Macdonald, was more outgoing, and quite taken with railroading. At the siding of Laggan, she stole the show.

Lady Agnes rode in the locomotive on the train from Calgary and, while a bigger unit was engaged for the mountainous section ahead, she became possessed of the idea of riding on its cowcatcher "from summit to sea." Despite the fact that the Prime Minister thought it a ridiculous idea, she made good on her word and, as can be imagined, caused a tremendous stir in the newspapers. Lady Agnes even wrote a magazine article entitled "By Car and by Cowcatcher." Cowcatcher riding then became the rage, much as flagpole sitting and wing walking would in later generations.

The steep hike to Lake Agnes is one of the most popular in the Rockies. The lake is probably named for the wife of Canada's first Prime Minister. A tea house operates on the lakeshore during the summer months.

most popular excursion in the Rockies. The presence of a tea house on the lakeshore is probably the principal draw, but the visitor would be wise to take a leisurely pace on this unrelentingly steep, 3.4 km hike, and to pause often to observe the interesting features of the landscape as they unfold.

The Lake Agnes trail branches from the Lake Louise lakeshore trail just beyond the Chateau and immediately begins its ascent through the damp lower subalpine forest. The dominant trees are Engelmann spruce and subalpine fir, with an undergrowth of feather mosses. The first switchback is reached in 1.6 km. Through a break in the forest, Lake Louise is visible directly below. Bear in mind that at this point you are slightly less than half way to your destination.

Beyond the viewpoint a gradual transition to upper subalpine forest takes place. The trail crosses a swath which formerly contained a wooden pipeline, used when Lake Agnes was the water source for the Chateau. At the horse/hiker barrier, the hiker turns left, and in few minutes reaches "the goat's looking glass" — Mirror Lake. The appropriately named Big Beehive forms the backdrop for the lake. Goats don't frequent this well-traveled area much any more, but the surrounding mountainsides contain a sizeable population of this animal.

Climbing away from Mirror Lake, the trail enters an open area

waters. The other lake, subsequently named Lake Agnes for the wife of Canada's first prime minister, is as fine an example of a glacial tarn and cirque as will be found in the Rockies. Together, the lakes were called "the lakes in the clouds" in Canadian Pacific Railway promotions at the turn of the century.

The hike to Lake Agnes is the

in the forest — the bottom of a kilometre long avalanche path on Mt. St. Piran. Snow avalanches sweep the mountainside here annually, precluding the growth of mature trees. The jumble of dead trees and branches down-slope from the trail testifies to the power of these avalanches.

Mt. St. Piran was named for the English birthplace of the origi-nal Chateau manager, Willoughby Astley, who supervised the con-struction of many trails in the area — including this one. Higher on the mountainside, the trail enters stands of Lyall's larch that mark the beginning of the treeline for-est. Mt. Aberdeen and the gla-cier-capped summit of Mt. Temple are visible to the south.

Bridal Veil Falls is reached in a half a kilometre, and immediately above is the tea house on the lake-shore. Walter Wilcox described Lake Agnes as "a wild tarn impris-oned by cheerless cliffs." Despite the number of visitors in the pres-ent day, the view from the tea house is still an impressive scene.

Directly across the lake is the pinnacle of Devil's Thumb. The backdrop is provided by Mt. Whyte (viewer's left), and Mt. Niblock, each of which is almost 10,000 feet high. The mountains are named for a vice-president and superintendent of the Cana-dian Pacific Railway, respectively. Apparently Whyte and Niblock enjoyed the fishing in Lake Ag-nes. Their success may have been too great, for fish repopulate slowly in the cold water at these

elevations, and are scarce in the lake now. As a result fishing is no longer allowed.

If you're feeling tired, it may be the effects of the climb. Since leaving the Chateau, you've gained 307 metres, roughly the equivalent of a 100 storey office building. Lunch, refreshments and snacks are available in sea-son at the tea house. The original structure was built in 1905 by the C.P.R. The present building is a privately owned reconstruction completed in 1981.

The hoary marmot and pika are animals encountered in the

A series of slab waterfalls called The Giant Steps are one of the scenic highlights of a hike into Paradise Valley near Lake Louise.

Porcupine

The much-maligned porcupine is a perfect example of the often peculiar ways in which nature ensures the survival of a given species. So slow moving it could not possibly outrun any predator, the porcupine compensates by wearing a cloak of quilled armour that deters all but the most serious and agile would-be attacker — with the possible exception of the family dog.

The 30,000 yellow and black quills are in reality hairs, and cover all but the animal's face, feet and underside. They are hollow and barbed, and cannot be shot as lore would have it. The quills detach easily, barbed end first, and work their way quickly into the attacker's skin.

A Chippewa legend tells how the porcupine originally did not have quills, and often fell prey to bears. One day a porcupine broke a branch from a hawthorn bush and laid this on his back. Seeing the thorns, the bear left the porcupine alone. The wolf, however, did not, and ended up with a muzzle full of thorns.

Most of the porcupine's diet is made up of the tender layer beneath tree bark. Coniferous trees denuded of their bark in rings are a certain sign porky is about. The injury is often fatal to the tree. Recently, the porcupine has become accustomed to artificial additives in its diet. Delicacies include chemically treated woods, salt-stained boots and backpacks and, remarkably, tires, trim and brake lines on parked vehicles.

The porcupine is mostly nocturnal, and the average camper's experience of this animal will consist of a loss of sleep. Porcupines are quite vocal, with a bizarre repertoire that includes some sounds that are nearly human in character. The effect is enhanced when a group of the animals convene, as is frequently the case. When not serenading, porky will keep you awake by noisily chewing on nearby outhouses or signs.

Porcupines do not hibernate, but nestle in boulderfields or undergrowth. Plywood is a major feature of winter diet, and each spring park maintenance crews inventory the damage to campground buildings in the high country.

Campers in porcupine habitat are advised to wear shoes at all times, and to keep dogs leashed and under strict control.

rocks along the lakeshore beyond the tea house. Red squirrel, least chipmunk, Columbian ground squirrel, golden mantled ground squirrel, Clark's nutcracker and gray jay compete for your attention nearby. Please refrain from feeding them.

For those with energy remaining, the outing can be extended with hikes to Little Beehive, Big Beehive, or the other tea house at the Plain of Six Glaciers. Otherwise, it's all downhill back to the Chateau Lake Louise.

Paradise Valley

The first recorded visit to Paradise Valley was made by Samuel Allen, Walter Wilcox and companions from Yale in the summer of 1894. As is often the case with exploration, the discovery was made in a roundabout fashion: the schoolboys came in through the back door, by a route which crossed a high mountain pass from The Plain of Six Glaciers to the north.

On that particular day the weather had been gloomy as they toiled up the pass. But from its crest, through thinning clouds, came a glimpse of an idyllic, meadowed valley. Struck by the contrast, Allen bestowed the Native name "Wastach," which means "beautiful." Wilcox called it Paradise Valley. "Wastach" was later applied to a pass at the far end of the valley. The towering mountain at the valley's head was

The gondola lift operated by Lake Louise Ski Area provides a splendid panorama of Lake Louise and the surrounding mountains.

Lake Louise: Ten Questions

How far away is Mt. Victoria?
It is 10 km to the cliff beneath the Upper Victoria Glacier, and an additional kilometre to the mountain's summit.

Why do I keep hearing thunder?
Thunder is uncommon at Lake Louise. You are probably hearing the rumble of snow and ice avalanches from the Upper Victoria Glacier. Sound from these events takes 30 seconds to reach the Chateau, so you may hear the avalanche but miss seeing it.

What's that yellow scum on the water?
Yellow tree pollens collect on the water during July and August.

How cold is the water?
Not far from freezing point. The annual high temperature of 4°C is reached in early August.

Does the lake freeze?
Yes, usually from early November until early June. The Chateau maintains skating rinks on the lake surface for much of the winter.

How much snow falls here each year?
About 418 cm, or 165 inches.

Can you walk around the lake?
A developed trail exists on the northwest shore only (viewer's right).

Where do the Chateau staff live?
Most of the staff live in five residences behind the Chateau. Some live in Lake Louise townsite.

Who lives in the house by the bridge?
The house was occupied by the Swiss Guides until the 1940's. Since then it has been the residence of the Chateau manager.

Is it safe to drink the water?
The Chateau takes its water from the lake, but it is treated before consumption. It would not be wise to drink the lake water near shore.

named Hungabee Mountain — "The Chieftain."

Throwing caution to the wind, the party descended into the trackless, new valley, even though they were not certain how to get out of it and back to the chalet at Lake Louise. Two of them were benighted and their campfire, which didn't give much comfort when they needed it, later rekindled and set much of the valley ablaze.

Today hikers and backpackers use several trails to access Paradise Valley, most commonly departing from the Moraine Lake Road at Paradise Creek. Features of this area include Annette Lake and the north face of Mt. Temple, Horseshoe Glacier, stands of Lyall's larch and a series of slab waterfalls known as the Giant Steps. Hiking circuits can be made to Lake Louise via Saddleback Pass, and to Moraine Lake via Sentinel Pass. One of the most accessible backcountry campsites in Banff National Park is also located in the valley

Skoki Valley

The front range valleys east of Lake Louise include some of the most picturesque alpine terrain in Banff National Park. Within a day's hike of the trailhead are over a dozen lakes, appealing subalpine and alpine meadows, and half a dozen valleys to explore.

The trailhead is at the Fish Creek parking lot, adjacent to the Lake Louise Ski Area. Beyond Temple Lodge the trail climbs gently through the upper subalpine forest to Boulder Pass, the

Rustic Skoki Lodge was one of the first ski resorts in western Canada. The lodge is reached by an 11 km ski or hike from the Lake Louise Ski Area.

gateway to the valleys beyond. The Vaux family visited this area in 1906, and various other exploratory forays were made by mountaineers during the next twenty years, including those from the Alpine Club of Canada annual camp in 1915. Walter Wilcox came this way in 1922, as did Charles Walcott of the Smithsonian Institute.

In 1911, a group of American mountaineers climbed in the area, naming many of the features, including the Skoki Valley. "Skoki" (SKOWE-key) is a Native word meaning "marsh." In 1930, local ski enthusiasts constructed a lodge in the valley. It became one of the first ski resorts in western Canada. Skoki Lodge is operated by the Lake Louise Ski Area today, and houses hikers and skiers in a rustic atmosphere.

Moraine Lake

Like most people, mountaineers and explorers have their good days and their bad days. The names they bestow on the landscape may reflect the euphoria of discovery, or the dreariness of another difficult day on the trail. The austere nature of the valley containing Moraine Lake was in marked contrast to the lush green of Paradise Valley to the north, so Walter Wilcox coined the name "Desolation Valley."

The upper valley floor is indeed desolate. The ice-mantled, shaded north faces of the Wenkchemna Peaks are a sombre and imposing sight, towering over

1,200 metres above the Wenkchemna Glacier. Various processes of erosion break apart these massive cliffs, and the rubble collects at the base in funnel-shaped piles called talus (TAY-lus) cones. The prominent, ice-filled couloir at the far end of the lake is often used by climbers as an approach to the mountaineering routes above. Not surprisingly, fatal accidents involving climbers and rockfall sometimes occur in this location.

With all the excitement attending mountaineering in the immediate vicinity of Lake Louise in the late 1890's, it seems odd Moraine Lake went unvisited between the first time it was glimpsed in 1893, and 1899, when Walter Wilcox became the first to reach the lake's shore. Later he wrote: "No scene has given me an equal impression of inspiring solitude and rugged grandeur."

A magazine article written by Wilcox turned Moraine Lake into a popular destination overnight.

The rockpile that dams Moraine Lake is likely debris from a large rockslide. The blocks in the rockpile are Gog quartzite, which forms the lower two thirds of the cliffs on the Wenkchemna Peaks. In the background is the Tower of Babel.

Opposite: Moraine Lake.

The Wenkchemna Peaks form an impressive backdrop for Moraine Lake. In this view, the outflow of the lake is in the foreground, with some of the quartzite blocks of the rockpile on the left.

As a result the inspiring solitude has been nearly impossible to find ever since, although the rugged grandeur prevails.

The Moraine Lake Road is not plowed in winter, when the lake is the sole domain of cross-country skiers and a few mountaineers. The Canadian Pacific Railway constructed a bungalow camp at the lake in the 1920's, the forerunner of today's privately owned Moraine Lake Lodge, where meals, accommodation and boat rentals are available.

Moraine Lake Rockpile

Walter Wilcox, the first visitor to Moraine Lake, was a keen and knowledgeable observer of the landscape. He named the lake on the assumption that its waters are dammed by a moraine deposited by the Wenkchemna Glacier — a manner in which many other lakes in the Rockies have been formed.

Wilcox was probably incorrect. It seems likely the Moraine Lake rockpile was deposited by a rockslide from the cliffs to the south. The boulder fields attest to the fact that the cliffs are in a continual process of tumbling down, and one can almost trace the path of this rockslide in the scarring on the hillside.

Another theory states the rockpile may have been a rockslide that landed on the glacier while the ice was still advancing. The boulders were transported to this point as surface moraine, and deposited when the glacier receded. Yet another theory states

Massive Mt. Temple, the third highest mountain in Banff National Park, dominates the view south from Lake Louise.

the rockslide came to rest on top of an existing moraine. Whether dammed by rockslide or moraine, the name Moraine Lake is still appropriate. Fine examples of moraines are visible at the far end of the lake, and part of the Moraine Lake Road is built along the

Charles Fay

Samuel Allen's "Peak 1 — Heejee" is now known as Mt. Fay, named in honour of Professor Charles Fay of Boston. At the turn of the century, Fay and his companions from the Appalachian Mountain Club made annual pilgrimages to the Rockies, accomplishing first ascents of many high mountains: Hector, Lefroy, Victoria, Goodsir South, Vaux, Chancellor and Balfour. The Club's journal, *Appalachia*, served as a forum in which the mountaineers' adventures were communicated to the world, thereby greatly increasing the popularity of the Rockies with climbers from the United States and Europe.

As well as being the founder of the Appalachian Mountain Club, Fay established the American Alpine Club in 1902. He made 25 visits to the Rockies, including one at the age of 84, in 1930, the year of his death.

Mt. Fay was first climbed in 1904. Today, the prominent ice bulge on the mountain's north face is one of the most popular alpine climbs on the continent.

crest of a lateral moraine.

Moraine Lake is less than half the size of Lake Louise, and is relatively shallow. There is considerable seasonal variation in the volume of water it contains, and by autumn in some years the level is so reduced that barely a trickle escapes at the outlet.

The Wenkchemna Peaks

Mountaineers Samuel Allen and Walter Wilcox first saw Moraine Lake and the mountains surrounding it during an attempt on Mt. Temple in 1893. The following summer, Allen once again observed the mountains during a crossing of Sentinel Pass, and elected to name them using the Stoney Native numbers from one to ten, with Wenkchemna meaning "ten."

Allen's nomenclature was somewhat arbitrary, as there are more than ten peaks in the valley containing Moraine Lake. Most

Coniferous, But Not Evergreen

One of the most popular hikes in the vicinity of Moraine Lake leads to Larch Valley, which is nestled between Pinnacle Mountain and Mt. Temple. The valley is named for the tree Lyall's larch — an altogether uncommon coniferous tree that grows in scattered mountainous areas of southern Alberta and British Columbia.

The branches of the larch are often gnarled and covered in small, black knobs, from which the clusters of bright green needles grow. What is peculiar about this coniferous tree is that the needles are shed annually. This shedding is an adaptation feature that conserves hard-to-obtain nutrients in the winter. Before dropping off in early October, the needles turn yellow and gold. Under the blue skies of an Indian Summer day, and with the Wenkchemna Peaks as a backdrop, Larch Valley is a photographer's paradise — and in recent years it has been a very popular destination.

Because of the elevation at which they are found, larches are very slow-growing trees. Large specimens can be many hundreds of years old. The treeline forest is not dense, and open glades of flower-filled subalpine meadow add to the area's attraction in summer.

Strong hikers can climb beyond Larch Valley to the crest of Sentinel Pass, which is, at 2611 m, the highest point reached by trail in the mountain national parks. On the opposite side of the pass is Paradise Valley and the rock spires that give Pinnacle Mountain its name. The largest of these is called the Grand Sentinel. Sentinel Pass marks the base of the "regular route" on Mt. Temple — the route used by Samuel Allen and Walter Wilcox in the first ascent, 1884.

The short hike to Consolation Lakes offers an easy and quiet alternative to all the activity at Moraine Lake. Fine views of the lakes, the glacier-capped summits of Mts. Bident and Quadra, and colourful larch trees are the hiker's reward.

of his names have now been replaced with contemporary ones, but peaks nine and ten — Neptuak and Wenkchemna — recall a colourful aspect of local history. Other Native names bestowed by Allen are still in use in the Lake O'Hara area.

Popularly called "The Ten Peaks," the name Wenkchemna Peaks was officially adopted in 1979. The peaks were featured on the back of the Canadian twenty dollar bill for a period of twenty years.

Mt. Temple
3543 m/11,626 ft

The bulky form of Mt. Temple dominates the northwest edge of the Valley of the Ten Peaks. Mt. Temple is one of the largest mountains in the Rockies, occupying 15 sq km. It is also the eleventh highest in the range, and third highest in Banff National Park. The mountain was named for Sir Richard Temple, patron leader of a scientific expedition that visited the Rockies in 1884. The summit glacier was named Macdonald Glacier after Canada's first Prime Minister.

Walter Wilcox and Samuel Allen made the first ascent of Mt. Temple in 1894, the first time a summit over 11,000 feet had been reached in Canada. It was seven years until a higher mountain was climbed. Their climbing route, not visible from Moraine Lake, is the "regular route" on the mountain today.

Pika

The tiny pika is largely heard but not seen. It makes a home in rocky areas, where it is well camouflaged. With a minuscule tail, big round ears and a gray coat, this member of the rabbit family looks like a tennis ball with ears.

Active during daytime, the pika gathers grasses, lichens, leaves and wildflowers from the slopes nearby, and dries them on the boulders. This hay is stashed underground. The pika does not hibernate. During the winter it uses rocky corridors under the snow to reach its food caches.

Large boulderfields may feature a colony of pikas, who take turns acting as lookouts. The characteristic, shrill "eeeep" warns their fellows of approaching danger. The sound is audible for a great distance, but the pika is tiny and usually remains unseen. Eagles and hawks can pick off the pika from above. More dangerous are martens, ermine and weasels, which hunt the pika through its bouldery home.

In the 1960's, climbers began to pit their skills against the mile-high, glacier-capped north face of Mt. Temple, which rises above Paradise Valley. A large number of routes have since been established, some combining a high degree of difficulty and danger.

Consolation Valley

"Suddenly a long stretch of water opened before us and disclosed a beautiful scene. Beyond the pretty banks of the stream, lined with birch and willow bushes, appeared in the distance an Alpine peak, fringed in a narrow border of ice near its tooth-like crest ... Everything in these beautiful surroundings helped to make one of the most beautiful pictures I have ever seen in the Rockies."

Two days after his initial visit to Moraine lake, Walter Wilcox and companion Ross Peecock explored this valley, seen by Wilcox and Allen in their attempts on Mt. Temple. The beautiful new valley contrasted with the austere Desolation Valley, and gave rise to the quoted passage. Thus Consolation Valley was named.

Today you can follow Wilcox's path to Consolation Valley and easily reach the Lower Consolation Lake, to enjoy the same grand view. The "tooth-like crest" is comprised of Mt. Bident and Mt. Quadra. Along the way you pass the Tower of Babel, the prominent flat-topped peak immediately east of the Moraine Lake rockpile. A rough trail continues to the Upper Consolation Lake. This is a route for those who don't mind wet feet and are adept at boulder-hopping.

The upper valley is no less a chaos of moraine and rubble than exists at Moraine Lake, but the larch-covered slopes of Panorama Ridge to the viewer's left are the consolation—a delight to the eye —especially in autumn when the larch needles turn gold.

Yoho

Yoho National Park

The origin of Yoho National Park is intrinsically connected to the Canadian Pacific Railway, which was completed through the area in 1884. The railway built its first hotel, Mount Stephen House, at Field in 1886. The rationale was that a dining room at railside would eliminate the need to haul heavy dining cars up and down The Big Hill. Soon the town of Field became a destination point for climbers, artists and scientists wishing to explore the surrounding region, and the railway found itself in the hotel business as well.

Later in 1886, a 16 sq km area of land near the foot of Mt. Stephen was set aside as the Mount Stephen Reserve, forerunner of Canada's second national park.

"Yoho" is a Native expression of awe and wonder. In 1898 German explorer Jean Habel (AHH-bull) published an account of explorations in the Yoho Valley, and in his descriptions the scenery lived up to the name. Pressure mounted from the railway, the outfitters and the explorers to enlarge the protected area. This was accomplished in 1901, with the founding of the Yoho Park Reserve. National Park status fol-

Solar halo and shadow bands over Cathedral Crags, seen from the bottom of Yoho's "Big Hill".

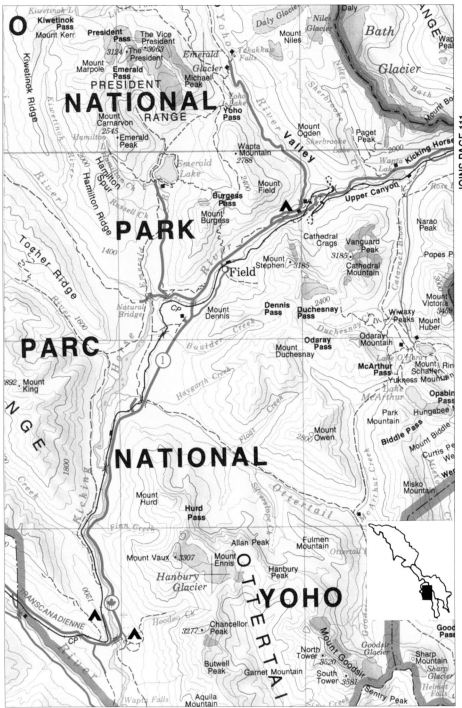

lowed in 1911, along with reductions in area. Since the passing of the National Park Act in 1930, the park's area has been stable at 1,313 sq km.

Kicking Horse Pass
The National Dream

In July 1871, the province of British Columbia entered into Confederation. Eastern Canadians

"Hell's Bells" Rogers

"Every man present had learned, in three days, to hate the Major with real hatred. He had no mercy on horses or men — he had none on himself. The labourers hated him for the way he drove them and the packers for ... the way he abused the horses — never gave their needs a thought."

Outfitter Tom Wilson was describing Major A.B. ("Hell's Bells") Rogers, the man in charge of finding a route through the Rockies and Columbia Mountains for the Canadian Pacific Railway. Colourful, obstinate and seemingly indestructible, Major Rogers was noted for his profanity, the amazing length of his moustache, and his diet of chewing tobacco and raw beans. He was also a competent railway surveyor, having proven himself in the U.S.

In July of 1881, surveying parties organized by Rogers were converging on the Continental Divide. From a camp in the Bow Valley, Rogers sought a volunteer to accompany him on an exploration towards Kicking Horse Pass. None except Wilson dared, for fear of "being starved to death or lost in the woods." Rogers' real motivation was uncertainty over the whereabouts of his nephew Albert. Rogers had instructed Albert to find a way over the divide from the west

— something that hadn't been done since James Hector's eventful first crossing in 1858.

When Wilson and Rogers came upon the swollen waters of a glacially fed creek below Kicking Horse Pass, Wilson suggested they camp and cross the creek next morning when the torrent would be lower. Rogers would have none of that, and plunged into the creek on his horse. Both were quickly submerged in the icy waters. And so Bath Creek was named.

For years afterwards, whenever Bath Creek was in spate, its waters murky with glacial till, it would be remarked that the Major was taking another bath. Albert Rogers was located several days later by Wilson on the west side of the pass, exhausted from the rigours of his journey in the valley of the Kicking Horse.

Major Rogers' chief claim to fame was the discovery in 1882 of the pass across the Selkirk Range that now bears his name. For his work in locating the line of the railway, he was awarded a $5,000 bonus cheque, which he framed and never cashed. Rogers died in 1889 from injuries sustained in a fall from his horse, while surveying a line for the Great Northern Railway in the U.S. Another pass there also commemorates his name.

had been very anxious that British Columbia be included to prevent the province from coming under U.S. control, with a consequent loss of resource wealth and access to west coast shipping. Part of the deal negotiated between Canada and its newest province called for a railway connection to the rest of the country.

The construction of Prime Minister John A. Macdonald's "National Dream" of railway steel from coast to coast was a saga that took 14 years to play out. The characters, intrigue, scandal and wrangling involved are the stuff of Canadian legend. The financial cost was not one the fledgling country could bear, so a syndicate of wealthy bankers, railway builders and Hudson's Bay Company stockholders was formed — the Canadian Pacific Railway. These dedicated men eventually spirited the railway through crisis after crisis and, mortgaged to the hilt, oversaw its construction between 1881-85.

The difficult terrain on the west slope of the Kicking Horse Pass made it a poor choice for the route of the railway. Yellowhead and Howse passes offered much easier prospects for railway construction. The Yellowhead route had the backing of many surveyors, including the original Engineer-in-Chief of the Canadian Pacific Railroad, Sandford Fleming. Of his journey over Kicking Horse Pass in 1883, Fleming wrote: "I do not think I can ever forget that terrible walk; it was the greatest

trial I ever experienced."

However, the purpose of the railway was to help bind the young country together, and to introduce settlement into the prairies. If the railway line was constructed through Yellowhead Pass to the north, a large amount of prairie land adjacent to the U.S. border would come under American influence, and resources would possibly be lost from the Dominion. The selection of Kicking Horse Pass in 1881 was ultimately a desperate political and economic one, and the difficulties presented by the surveyor's line would be dealt with later. As we shall see on The Big Hill, the Canadian Pacific Railway is still dealing with the consequences of this decision.

Yoho, Canada's second national park, protects 1,313 sq km of the western slopes of the Rockies. The park's theme is "rockwalls and waterfalls." The photograph shows a mountaineer's view of Field and the Kicking Horse Valley, from the summit of Mt. Stephen.

Many of the east/west passes in the Rockies feature lakes near their crests. Melting lobes of ice at the end of the Wisconsin Glaciation, 11,000 years ago, created the hollows in which runoff and other meltwater now collects. Wapta Lake, slightly west of Kicking Horse Pass, is one such lake.

Hector's Close Call

The Palliser Expedition of 1857-60 had been sent to central and western Canada by the British government, to explore the region for future settlement, resource wealth and transportation routes. It was a big undertaking in an unknown land. Captain John Palliser was fortunate that one of his charges, James Hector, a 23-year-old Scots geologist, was up to the task. Many of the expedition's discoveries regarding the topography of the Rockies were the result of Hector's ambitious travels. (See picture, p. 187)

Hector wanted to find a route across the Rockies to the Columbia River. From the Bow Valley in 1858, he crossed the Continental Divide at Vermilion Pass, but instead of following the Vermilion and Kootenay Rivers on a certain route to the Columbia, his Native guide led him north over the Beaverfoot Divide to the Kicking Horse Valley. It was there, near Wapta Falls, that Hector was kicked in

the chest by a pack horse and rendered unconscious. His men assumed he was dead, and were preparing to bury him, when to their astonishment (and his!) Hector revived. The incident gave the river, valley and pass their contemporary names. Previously the river had been known as the Wapta — Stoney Native for "river."

Returning from Wapta Falls, Hector's party made an arduous crossing of Kicking Horse Pass, from west to east. Undeterred, Hector kept going: north over Bow Pass, west to Howse Pass, and east to Fort Edmonton for a few month's rest, before embarking in the dead of winter for Athabasca Pass.

Native peoples avoided Kicking Horse Pass. The Kootenay Trail, their route across the Continental Divide, veered north from the Kicking Horse Valley, west of the present day town of Field. It then crossed the gentler Amiskwi and Howse Passes to the North Saskatchewan River and Kootenay Plains.

Where Waters Divide

A navigable break that leads across a mountain range is known as a mountain pass. Most mountain passes separate river systems, and are also part of a watershed divide. If a watershed divide separates waters flowing to different oceans, it is part of the Continental Divide. Kicking Horse Pass is on the Continental Divide, separating waters that flow to Hudson Bay and the Atlantic via the Bow and Saskatchewan Rivers from those that flow to the Pacific via the Kicking Horse and Columbia Rivers.

The quest for feasible passes across the Continental Divide was crucial to surveying the line for the Canadian Pacific Railway. There are hundreds of passes in the Rockies, but most are rugged and remote, and today only three on the Continental Divide are crossed by roads in the mountain national parks.

The Great Divide

A Natural Boundary

From the Yoho junction of the Trans-Canada Highway with the Great Divide Parkway, it is worthwhile to backtrack three kilometres to The Great Divide, along the route of the original roadway in Yoho. Divide Creek wanders onto the crest of the Continental Divide and branches. From this point its waters flow to two oceans, 4,500 km apart. Water flowing east into Alberta feeds the Bow and Saskatchewan river systems, and reaches Hudson's Bay. Water flowing west into British Columbia feeds the Kicking Horse and Columbia Rivers, and reaches the Pacific Ocean. You can stand with the provincial boundary between your feet. Just beyond the dividing point are the main tracks of the Canadian Pacific Railway.

The Great Divide has been a tourist attraction since the arrival of the railway. But at times Divide Creek has deviated slightly from its course, and not divided! It seems the C.P.R. made efforts to ensure the creek lived up to its name, for in the Yoho Park library there are letters between the park

Mountain passes crossed by road in the Rockies

Pass	Elevation	Highway	Watersheds	First Recorded Crossing
Kicking Horse	1625 m	Trans-Canada Highway, CPR	Bow (Atlantic) Kicking Horse (Pacific)	Hector, 1858
Vermilion	1651 m	Kootenay Parkway	Bow (Atlantic) Vermilion (Pacific)	Hector, 1858
Yellowhead	1125 m	Yellowhead Highway, CNR	Miette (Arctic) Fraser (Pacific)	Unknown, ca. 1820
Bow	2069 m	Icefields Parkway	Bow (Atlantic) Mistaya (Atlantic)	Hector, 1858
Sunwapta	2035 m	Icefields Parkway	North Saskatchewan (Atlantic) Sunwapta (Arctic)	Wilcox, 1896

At the Great Divide, Divide Creek branches east into Alberta and west into British Columbia. This one tiny stream feeds two oceans 4,500 km apart.

superintendent and the regional manager of the C.P.R. wherein the latter is admonished for the railway's landscaping efforts.

A cairn at The Great Divide commemorates explorer James Hector, who made the first crossing of Kicking Horse Pass in 1858. Another cairn and plaque describe the work of the Interprovincial Boundary Survey.

Lake O'Hara
"The Fairest of Mountain Lakelet Tarns"

So mountaineer James Outram described Lake O'Hara in 1900. Ever since the first accounts extolling the beauties of Lake O'Hara appeared around the turn of the century, countless other visitors have concurred. At no other location in the Rockies is the visitor immersed so easily in such a wonderful example of a glaciated landscape.

Lake O'Hara's chief attractions are its many lakes, and the splendid diversity of alpine and subalpine terrain offered in its compact area. Adding to the lure is motorized access. Bus transportation is available to a campground and lodge, the staging area for more than 30 hiking trails, which total over 80 km in length.

The area features over 25 named lakes, the second largest of which is Lake O'Hara. Surveyor J.J. McArthur first saw the lake in 1887. From him, Robert O'Hara, a retired British Colonel, heard of the region. He made annual visits for a number of years thereafter. The Alpine Club of Canada held one of its first annual camps near

the lake in 1909, and the Canadian Pacific Railway built a bungalow camp in the 1920's. In 1926, most of the cabins were moved to the lakeshore, the forerunners of today's privately owned Lake O'Hara Lodge. Two other cabins in the meadows are still operated by the Alpine Club of Canada. In 1989, a day-use shelter was constructed near the lake for the benefit of those needing a place to dry out during the frequent spells of poor summer weather.

Lake O'Hara is located directly across the Continental Divide from Lake Louise. Some of the mountains that form O'Hara's backdrop are familiar in name, if not appearance, from this perspective. Many names in the area are from the Stoney language, and were bestowed by mountaineer Samuel Allen between 1893 and 1895.

The number of visitors to the Lake O'Hara area is controlled in an attempt to reduce impacts on the fragile subalpine vegetation. Visitors must make reservations in advance to stay overnight in the campground, cabins or lodge, and to ride the bus. The access road is not open to public vehicles. The area may also be reached via an 11 km fireroad, or a trail hike along Cataract Brook.

Lake O'Hara is one of the most picturesque and popular hiking areas in the Rockies. Numerous alpine lakes are the principal highlights of this rugged, glaciated landscape.

The Big Hill

From Wapta Lake to the flats east of Field, the Kicking Horse River drops 330 m in six kilometres. The terms of the Canadian Pacific Railway's agreement with the government required that in no place could the grade of the railway line exceed 2.2 per cent. The terrain of Kicking Horse Valley dictated a grade two and a half times as steep.

To construct the railway to specifications on The Big Hill would have required many tunnels and at least an extra year. The C.P.R. needed to be in business as soon as possible, to begin paying off the incredible debt it was incurring. General manager William Cornelius Van Horne decided to adopt a "temporary solution" — a grade of over four per cent — which would be rectified when the financial situation allowed. It was the steepest grade ever constructed on a regularly operated commercial railway line and, as one C.P.R. executive commented, became "a heavy cross to bear through the years."

Runaway trains can occur on grades exceeding one per cent. The very first construction train that attempted to descend The Big Hill ran away and plunged into the canyon, killing three workers. It would not be the last such disaster. A system of manual safety switches was installed to divert runaway trains onto spur lines, where as one worker remarked: "Wrecks could take place without hindering traffic on the main line." Four blasts on the whistle from an approaching train meant it was out of control.

One engineer, finding himself with a runaway on his hands and not wanting to face a certain wreck on a spur line, signalled all the switchmen to let him through, and actually survived the ride to Field. For his heroism, and disregard for the rules, he was unceremoniously fired — by a telegram marked "rush."

Lady Agnes Macdonald, wife of Prime Minister John A. Macdonald, rode down The Big Hill on the cowcatcher of a locomotive in 1886, remarking it presented a "delightful opportunity for a new sensation." One can imagine the cringes of the train's crew.

Uphill trains had their problems, too. Some locomotives exploded under the stress. The steep grade required four locomotives to haul a 15 car train, and additional "pusher" locomotives were sometimes dispatched to help trains stalled on the hill. It took an hour for the trains to climb from Field to Wapta Lake. With all the wear and tear, a roundhouse and yard were built at Field in 1898 to service locomotives and rolling stock. The turn-table can still be seen today.

The large number of steam engines working at full capacity had a pronounced effect on the immediate area. A thick deposit of coal soot collected on everything. The town of Field was drab and dirty, and residents didn't bother to paint or decorate their homes, or to hang out their laundry! This condition persisted until the arrival of the diesel age in 1956. Coal cinders are still visible at railside today.

As if all this wasn't bad enough, the railway line passed through many avalanche paths on Cathedral Mountain and Mt. Stephen, and winter snow and ice avalanches would frequently bury the tracks, and derail unfortunate trains in their path. This happened as recently as 1986, finally prompting the C.P.R. to construct, at considerable expense, the concrete snow shed visible at the bottom of the hill. Mud slides and flash floods also occur along this section of the line. On average, these inundate both the railway and the Trans-Canada Highway once every two years.

Despite all the horrors and headaches on The Big Hill, in the 24 years before the Spiral Tunnels were constructed there was not a single accident involving a passenger train.

Spiral Tunnel Viewpoint

William Cornelius Van Horne's "temporary solution" to the problems posed by the grade of The Big Hill was finally rectified in 1909 with the completion of the Spiral Tunnels. These two ingenious tunnels combine to create a figure eight deep within Mt. Ogden and Cathedral Mountain, adding nearly seven kilometres to the length of the line and reducing

the overall grade to 2.2 per cent.

The lower tunnel in Mt. Ogden is 900 m long, has a curvature of 226°, and drops 15 m. The upper tunnel in Cathedral Mountain is 1,000 m long, has a curvature of 288°, and drops 16 m. One thousand men were employed for almost two years in the construction of the tunnels, working concurrently from either end. The error in alignment where the tunnel sections met in the centre was less than five centimetres (two inches). The tunnels cost $1.5 million.

Although they're a tremendous improvement, the tunnels have not been without their problems. During the days of steam engines, condensation caused icicles to build up on the tunnel roof and walls. In an attempt to alleviate this problem, manually-operated doors were installed on the upper tunnel to keep cold air out. Between 1954 and 1962, the interior of the tunnels was lined with concrete and steel arches, to

Engine 314 derailed while coming down The Big Hill. It was subsequently repaired. On a later uphill journey the locomotive exploded, killing three of the crew.

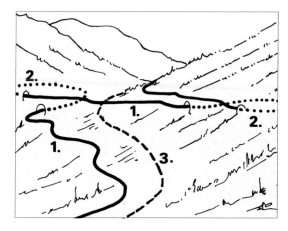

The steepness of the grade on The Big Hill was finally rectified in 1909, with the completion of the ingenious Spiral Tunnels. These two tunnels combine to make a figure eight, adding seven kilometres to the length of the line, and reducing the grade to the specified maximum.

In the above diagram, the solid line (1) represents the exposed section of railway track, the dotted line (2) represents the tunneled part of the railway track, and the dashed line (3) indicates the Trans-Canada Highway.

prevent rocks from falling onto the tracks. Ice build-up from seeping water is still a problem in the tunnels today.

From this viewpoint, the Lower Spiral Tunnel in Mt. Ogden is visible. Locomotives on long freight trains will be seen exiting from one portal, while the last cars of the train are still entering the tunnel at the other portal. On average, 20–30 trains travel through the tunnels each day. If you really want to see a train here, have patience. The Upper Spiral Tunnel in Cathedral Mountain can be seen from a viewpoint on the Yoho Valley Road.

Motorists and pedestrians are advised the Spiral Tunnel Viewpoint is the most heavily visited roadside pull-off in any Canadian national park. The intersections are dangerous. Observe the posted speed limit and lane markings, and signal your intention to turn well in advance.

Climbers and Controversy

In 1896, Jean Habel (AHH-bull), a German professor and mountaineer, rode the railway west to Field. On The Big Hill a pyramid-shaped peak, which he named Hidden Mountain, caught his eye, and he resolved to return the following year and climb it.

Habel's party journeyed from Emerald Lake, across Yoho Pass, to reach the Yoho Valley roughly opposite Takakkaw Falls. They then proceeded north in the valley, discovered Twin Falls, and eventually ascended onto Yoho Glacier. At this point the party decided to retreat.

Outfitter Tom Wilson vehemently insisted he first explored the Yoho Valley in 1894 while prospecting for minerals. He claimed to have suggested and organized Habel's journey for him, with the idea that, in return, Habel would publish a description of the scenery for public consumption. Some feel that in claiming another "first" in the area, Wilson was jealously guarding his domain. But there may be truth in his version of the events.

Wilson did outfit the Habel party in 1897, and the guide on the trip, Ralph Edwards, stated it was Habel's intention to climb Mt. Balfour, not Hidden Mountain. Despite all these discrepancies, the outcome was that Habel's published account of the exploration, which appeared in the mountaineering journal *Appalachia*, succeeded in attracting public attention, and was instrumental in the subsequent expansion of the Mt. Stephen Reserve.

The argument of who first explored the Yoho Valley is somewhat academic. Along the Yoho Valley Road, evidence has been found of Native campsites that pre-date the controversy by hundreds of years.

Habel made another exploration in the Rockies, to the upper reaches of the Athabasca River, north of Columbia Icefield, in 1901. He died shortly thereafter. Mountaineer J.N. Collie renamed "Hidden Mountain" as Mt. Habel, but anti-German sentiment after the First World War prevailed, and the name was changed again to Mount des Poilus (daypwah-LOO), to commemorate French foot soldiers.

Monarch Mine

As the presence of mine openings on Mts. Stephen and Field attest, resource extraction has been allowed in the past in the mountain national parks. Coal mining and logging in Banff and Jasper, talc and ochre mining in Kootenay, and ore mining and logging in Yoho have all been phased out now, but form interesting chapters in the human history of the Rocky Mountains.

During travels in the Kicking Horse Valley in 1882, Tom Wilson found ore at the base of Mt. Stephen. He sent a sample off for analysis and was informed the ore was valuable, but that expensive procedures would be required to extract it. Wilson staked a claim and, being without the finances to mine it, turned it over to others. The claim was resold, and eventually became the Monarch Mine.

For 60 years, various companies worked the mine for lead, zinc, silver, and traces of iron, silica, sulphur and gold. A mill was built at the base of The Big Hill, hydro-electricity was generated from nearby Monarch Creek, and a 160 m aerial, gravity tramway was used to bring ore down from the mountainside.

The Kicking Horse Mine opened on Mt. Field in 1910, and a similar arrangement was constructed in 1937 to bring the ore to roadside, from where it was trucked to the Monarch mill. To support all the activity, a small

A Hero Remembered

The name of Partridge railway siding on The Big Hill does not commemorate a species of bird, but engineer Seth Partridge. One night in August 1925, Partridge was manning a pusher engine on the upper line on Cathedral Mountain, when he heard an avalanche of mud, water and rocks sweeping the mountainside above.

Partridge knew there was a siding house directly below in which men were sleeping. He stopped his locomotive and quickly descended the mountainside on foot to warn the men of the danger. When he reached the siding house he was too breathless to yell, but managed to get everyone outside before the slide hit, demolishing the building. For his brave and heroic act, Partridge was awarded $1,000 by the American magazine *Liberty*.

Mt Stephen and the Kicking Horse River, from just below Meeting of the Waters.

tonnes of ore were extracted, with production peaking in the mid 1940's.

Wooden balconies and ladders, and entrances to the mine shafts, are visible from the bottom of The Big Hill. The mine entrances are now permanently sealed.

Logging took place in Yoho at various locations from 1884 until the end of operations in the Amiskwi Valley in 1968. In the early 1950's, this remote valley supported a logging community as large as the present day town of Field.

Meeting of the Waters

Meeting of the Waters is where the Kicking Horse River receives a major tributary, the Yoho River. (In reality, the Yoho is the larger of the two at this point.) The Yoho is thick with glacial till, which gives its waters a dirty, gray appearance, while the waters of the Kicking Horse are much clearer.

This is unusual, as both rivers are glacially fed. The difference is produced by natural settling ponds further upstream on tributaries of the Kicking Horse. Most of its waters pass through Sherbrooke Lake and Wapta Lake, and much of the till it carries drops from the flow to the lake bottoms.

Switchbacks

To by-pass a canyon in the Yoho River, the road now makes a zigzag climb up the slope to the west. Buses cannot negotiate the sharp

mining community called Cathedral developed near the present day Kicking Horse campground. The mines operated intermittently until 1952 and employed up to 120 workers. Over 930,000

The Yoho Valley Road

At the bottom of the Big Hill, turn right for the Yoho Valley Road and Takakkaw Falls. The Yoho Valley Road cannot be safely negotiated by large recreational vehicles, or cars pulling trailers. A trailer drop-off site is provided. The road is not plowed between October and June.

bend, and are forced to reverse along one length of the switchback. Use caution here, and yield the right of way to any vehicle negotiating the middle bend. Mountain goats are sometimes seen in this vicinity.

Cathedral Crags
3073 m/10,149 ft

The pinnacled summits of Cathedral Crags are featured in the view south from this part of the Yoho Valley Road, concealing the higher summit of Cathedral Mountain. The Crags were first ascended by James Outram in 1900.

The ice of Cathedral Glacier can be seen in the notch to the left of the Crags. A lake that forms beneath the ice occasionally discharges through the notch with disastrous results, sweeping the mountainside with a slurry of debris, inundating the railway and highway below. This phenomenon is known as a jokulhaup (YOWE-kull-up). A pumping station was installed on the glacier after the last such event in 1984, in an attempt to keep the lake from reaching the critical level.

Mountaineering is popular in the Little Yoho Valley and on the Wapta and Waputik Icefields, during summer and winter months. This view is from the summit of Mt. des Poilus, Jean Habel's "Hidden Mountain."

C.P.R. Sites

Two interesting sites connected with the Canadian Pacific Railway can be viewed near the bottom of The Big Hill. The Old Bake Oven in Kicking Horse campground is a Dutch oven used at a railway construction camp in 1884. The wreck of a runaway locomotive can be reached in a half hour walk from the campground, along the Walk-in-the-Past trail.

Cathedral Crags and Cathedral Mountain tower over the Trans-Canada Highway at the bottom of Yoho's "Big Hill." These mountains are also visible looking south from the Yoho Valley Road.

Takakkaw Falls

Takakkaw (TA-kuh-kah) Falls is one of the most impressive sights at roadside in the Rockies. With a combined drop of 254 m, the falls rank as one of the highest in both Canada and the world. The name "Takakkaw" is Cree Native for "it is wonderful!" and, looking at these falls, it is easy to understand that sentiment, and how Yoho came by its motto: "rockwalls and waterfalls."

Takakkaw is fed by the meltwaters of Daly Glacier. The amount of water in the falls varies with the time of year and time of day, and will be at maximum late on a hot summer afternoon in July and August. Boulders carried in the stream flow can often be heard tumbling down the cliff. The Waputik (WAH-poo-tick) Range is above Takakkaw Falls. Waputik is Stoney Native for "white goat," and mountain goats are often seen along the base of the cliffs nearby.

In January 1974, four local climbers succeeded in climbing the frozen Takakkaw Falls, the most difficult such route completed at that time. This event heralded the arrival of waterfall ice climbing as a significant winter activity in the Rockies.

Yoho Valley

Although the Takakkaw Falls parking lot is the ultimate destination on the Yoho Valley Road for those seeing the Rockies by vehicle, it marks a prominent point of departure for many exploring on foot. With its waterfalls, lakes, and relatively quick access to the

Takakkaw Falls is one of the highest waterfalls in Canada. The name is a Native expression, meaning "it is wonderful!"

upper subalpine and alpine ecoregions, the hiker's experience of the Yoho Valley is one of a complete overview of the many facets of Rockies scenery.

For strong hikers with a full day to spend, Yoho Lake, the Iceline Trail, Twin Falls and Yoho Glacier are each recommended hikes. For those with more time, many of the trails interconnect, and multi-day loop hikes can be created, using the six backcountry campsites in the area.

The summits adjacent to the Yoho Valley have been popular with mountaineers since 1901, when James Outram teamed up with the conqueror of the Matterhorn, Edward Whymper, to make first ascents of most of the major peaks in the area.

Kicking Horse River, Trans-Canada Highway

The Kicking Horse River has its origins in the melting snow and ice on the Wapta and Waputik Icefields, and the glaciers in the Lake O'Hara area. Glacial meltwaters contain a high concentration of rubble known as till. At the bottom of The Big Hill, most of

Twin Falls in the Yoho Valley were first visited by the party of German explorer Jean Habel in 1897.

the larger till particles carried by the rambunctious river drop out of the flow, and form a gravelly outwash plain. The daily and seasonal variations in the glacial melt produce an ever-changing braided stream.

The Kicking Horse River has been called one of the biggest gravel-producing rivers, by volume, in the world. This outwash plain, one of several in Yoho, is over eight kilometres long. Mats of a wildflower, yellow mountain avens, thrive on the gravels. The twisted, dandelion-like seed pods appear in mid-summer.

The Kicking Horse River is the principal watercourse in Yoho and is the "home" valley for wildlife that live in the park year-round. In summer you may see

Lofty Mt. Stephen dominates the Kicking Horse valley in the vicinity of Field.

white-tailed deer, mule deer and black bear; in winter, elk, coyote and wolf.

In recognition of its unique natural history, and the role it played in the development of transportation in this country, the portion of the Kicking Horse River within Yoho National Park was designated a Canadian Heritage River in 1989. A plaque may be viewed at the Information Centre in Field. The designation stops at the west boundary of the park. The government of British Columbia refuses to participate in the Heritage Rivers Program.

Mt. Stephen
3199 m/10,495 ft

From the town of Field, Mt. Stephen appears to be one of the highest mountains in the Rock-

ies. Although it is not, the vertical relief from base to summit is 1940 m/6400 ft, a figure matched by few other mountains this close to the road.

The same sequence of sedimentary formations that comprise the cliffs of Castle Mountain occurs again in Mt. Stephen. It was in the shales of the Stephen Formation, near mid-height on the mountain, that fossils were discovered in 1877. The Stephen Fossil Bed and its trilobites subsequently became world famous.

Dominion Land Surveyor J.J. McArthur and his assistant made the first ascent of Mt. Stephen in 1887, the first time a summit over 10,000 ft had been climbed in Canada. In his surveying work, McArthur became an accomplished mountaineer, making

Study of the weird and wonderful soft-bodied fossils of the Burgess Shale is leading to radical scientific revisions of the history of life on earth.

many first ascents of prominent mountains in the central Rockies.

For several decades, Mt. Stephen, along with Mts. Lefroy and Victoria at Lake Louise, and Mt. Sir Donald at Rogers Pass, were "must" ascents for any mountaineer visiting western Canada. The Canadian Pacific Railway stationed Swiss Guides at Mt. Stephen House in Field, to lead aspiring alpinists to the summit.

The mountain was named for Sir George Stephen, first president of the C.P.R.

The Burgess Shale

Towards a New View of the Past
Charles Walcott of the Smithsonian Institute discovered another outcrop of the fossil-rich Stephen Formation above Field in 1909, on the ridge connecting Wapta Mountain and Mt. Field. These sites and others discovered more recently are commonly referred to as the Burgess Shale, an old name for the Stephen Formation.

The creatures fossilized in the Burgess Shale owe their remarkable state of preservation to the fact that they lived in water at the base of a cliff, and were annihilated by mudslides that swept over the cliff. Entombed in thick

Home Ownership in the National Parks

Residence in the national parks is restricted to those who have a "need to reside" — employees of the parks and vital services. As all land in the parks is owned by the Crown, private ownership of lots is not permitted. Instead, homeowners, businesses and hotels lease their land from the Canadian Parks Service, and pay annual land taxes.

Banff, Jasper and Field are officially called "townsites," and private homes are allowed, although the number of lots available is limited. Lake Louise is officially a "visitor centre," and private homes are not permitted. All accommodation there is government- or business-owned, and allotted solely for occupancy by essential staff.

silts, they never decayed. The cliff is known as the Cathedral Escarpment, and may mark the shoreline of an ancient sea that covered the area 530 million years ago. It is to this era — known to geologists as the Cambrian — that these fossils date. By comparison, the dinosaurs disappeared a scant 66 million years ago.

Walcott made repeated visits to his fossil quarries until 1917, and took a grand total of 80,000 fossil specimens back to the Smithsonian Institute in Washington D.C. His administrative duties there precluded a comprehensive evaluation of all he had found, but in the descriptions Walcott did make of his samples he attempted to fit all of the fossil species into categories already known from the fossil record elsewhere in the world.

Closer inspection has revealed the Burgess Shale fossils contain much diversity, and creatures not known from any other sites. New research on Walcott's specimens, which began in the 1970's, continues today. Over 150 species have been identified. Many of these creatures have since disappeared from the face of the earth. This indicates a reduction in the variety of lifeforms has taken place over time — a marked shift from the concept of an increase in diversity normally associated with evolutionary theory. This discovery may lead to a radical scientific revision of the history of life on earth.

The Burgess Shale sites have been designated as areas of special preservation, and access is only permitted on guided hikes, or by permission of the park superintendent. Call the park in advance for details. Displays portraying the fossils can be viewed beneath the flagpoles at the beginning of the Yoho Valley Road, and in the Information Centre in Field.

Field

The community of Field developed from a railway construction camp in 1884, and was named for Cyrus Field, promoter of the first trans-Atlantic communications cable, who visited the area that year. Originally, Field occupied both sides of the Kicking Horse River, but many buildings on the north side were totally destroyed by an avalanche from Mt. Burgess in 1909 — a good incentive for relocation!

Field's heyday was the turn of the century, when scientists, artists, climbers, railway workers, miners and outfitters rubbed elbows while using the town as a base for their ventures. Mount Stephen House, the Canadian Pacific Railway's first mountain hotel, was constructed in 1886, and drew visitors from around the world. In the summer of 1912, it registered almost 8,500 guests. It was at Mt. Stephen House that the seed idea for the Alpine Club of Canada was proposed in 1906. The club held its first annual camp at Yoho Pass that summer.

The Natural Bridge marks the point where the Kicking Horse River encounters a resistant limestone formation in the bedrock. The river has eroded a small channel through the lip of the formation, creating the "bridge."

With the coming of the automobile, the C.P.R. shifted its hotel interests to "bungalow camps." Mt. Stephen House was sold to the Y.M.C.A in 1918, and operated as a hostel until being demolished between 1953 and 1963.

Field's climate is the subject of much derision amongst residents of other Rocky Mountain communities. The summers are wetter than on the eastern slopes, and the town spends much of the winter in the icy shade of Mts. Stephen and Dennis. Winter inversion fogs frequently trap the valley bottom in chilling cloud, and a vicious, local east wind called the Yoho Blow sometimes howls in winter months across the Kicking Horse Flats, sending the snow flying and the wind chill plunging.

Still, some 300 people make Field their home. The community is the administrative centre for Yoho National Park, and most of its residents find work with the park, the railway or the hotels in the area.

Natural Bridge

Three kilometres west of Field, turn right for the Emerald Lake Road and Natural Bridge.

Downstream from the Kicking Horse Flats, the Kicking Horse River has eroded a narrow canyon through the weak shales. At Natural Bridge, the river encounters a fairly resistant formation of limestone rock, which is oriented perpendicular to the flow of the water. At one time, this would have produced a small waterfall here. The river has succeeded in eroding a channel downwards through the limestone, just upstream from its edge, thus creating the bridge. At high water the river flows over all the surrounding rock, and covers the Natural Bridge.

William Cornelius Van Horne

The Van Horne Range, running northwest from the Kicking Horse Valley beyond Field, commemorates William Cornelius Van Horne. Van Horne was appointed General Manager of the Canadian Pacific Railway in 1881, and later became its president and chairman of the board.

Much to the chagrin of the Canadian press, Van Horne was an American directing a Canadian venture. His career read like the ultimate success story. In twenty years he had worked his way from telegraph operator of the Michigan Central Railway to chief of one of the largest of railway undertakings, the C.P.R. At the age of 38 he was touted as "one of the greatest railway generals in the world." He needed to be. He was about to oversee construction of a railway committed to crossing two mountain passes that had not yet been surveyed.

Van Horne was a bear of a man, with a remarkable memory and no apparent requirement for sleep. In his rise to the top he took no rest, either, from learning about his profession, preferring instead to acquaint himself with other railway jobs by working them on his days off. As a result he knew every aspect of railroading, from yardwork to scheduling to driving locomotives. In all matters, Van Horne paid tenacious attention to detail, saving pennies here and minutes there, making railroads pay.

Van Horne's crowning achievement with the Canadian Pacific Railway was the creation of a hotel business, and the establishment of working relationships with an array of mountaineers, artists and scientists who visited the Rockies. These travellers publicized their exploits, thus repaying the C.P.R. by generating more tourist business.

Van Horne was forthright in his support of proposals to establish Banff and Yoho National Parks. Although he was primarily motivated by commerce, we can be thankful to this dynamic man for the direct role he played in helping create Canada's national park system.

Black-tipped groundsel, paintbrush and fireweed fill meadows in the logged and burned forest of the upper Amiskwi Valley, 25 km northwest of Field.

Amiskwi Valley

A gravel road continues beyond Natural Bridge to a pleasant picnic area at the junction of the Kicking Horse, Amiskwi (a-MISS-kwee) and Emerald Rivers. Along the way, the road passes a mineral lick frequented by moose, deer and, very occasionally, mountain goats. At the meeting place of the rivers, it is interesting to observe the river colouration produced by the intermixing of the three streams — the silty Kicking Horse, the less silty Amiskwi, and the clear Emerald.

The Amiskwi Valley is the second largest in Yoho, stretching 40 km to the park's north boundary. It was part of the Native Kootenay Trail between interior B.C. and Kootenay Plains, east of the Rock-

Emerald Lake is one of many lakes in the Rockies created by natural dams of glacial rubble, deposited at the end of the Wisconsin Glaciation, 11,000 years agao. Hiking, fishing, trail riding and canoeing are popular activities at the lake.

Left: The Canadian Pacific Railway constructed the original Emerald Lake Chalet in 1902. The present lodge was constructed in 1986, incorporating some of the original logwork.

ies. An archaeological excavation nearby uncovered bison bones and iron-stained mud called ochre, two items that indicate Native peoples camped in this area. Logging took place in the valley from 1948 until 1968, and much of the vegetation in the upper valley is presently regenerating from forest fires connected

with this industry.

Amiskwi is a Native word for "beaver." The river had originally been called the Beavertail by explorer Mary Schäffer. From the Amiskwi River bridge, fire roads continue into the Amiskwi Valley and along the Kicking Horse River. Today these gated roads are used primarily by mountain bikers.

Emerald Lake

As with many large lakes in the Rockies, the waters of Yoho's largest lake are dammed by an old glacial moraine, atop which sits the lodge. Most of Emerald Lake's waters are glacial in origin, and the remarkable colour of the water is caused by fine particles of suspended till called rock flour, which reflect the blue/green spectrum of light.

Trails radiate from the Emerald Lake parking lot. It is possible to make both shoreline (two hours) and high level (full day) circuits around the environs of the lake. A branch trail leads from the Emerald lakeshore to the impressive glacial amphitheatre of Emerald Basin. Another trail climbs past Hamilton Falls to Hamilton Lake in the upper subalpine ecoregion. The meadows at Hamilton Lake are filled with the blooms of glacier lily and anenome in July.

The original Emerald Lake Chalet was constructed by the Canadian Pacific Railway in 1902. The present Lodge and cabins were completed in 1986, utilizing some of the original logwork. Beyond the wooded saddle,

All in a Summer's Work

The year 1882 was a momentous one for Tom Wilson. In his work surveying with the Canadian Pacific Railway he discovered Lake Louise, crossed Bow and Howse passes, and found ore on the slopes of Mt. Stephen. At the end of the summer he topped it off by discovering Emerald Lake.

Wilson had left horses in a pasture near the present town of Field. The horses went looking for better feed, and Wilson tracked them across Natural Bridge to Emerald Lake.

"Emerald" is an obvious name for the lake, but it was not bestowed by Wilson. He had already used that name for the lake now known as Louise. In 1884, the name of Lake Louise was changed, and Emerald was given to this, Wilson's other gem of a discovery.

Highest Mountains in Yoho

across the lake from the lodge, is Takakkaw Falls and the Yoho Valley.

The Emerald Lake Road, then known as "Snow Peak Avenue," was completed in 1904. It continued around the west side of the lake as a corduroy carriage road. Portions of the original road in the vicinity of Natural Bridge are now known as the Tally-Ho Trail, and are used by hikers, cyclists and skiers.

Sport fishing, trail riding and canoeing are popular activities at the lake. Emerald Lake Sports provides rentals and guiding services. Along with moose and the occasional black bear, wildlife you may see in the vicinity includes American marten, swallows, osprey and common loon.

The twin peaks of Mt. Goodsir are 20 km southeast from here, along the Trans-Canada Highway at the head of the Ottertail River. Although they are the highest mountains in Yoho, they are virtually concealed from view to all but hikers and mountaineers. The best view of them from a highway is a distant one from the south, on the Kootenay Parkway.

The Goodsirs are notable exceptions to the generally lower and more gentle topography of the western main ranges. With an elevation of 3562 m/11,686 ft, South Goodsir is the ninth highest summit in the Rockies. Charles Fay participated in the first ascent in 1903. North Goodsir, only 37 m lower, was first climbed

The twin towers of Mt. Goodsir, Yoho's highest mountain, are at the head of the Ottertail Valley, 20 km south of Field. Concealed from motorists' view, these peaks are familiar landmarks to mountaineers.

Opposite top: Mt. Burgess rises above Emerald Lake. The teahouse at the Emerald Lake Lodge is very popular in the summer.

in 1909. James Hector of the Palliser Expedition named the Goodsirs in 1858, for a professor at the University of Edinburgh.

The Ottertail Range, which includes the Goodsirs, is home to many of Yoho's estimated population of 400 mountain goats. Mt. Hurd, the northern outpost of the Ottertail Range, shows evidence of a 1971 forest fire, which was started by lightning.

Western Wood Lily

Blooming during early summer in the montane forest, the western wood lily's large, orange flower immediately catches the eye. The flower is speckled inside with black dots on a yellow background.

It is illegal to pick the western wood lily. As this act is usually fatal to the plant, it is becoming less and less common. Please leave the blossoms for others to enjoy. The western wood lily is the provincial emblem of Saskatchewan.

Deerlodge

The turn-off for Hoodoos Campground provides access to two points of interest. Built in 1904, Deerlodge was the first park warden patrol cabin in Yoho. Warden John Tocher lived here from 1920-26, when the railway was the only connection to the outside world. He brought the cookstove to the cabin from nearby Leanchoil siding by slinging it between two horses and crossing the Kicking Horse River at low water in autumn.

The building stands in a climax montane forest notable for incredibly large black cottonwood poplar trees. Deerlodge has been vacant for many years. The cabin was restored in 1961 and may be inspected during the summer months. There are eight warden cabins in use in the park today. The nearby Nature Trail encircles a montane wetland.

Leanchoil Hoodoos

The Leanchoil (lee-ANN-coil) Hoodoos were created by the same process as those near Banff townsite. What makes these hoodoos so special is that most, true to the proper definition of a hoodoo, still retain their capstones. This indicates they are most likely of recent origin. Geologists have referred to the Leanchoil Hoodoos as the best examples of this formation in the world. The hike to the hoodoos is very steep, but it's also fairly short.

Leanchoil is another Scottish name connected to the construc-

tion of the Canadian Pacific Railway. The mother of Donald Smith, a Canadian Pacific Railway stockholder, lived in a manor named Leth-na-Coyle in Scotland. The name was applied to the railway siding just west of here.

Mt. Vaux
3319 m/10,890 ft

In a curious twist that foreshadowed events to come, James Hector named Mt. Vaux (VOX) in 1858 for William Vaux, a friend of the leader of the Palliser Expedition. In 1887 the Vaux family of Philadelphia (distantly related) arrived in the Rockies, beginning a love affair with the mountains which lasted over 40 years. Summer after summer, family members returned here, and to the Selkirk Mountains near Rogers Pass. Their interests were more than recreational. The Vaux family were talented photographers, amateur scientists and artists, and much of the early record of this landscape results from their work.

The Vaux family made systematic measurements of the Great Glacier at Rogers Pass, and the Yoho and Victoria Glaciers in the Rockies, and published monographs of their studies, documented with black and white photographs. Mary Vaux was accompanied by explorer Mary Schäffer on many travels. In 1914, Vaux married Charles Walcott, of Burgess Shale fame. Mary was skilled at painting Rocky Mountain wildflowers and, with Walcott's assistance, a collection of her work was published by the Smithsonian Institute in 1925.

Capstones on the Leanchoil Hoodoos have protected the resistant pillars of glacial debris, while the surrounding material has weathered away. These are considered to be some of the best examples of hoodoos in the world.

The Vaux family of Philadelphia made repeated trips to the Rockies around the turn of the century. They were talented photographers, artists and amateur scientists, and left a rich legacy of images and writing concerning the early days of exploration in the Rockies. The photograph shows some members of the Vaux family on Victoria Glacier at Lake Louise in 1900.

The summit of Mt. Vaux rises almost 2200 m/7200 ft above the Trans-Canada Highway, the greatest vertical relief of any mountain at roadside in this part of the range. Charles Fay and James Outram were in the first ascent party in 1901. Neighbour-ing Chancellor Peak (viewer's right) is but 39 m lower. Outram was in its 1901 first ascent party, too.

The avalanche path on Mt. Vaux is one of the largest in the Rockies, sweeping almost 2,000 vertical metres of mountainside.

The Golden Canyon

Beyond the west boundary of Yoho, the Trans-Canada Highway follows the Kicking Horse to its junction with the Columbia River at Golden. The valley is V-shaped, and the river has eroded a spec-tacular canyon through the weak shales and limestones. In places the road snakes along ledges carved from the mountainside above the canyon. The driving requires great attention and care.

The mountains on the south side of the valley are part of the western ranges, the oldest mountains in the Rockies. Look for deer, bighorn sheep and coyote along this section of the highway.

Wapta Falls
Yoho's Niagara

The 30 m drop of Wapta Falls is minuscule compared to other waterfalls in Yoho. However, what these falls lack in height they make up for in breadth. Most of the surface runoff and glacial meltwa-ter in the park passes over the brink of this cataract, with a peak summer flow of 255 cubic metres a second.

Just upstream from the falls, the Beaverfoot River joins the Kicking Horse. It was near this junction that James Hector was

Most of the meltwater and surface runoff in Yoho passes over the brink of 30 m high Wapta Falls. At high water, the roar of these falls is audible from the trailhead, more than two kilometres away.

kicked by a pack horse in 1858, a fateful incident that gave name to Kicking Horse Pass. "Wapta" is a Native Stoney word for "river," and was used alternately for the Kicking Horse River until the turn of the century.

The round-trip hike to Wapta Falls is less than five kilometres, and is within the capabilities of the most modest of hikers. In the airborne mist at trail's end, one can obtain a refreshing, close-up view of the falls.

The access road to Wapta Falls parallels the Leanchoil Marsh, an Environmentally Sensitive Site with abundant aquatic vegetation. The marsh is home to beaver, muskrat, great blue heron and moose.

The Kootenay Parkway

Floe Lake lies at the base of The Rockwall, a 900m high limestone cliff that forms part of the western boundary of Kootenay National Park. The lake is one of the many highlights along the Rockwall Trail, a popular backpacking route.

The idea for a road across Vermilion Pass, linking the Bow and upper Columbia Valleys, originated in 1910 with Robert Bruce, a businessman from Invermere, British Columbia. Bruce's motivation was commerce — he predicted the development of a fruit growing industry in the Columbia Valley. Eventually, his plan led to the creation of Kootenay, Canada's tenth national park.

Bruce promoted his idea to a receptive Canadian Pacific Railway, and a deal was made whereby the Federal Department of the Interior would build the portion of the road between Banff and Vermilion Pass. British Columbia and the C.P.R. would construct the rest.

Construction began in 1911, and soon went over budget. By November 1914, Banff and Vermilion Pass were connected, but only two difficult stretches had been completed in British Columbia, totalling less than a third of the 90 km section. With the outbreak of the First World War, the project was suspended.

Bruce continued lobbying for the road. In 1916 he suggested

JOINS PAGE 111

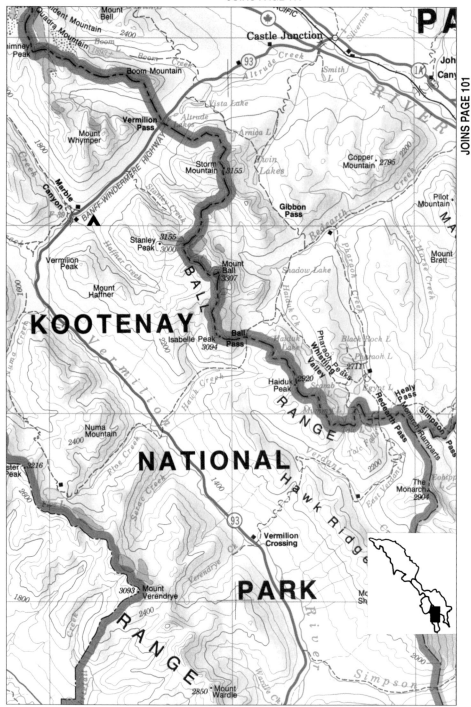

JOINS PAGE 101

Boom Lake is a popular hiking destination, reached along an easy trail from the Kootenay Parkway near the Banff/Kootenay boundary. The lake's name comes from a natural log boom of avalanche debris, which has collected near the outlet.

the National Parks Branch complete the construction in return for lands adjacent to the road being set aside as a national park. By 1919, the necessary federal-provincial agreement was reached, and a strip of land eight kilometres (five miles) wide on either side of the highway was conveyed. With an area of 1,406 sq km, Kootenay National Park was officially established on this land in 1920. The Banff-Windermere Highway was completed four years later.

Four thousand five hundred vehicles travelled the route in the first year. The automobile had arrived to stay in the mountain national parks. The Kootenay Parkway is now open year-round, and is the only through-road in Kootenay National Park.

Kootenay is a park of tremendous diversity, incorporating Rocky Mountain and Columbia Valley climates, four distinct mountain topographies, 256 animal species, and 993 species of plants. It is certainly the only park in Canada in which both cactus and glacier can be found. The name "Kootenay" is a Native word meaning "people from beyond the hills."

Vista Lake

Puzzling features of topography often give insights into the natural history of a landscape. Vista Lake lies in the relatively deep valley of Altrude Creek, which drops steeply from the Continental Divide. How could this valley have been eroded to such a depth in such a short distance, with so little an amount of water apparently flowing through it?

At the end of the Wisconsin Glaciation, 11,000 years ago, a lobe of glacial ice retreated to near the crest of Vermilion Pass. This ice rapidly melted as the earth warmed, releasing a large volume of water that cut the valley of Altrude Creek through the mass of rubble deposited by earlier glaciations. This discharge of water was so strong that the underlying bedrock was exposed. In it, the basins that now contain Vista Lake and the Altrude Lakes were eroded.

The Altrude valley was originally known as the Little Vermilion. In 1939 a change of name was sought. A surveying party working at the pass combined the Latin words for "high" (altus) with "beautiful" (pulchitrude), to come up with the odd, but appropriate, name. The Altrude Lakes are partially concealed from view, close to Vermilion Pass.

The Bungalow Camps

Restrictions on automobiles in Rocky Mountains Park were lifted in 1915, and by the 1920's it was clear the future of tourism in the mountain national parks would be more connected to automobiles than trains. The Canadian Pacific Railway immediately began to construct and promote "auto bungalow camps" at a number of scenic locations in the Rockies: Johnston Canyon, Castle Mountain, Storm Mountain, the

Rustic Storm Mountain Lodge had its origins as an auto "Bungalow Camp" constructed by the Canadian Pacific Railway in the 1920's.

Kootenay Valley, Radium Hot Springs, Moraine Lake, Wapta Lake, Lake O'Hara and Emerald Lake. The increasing number of auto-tourists also resulted in construction of roadside campgrounds in the parks.

The railway divested itself of the bungalow camps by the late 1940's. Many of the facilities have evolved into the commercial accommodations still present at these locations. Storm Mountain Lodge is an example.

Continental Divide
1640 m/5382 ft

The crest of Vermilion Pass marks the Continental Divide and the boundaries between Alberta and British Columbia, and Banff and Kootenay National Parks. From here waters flow east to the Bow River and eventually the Atlantic Ocean, and west to the Vermilion, Kootenay and Columbia Rivers, and on to the Pacific Ocean.

Like the Kicking Horse and Yellowhead passes further north, Vermilion Pass is parallel to the prevailing southwest winds. As a

In July 1968, much of the forest in Vermilion Pass was consumed by fire. Although the landscape looks devastated, fire is an essential process which regenerates growth. In a few decades this area will be appear as a healthy forest again.

result, a great deal of poor weather channels through the pass — a fact that gave rise to the name of Storm Mountain, immediately south.

The first European to cross Vermilion Pass was James Hector of the Palliser Expedition in 1858. The pass was not given serious consideration as a route for the Canadian Pacific Railway. Hindsight suggests it would have been a much more prudent choice than Kicking Horse Pass.

Vermilion Pass Burn
The Role of Fire

On July 9, 1968, a bolt of lightning struck in the forest just west of Vermilion Pass. The resulting forest fire consumed over 2,400 hectares in a four day period, before a combination of fire-fight-ing efforts and wet weather brought it under control. In the time since, the process of succession has begun, naturally reforesting the scorched earth.

With the shading forest canopy removed by the fire, the lodgepole pine, its seeds cracked open in the blaze, has quickly colonized areas of the burn, forming a dense doghair forest. Other, open areas have been covered by common fireweed, twinflower, paintbrush and sun-loving wildflowers. Deer, elk and moose find abundant food in the new growth, and black bear and grizzly bear have returned to the area.

Competition between the pines will result in a natural thinning. This will allow shade-tolerant spruce and fir, which have begun growing beneath the pines, to again become the dominant species in this forest, completing the succession. A hundred years or so from now, the descendants of these spruce and fir trees will have reached the end of their lives, and Nature will require another fire to rejuvenate growth.

Eventually, forests are supposed to burn. To see forest fires as devastation is a narrow view of an essential process. In the montane ecoregion, natural fire return cycles are on the order of 42-56 years; in the lower subalpine, 77-130 years; and in the upper subalpine, 180 years. A forest much older than these figures is in decline, and provides good habitat for relatively few species.

With the marked absence of

major forest fires in the mountain national parks during the last 50 years, vegetation in many areas is now over-mature. As well as reducing wildlife range, this means huge areas of the parks are now becoming tinder boxes, awaiting in some hot summer a conflagration like the one that occurred in Yellowstone National Park in 1988.

An experimental program to initiate prescribed burns in certain areas is presently being developed. The goal is to reintroduce the essential role of fire into the mountain landscape, without threatening roadways and structures. One such burn, set along the north shore of Lake Minnewanka in Banff National Park in 1988, was deemed successful.

The Vermilion Pass Burn can be explored from the Fireweed Trail at the Continental Divide.

Peaks and Publicity

Stanley Peak (3155 m/10,351 ft) was first climbed by Edward Whymper and guides in 1901. Whymper, the celebrated and tragic first ascencionist of the Matterhorn, was considered the finest product of Europe's "Golden Age" of mountaineering. Although 62 years old, and past his mountaineering prime, he had convinced the Canadian Pacific Railway to sponsor him and his sizeable entourage of Swiss Guides in the Rockies, in return for Whymper's publicizing the trip and helping plan hiking trails. It was hoped in his exploits

Whymper would conquer Mt. Assiniboine, the "Canadian Matterhorn," as well.

The arrangement was repeated in two subsequent seasons, but the railway grew less and less happy with Whymper's productivity. Assiniboine fell to his companion, James Outram, in 1901, and the outfitters who travelled with Whymper had difficulty handling his dour, and apparently alcoholic, temperament. The C.P.R. did receive some benefit from Whymper's scheme: he described the Rockies in one of his articles as being "fifty Switzerlands in one" — a slogan that the railway thereafter used frequently in its advertising campaigns.

The mountain directly opposite Stanley Peak, on the north side of the highway, was also first

Due to active fire suppression, there have been few large forest fires in the mountain national parks during the last 50 years. Prescribed burns have been used in Banff since 1983, in an attempt to re-introduce the essential role of fire into the parks. This spectacular burn was set along the north shore of Lake Minnewanka in 1988.

The glaciated, snow-mantled form of Mt. Stanley looms in contrast to the blackened timbers of the Vermilion Pass burn.

climbed by Whymper's party, and was subsequently named for him.

The worthwhile hike along Stanley Glacier trail leads through the Vermilion Pass Burn into the hanging valley below the north face of Stanley Peak. The trail offers close-up views of this alpine valley glacier and the recently glaciated landscape. Hoary marmot and white-tailed ptarmigan

are common in the upper valley, which is also noted for its fossils.

Marble Canyon

Marble Canyon is one of a half dozen limestone canyons in the Rockies that are easily accessed by interpretive trail from roadside. It has taken Tokumm Creek 8,000 years to create the canyon, which is 600 m long and 36 m deep. The interpretive trail leads along the canyon edge, and crosses several bridges above the depths. A natural bridge can also be seen.

The cool, damp air channelled by the canyon results in the growth nearby of a lower subalpine canyon forest. Several exotic species of vegetation normally found in arctic regions occur along the canyon edge. Please keep on the trail to spare these fragile plants, and to avoid the risk of a slip into the depths.

The first recorded visit to

Common Fireweed

Colourful common fireweed colonizes recently burned areas and gravelly, disturbed ground, often forming dense thickets. Numerous pink flowers grow at the top of a stem that may reach two metres in height. The flowers open low on the stem first, and in late summer it is common for flowers, buds and purple seed pods to be present on the same plant. Fireweed sheds a thick yellow pollen in mid-summer. The plant is the territorial emblem of the Yukon.

Mountain fireweed (River Beauty) is a smaller plant, with larger flowers. It generally grows at higher elevations and along glacial melt streams.

Left: Marble Canyon has been eroded through a limestone step at the mouth of Tokumm Creek valley. A pleasant and interesting self-guiding interpretive trail leads along the canyon edge, and several bridges span the narrow chasm. One of these bridges is 36 m above the creek.

Bottom: Edward Whymper (standing), who was in the first party to ascend the Matterhorn, with James Hector of Palliser Expedition fame, at Glacier House in 1903.

Marble Canyon was by outfitter Tom Wilson in 1889, although James Hector probably stopped here in 1858. "Tokumm" is a Stoney Native word for "red fox."

Paint Pots and Ochre Beds

The soils alongside this part of the Vermilion River are chiefly clay sediments which were deposited on the bottom of an ancient glacial lake. The red and yellow colours at the Ochre Beds result from saturation of the clay by iron-rich water, which percolates up from three mineral

Top: At the Ochre Beds, clay is stained red and yellow by iron oxide carried in spring water. To Kootenay Natives, the Ochre Beds were "the place where the red earth spirit is taken." They collected the clay, from which they derived a pigment used to make body paint. The springs from which the water issues are known as the Paint Pots. These attractions are reached by a short, easy hike.

Right: On the drive between the Paint Pots and Vermilion Crossing, glimpses of summits on The Rockwall may be obtained in the view west. One of the most spectacular is Mt. Verendrye, visible near Vermilion Crossing.

and baked in a fire. The resulting material was ground into powder and mixed with animal fat to form a body paint.

The "red earth" was a valuable trading commodity. The Kootenays stopped here on their way from the Columbia Valley to the Kootenay Plains east of the Rockies, to gather clay for trade with the Stoney tribe. Their route, The Kootenay Trail, went north over Ottertail Pass into Yoho, then on to the North Saskatchewan Valley. They returned home via the Kicking Horse, Beaverfoot and Kootenay Valleys.

In the early 1900's, a small industry developed here, exporting the coloured clay to Calgary to be used as a pigment base for paint. The extraction process was difficult and time consuming, and eventually the enterprise failed. Equipment remains at the site, beside mounds of clay heaped up for a mining season that was never completed.

The walk to the Paint Pots leads through a damp, lower subalpine forest, and includes the thrill of a suspension bridge crossing at the Vermilion River. Look for tracks of wolf, coyote, elk, moose, deer, American marten and bear in the clays of the Ochre Beds. The iron compounds in the water have stained many rocks in the riverbed, giving the Vermilion River its name.

springs — The Paint Pots. The water here does not filter far enough into the earth's surface to become super-heated, as with true hot springs. However, with a temperature of 10.7°C, the water is significantly warmer than the mean air temperature.

The Ochre Beds were an important site to Kootenay Natives from the interior of B.C. They called it "the place where the red earth spirit is taken." The coloured clay was formed into round cakes

The Rockwall

In a range the size of the Rockies, there are bound to be marked exceptions to the general descriptions applied to large areas. Amongst the typically rounded, shaly peaks of the western main ranges, The Rockwall is a spectacular exception—a sheer limestone cliff, over 900 m high in places, which extends along the west boundary of Kootenay National Park for over 40 km.

The Rockwall Trail parallels the base of this cliff for much of its length, passing the shores of Floe Lake and affording backpackers a highline view of one of the most spectacular areas in the Rockies. Floe Lake is so named because glaciers calve icebergs into its waters, creating ice floes.

The rewards for toiling over the trail's three high passes are expansive alpine meadows, larch forests, and views of the rugged, glaciated limestone peaks. A side trip to Helmet Falls, one of the country's highest waterfalls, is also possible. Some strong backpackers elect to extend this journey across two more passes to Lake O'Hara in Yoho National Park.

Mt. Verendrye
3086 m / 10,125 ft

The sharp spire of Mt. Verendrye (vurr-EN-dree) is one of the most impressive mountains along the Kootenay Parkway, and marks the

Mountain Goat

The mountain goat is the symbol of Kootenay National Park. British Columbia supports a larger population of this animal than any other area in the world. After elk, goats are the second most common large mammal in Kootenay, with current estimates of over 300 animals.

Mountain goats typically dwell in the alpine and upper subalpine ecoregions, browsing on open avalanche paths and grassy terraces which give quick access to steep, rocky escape routes. Attracted by the presence of mineral licks, goats will sometimes descend into the montane ecoregion, even to roadside.

The 70 goats that inhabit the slopes of Mt. Wardle frequent one such lick here on the Kootenay Parkway. In their craving for sustenance, these usually wary animals are quite tolerant of human presence. This be-

haviour should be respected, not exploited. Please do not climb the banks and approach the goats. Observe them from roadside. Park well off the road, and use caution with regard to traffic. For more information on mountain goats, please refer to the entry of Goats and Glaciers Viewpoint, on the Icefields Parkway.

Another mineral lick, used by moose, elk and deer, is slightly east of this point on the Kootenay Parkway.

southern end of The Rockwall. Verendrye was named by surveyor G.M. Dawson for the French-Canadian explorer who attempted to journey overland to the Pacific in the early 1700's. The mountain was first climbed in 1922. The area between Mt. Verendrye and Mt. Wardle to the west contains prime mountain goat habitat, and has been designated a special preservation area.

Mt. Assiniboine
3618 m/11,870 ft

The summit of the highest mountain in this part of the Rockies, Mt. Assiniboine (a-SINNI-boyne), is visible on clear days from the Kootenay Parkway, 2.5 km south of Vermilion Crossing. The mountain, located on the boundary of Banff National Park and Mt. Assiniboine Provincial Park, was named by surveyor G.M. Dawson in 1884 for the Native Assiniboine tribe. The name means "those who cook by placing hot rocks in water." Locally, the Assiniboine are called Stoney.

Hector Gorge

At this point, the southerly course of the Vermilion River is blocked by the Mitchell Range. Diverted westwards, the river has succeeded in eroding through the mountains to reach the Kootenay Valley. In doing so, it has created Hector Gorge, which separates the Vermilion and Mitchell Ranges. Hector Gorge is named for James Hector, who travelled here in 1858.

The Kootenay Parkway takes a shortcut not available to the river, and makes the climb over the end of the Vermilion Range, before descending to the Kootenay River. On the way it passes colourful Kootenay Pond.

Kootenay Valley Viewpoint

The expansive vista from this viewpoint reveals the grand scale of the Kootenay Valley, of which nearly a 80 km length is visible.

This view also puts forest fires into perspective. When you con-

---

The Little Emperor

In 1824, Sir George Simpson of the Hudson's Bay Company crossed Athabasca Pass, following the fur trade route to the Pacific coast. Seventeen years later Simpson had risen to the position of governor of the company, and was travelling again — this time around the world, on foot, horse, and boat. He crossed from the Bow to the Simpson Rivers over a crest known as Shushwap Pass, and then continued south of here to the Kootenay Valley. Simpson Monument recalls this journey.

Simpson apparently had a mean and demanding temperament, and drove his men and their horses hard — sometimes 100 km in a day. His servants called him "the little emperor" — presumably behind his back.

James Hector renamed Shushwap Pass as Simpson Pass in 1858, to commemorate Simpson's crossing. In 1904 a party camped on the pass found Simpson's initials and the date 1841, carved in a fallen tree.

The Simpson River valley is favourable habitat for lynx and cougar, two of the three species of wild cats in the Rockies.

JOINS PAGE 181

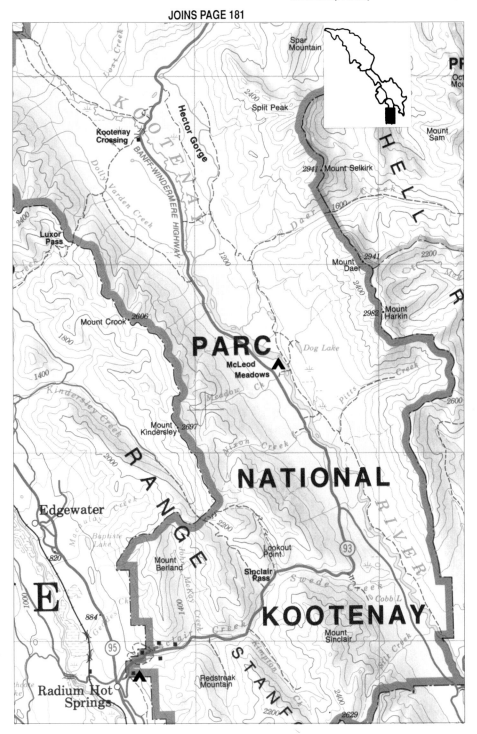

Spar
Mountain

Split Peak

Mount
Sam

2400

Kootenay
Crossing

Hector Gorge

BANFF-WINDERMERE HIGHWAY

2941 Mount Selkirk

Daer Creek

1600

2400

Luxor
Pass

1200

2941

Mount
Daer

2200

Mount Crook *2606*

1800

2982 Mount
Harkin

2400

PARC

Dog Lake

1400

McLeod
Meadows

Meadow Ck

Pitts Creek

2600

Mount
Kindersley *2697*

Nixon Creek

NATIONAL

2000

Kindersley Creek

RANGE

Edgewater

Macauldy Creek

Baptiste Lake

820

2200

RIVER

Lookout
Point

93

Mount
Berland

Holt McKay Creek

Sinclair
Pass

Swede Creek

Cobb L

1400

E

1000

884

KOOTENAY

Mount
Sinclair

95

Sinclair Creek

Radium Hot
Springs

Redstreak
Mountain

STANF

Silt Creek

2400

2200

2629

sider much of the forest in this valley is nearing the end of the succession cycle and needs to burn in order to rejuvenate, the problem confronting park managers as they contemplate prescribed burns is a large one.

Grouse

The ruffed grouse is the grouse species you are most likely to encounter while walking a roadside trail in the Rockies. Well camouflaged in its mottled coat, this bird will allow you to virtually step on it before flying away with an explosion of wing beating. The male is known for its drumming during courtship. This hollow, low frequency sound is produced by compression of air under rapidly beating wings. Both sexes have a crest of feathers on the head, white bars on the tail feathers, and a coloured spot above the eye. In the Rockies, the ruffed grouse prefers forest that includes poplar trees.

Grouse eat a variety of seeds, berries, insects and buds – even conifer needles. These birds and their eggs are hunted by many animals and birds of prey. Early explorers in the Rockies frequently dined on grouse – part of its Latin scientific name means "good when roasted"!

A few specimens of western larch grow near this viewpoint. This cone-bearing tree is not evergreen; its needles turn gold and drop off in the autumn. Western larch is altogether a rare tree in Canada, and Kootenay is the only one of the four mountain national parks in which it is found.

Sinclair Pass

The Sinclair Valley has the V-shape characteristic of erosion by water. The original topography of the Rockies contained many valleys like this, but the effects of glaciation rendered most of them U-shaped troughs. Elsewhere, rivers have now commenced the task of cutting new V's into the bases of the troughs. The Sinclair Valley escaped glaciation, and the V-shape we see is the product of tens of thousands of years of erosion strictly by water, an oddity in the Canadian Rockies.

Sinclair pass, creek, and canyon are named for James Sinclair, who in 1841 lead a group of 120 settlers from Manitoba along this route. Sponsored by the Hudson's Bay Company, their destination was Oregon, which they intended to colonize to support a claim by Britain. They eventually reached Oregon, but were ultimately unsuccessful in their aim. Sinclair's solitary visit to the hot springs in the lower canyon was the second recorded by a European.

Five hiking trails depart from the canyon, and offer the opportunity to explore this unique area in the Rockies.

The Redwall

The brightly coloured cliffs of The Redwall mark a fault in the earth's crust, along which there has been tremendous vertical displacement of sedimentary formations. The colour of The Redwall results from the oxidization of iron in the rock, caused by heat when the two sides of the fault ground against one another. It is along the fault of The Redwall that the waters of Radium Hot Springs percolate to the surface.

The grassy slopes beneath The Redwall are a favourite spot for bighorn sheep. Please drive slowly and carefully through this area.

Radium Hot Springs

Hot spring water is heated several kilometres within the earth's crust, and percolates back to the surface along faults and joints in the bedrock. At Radium Hot Springs, the Redwall fault provides a convenient vertical channel for the resurfacing water, which emerges at a temperature of 47.7°C.

As hot springs flow in the Rockies, those at Radium are fairly hot, but relatively lacking in mineral content. Sulphate and calcium are the most prevalent mineral compounds, and some algae is present. These combine to give the waters their unique sapphire colour. Unlike the other well-known hot springs in the Rockies, the Radium hot springs are virtually odourless.

What is most noteworthy about these springs is their radio-active content. The waters contain traces of radium, which was formerly attributed with healing and restorative powers. In the Victorian era, it was fashionable for the elite to take their vacations at hot springs, and the abundance of springs in the Rockies greatly increased the original appeal of the area to wealthy tourists.

The Redwall marks a fault in the earth's crust. The red cliffs have been coloured by iron, oxidized by heat generated in the faulting process. The waters of Radium Hot Springs return to the earth's surface along the Redwall fault.

Healing Waters

There is little record of Radium Hot Springs for some 50 years after the visits of Sir George Simpson and James Sinclair. Then in 1890, Roland Stuart, a British aristocrat, purchased a lease on the land from the Crown, and the rights to develop and market the waters from the springs — all for $160. He did little to develop his lease during the next 21 years, and for

most of this time a simple tent was the only facility provided bathers.

Stuart had grand visions for the area, and was an associate of businessman Robert Bruce, who in 1910 proposed the Banff-Windermere Road. There were easier routes this road could have taken to the Columbia Valley, but the presence of the hot springs, owned by a friend, saw the route planned for the road cross Sinclair Pass.

Stuart had trouble financing development of the springs. He was eventually able to convince John Harmsworth (of Perrier fame), a paralysed multi-millionaire from France, to test the waters. After four months soaking in the springs, the man was able to move his feet, and Stuart received

backing for development.

Being a man accustomed to the high life, Stuart squandered a great deal of the money, building only a concrete pool and a bath house with the rest. Meanwhile the British Columbia section of the Banff-Windermere Road project had also gone bankrupt, and Robert Bruce was lobbying the Federal government with his idea for a national park. Four years later, in 1920, Kootenay National Park was established. The government could not tolerate a private lease on national park land, and so expropriated Stuart's holding in 1922. Two years later, the Banff-Windermere Road was completed. Stuart eventually received $40,000 through a compensation hearing, at which some witnesses appraised the value of

the hot springs at half a million dollars .

To accommodate the increasing number of visitors, the hot pool was expanded and the Aquacourt constructed in 1950, with additional renovations taking place in 1968. Commercial accommodation near the hot springs dates from the 1920's.

Sinclair Canyon

The Sinclair Canyon is a narrow cleft in the rock step at the mouth of Sinclair Creek. Although Native peoples frequented the hot springs nearby — there are examples of rock art in the area — James Sinclair had been advised by a Cree guide to avoid the canyon. Sinclair's party used a Native trail that by-passed the canyon by climbing over the shoulder of Mt. Berland to the north, probably much the same way the Juniper Trail does today.

The section of road constructed in the canyon before the First World War was washed away by high water. The solution to the problem was essentially to pave the canyon floor and put the creek underground. And so the modern day motorist or pedestrian is able to travel in an intimidating place where for centuries few dared.

Development of Radium Hot Springs began in 1890, when Roland Stuart acquired a lease on the land. Stuart had dreams of bottling and selling the hot spring water, but did little more than provide a few crude shelters for visitors. When Kootenay National Park was created in 1920, Stuart's lease was expropriated, and the springs came under government control as part of the park.

Construction of the Kootenay Parkway through Sinclair Canyon began in 1911. The difficult project eventually saw completion in 1924, and was instrumental in the creation of Kootenay, Canada's tenth national park.

Rocky Mountain Trench

As it descends into the Columbia Valley, the Kootenay Parkway leaves the Rocky Mountains and enters the Rocky Mountain Trench. The Trench is a major rift in the earth's crust, and marks the division point between the Rocky Mountains and the older Columbia Mountains to the west.

Whereas the Rockies were created by compression, the Trench was created by stretching; its eastern wall fractured along a normal fault, and the valley bottom subsided. Today it contains the Columbia River.

The Trench lies strictly in the montane ecoregion. The benchlands and mountainsides are semi-arid, and dry coniferous forest prevails. Wetlands occupy much of the valley bottom, and provide important resting and breeding sites for migratory birds. The overall climate is much warmer and drier than in the Rockies. Radium, Invermere and Windermere are mid-winter (sometimes even mid-summer!) meccas for Rocky Mountain locals who are fed up with chill winds, snow and cloudy skies.

The vegetation around Redstreak Campground is typical of the Rocky Mountain Trench. Douglas fir, lodgepole pine, juniper, bearberry and grasses dominate. The steep, south-facing slopes provide critical winter range for hungry bighorn sheep and mule deer, and are frequented by the predators cougar, lynx and coyote.

Kootenay is the only national park in which the Rocky Mountain Trench vegetation is represented, and in recognition of this fact, drainages in the extreme south end of the park have been designated special preservation areas.

Columbia River

The 2,044 km long Columbia River is one of the major rivers of North America. Flowing to the Pacific from its source at Columbia Lake, 45 km south of Radium, the Columbia drains an area of 155,000 sq km in British Columbia and the northwestern United States. In doing so, it follows a very peculiar course. After flowing north for 300 km, it makes an abrupt hairpin turn to the south, past Revelstoke, through the Arrow Lakes, and across the U.S. border. Eventually its waters enter the Pacific Ocean beyond Portland, Oregon.

The Columbia River Treaty of 1961 greatly altered the wild nature of this river. More than 30 dams were constructed in British Columbia and the U.S. to control floodwaters and allow hydroelectric generation. Thousands of square kilometres of unharvested B.C. forest were inundated by the resulting lakes and reservoirs. This enormous manipulation of a water resource put an end to the migration of Pacific salmon on the Columbia. Formerly these fish made spawning journeys to the headwaters of the river.

The river was named by Captain Robert Gray for his ship, *The Columbia*. The lower reaches of the Columbia served as the boundary between British and American territory until the 1840's when, largely due to successful American colonization of the Oregon territory, Britain agreed to move the boundary north to the 49th parallel.

The Icefields Parkway

The Wonder Trail

*T*hrough dense primeval forests, muskeg, burnt and fallen timber and along rough and steeply sloping hillsides, a constant flow of travel will demand a broad, well-ballasted motor road ... this wonder trail will be world-renowned..
– A.O. Wheeler, 1920

Herbert Lake is one of many lakes along the Icefields Parkway. Its waters occupy a glacially scoured hollow. The lake is a fine setting for early morning and late evening photography.

Travellers have not always followed the present day route of the Icefields Parkway. In earlier days there were easier paths leading north from Lake Louise. The swampy nature of the Bow Valley, coupled with the many fallen timbers caused by forest fires in

the late 19th century, made travel to Bow Pass arduous. Natives and early explorers preferred a system of more open valleys, beginning at the Pipestone River, northeast of Lake Louise. These valleys led through the front ranges, to the Sunwapta Valley north of Columbia Icefield.

One of the first parties to use the Bow Valley instead of the Pipestone included American explorer Walter Wilcox and guide Bill Peyto, who passed that way in 1896. Other mountaineers followed, in their quests to ascend the high peaks along the Continental Divide, and the route of

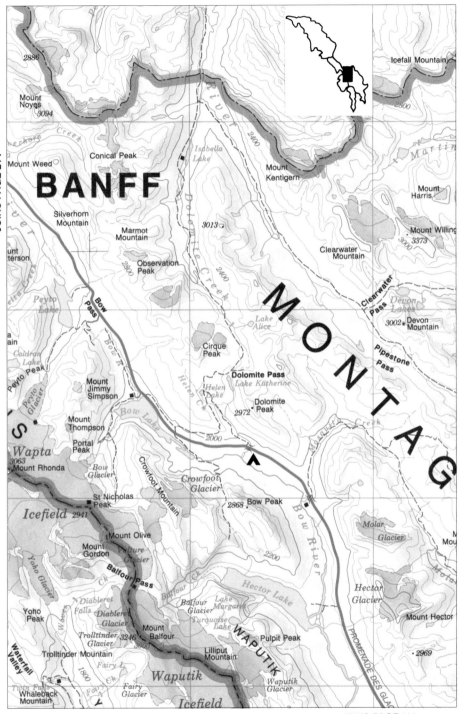

2886

Mount
Noyes
3094

Conical Peak

Mount Weed

BANFF

Silverhorn
Mountain

Marmot
Mountain

Isabella
Lake

2400

Mount
Kentigern

Icefall Mountain

2800

Mount
Harris

Mount Willing

3373

3000

ount
terson

unt
erson Creek

3013

Dolomite Creek

2600

2400

Observation
Peak

Clearwater
Mountain

MONTAG

Clearwater
Pass

Devon
Lakes

3002 Devon
Mountain

Peyto
Lake

Bow
Pass

Bow R.

Lake
Alice

Pipestone
Pass

Caldron
Lake

Peyto
Peak

Cirque
Peak

Helen Cr.

Dolomite Pass
Lake Katherine

Peyto
Glacier

Mount
Jimmy
Simpson

Helen
Lake

2972

Dolomite
Peak

Magquon Creek

Mount
Thompson

Bow Lake

2000

Wapta

Portal
Peak

3063
Mount Rhonda

Bow
Glacier

Crowfoot Mountain

Crowfoot
Glacier

Bow River

Molar
Glacier

St Nicholas
Peak

Icefield 2941

Mount Olive

Mount
Gordon

Vulture
Glacier

2868

Bow Peak

M
Mou

Yoho Glacier

Balfour Pass

2200

Hector
Glacier

Yoho
Peak

Diableret
Falls

Diableret
Glacier

Balfour Gl.

Balfour
Glacier

Lake
Margaret

Hector Lake

Mount Hector

2969

Trolltinder
Glacier

Mount
Balfour

3246

Turquoise
Lake

WAPUTIK

Pulpit Peak

PROMENADE DES GLA

Waterfall
Valley

Trolltinder Mountain

Fairy L.

Lilliput
Mountain

1800

Whaleback
Mountain

Fairy
Glacier

Fairy Cr.

Waputik

Waputik
Glacier

Icefield

JOINS PAGE 111

Mt. Hector is the most prominent mountain in the view north from Lake Louise, and is the highest mountain between there and the North Saskatchewan River. A group of American mountaineers accomplished the first ascent in 1895. An alpine valley glacier lies on the north side of Mt. Hector, and can be seen from Bow Lake.

the Icefields Parkway was eventually established.

The first complete journey from Banff to Jasper along this route was accomplished in 1904 by a party led by outfitter Jim Brewster. Three years later, explorer A.P. Coleman made a similar trip. From the experiences gained in this and earlier journeys, Coleman became one of the strongest proponents of a developed road between Lake Louise and Jasper, along the route he called "The Wonder Trail."

Construction of the forerunner of the Icefields Parkway began in 1931, as a make-work project during the Great Depression. Crews worked towards each other from Jasper and Lake Louise. When in full swing, the construction involved 625 men. Very few pieces of machinery were used in overcoming the obstacles presented by the difficult terrain.

The crews met on the hill at the Big Bend in 1939. Their finished product was a 6.5 m wide gravelled road, 230 km in length, which in no place exceeded 8% in grade. The Parkway was first used by autos in 1940, and echoing the words mountaineer Edward Whymper spoke forty years earlier, was heralded in the *Banff Crag and Canyon* as being "twenty Switzerlands in one."

When the road was upgraded to its present standard in 1961, most of the original grading was retained – a tribute to the quality of the original construction. Sections of the abandoned road bed are being allowed to naturally revegetate, and can be seen at

various locations. The Parkway celebrated its 50th year in 1990, and the Canadian Parks Service held a reunion at Jasper Park Lodge for those who had worked on the road.

Miette Formation

The striking purple, brown and orange rocks at the junction of the Icefields Parkway and Trans-Canada Highway are slates of the Miette (mee-YETT) Group. Slate is formed from fine sedimentary particles that settled out on ancient sea floors as clay. Under pressure, the clay became shale. Under even greater pressure and resulting heat, the shale was transformed into thin layers of slate — a metamorphic rock. (Metamorphic means "changed.")

At between 570 and 730 mil-lion years of age, the formations of the Miette Group are among the oldest commonly visible in this part of the Rockies. These formations accumulated to a maximum thickness of eight kilo-metres, making the Miette the thickest deposit underlying the Rockies.

Miette slate is also visible west of Jasper along the Miette River (which gave the formation its name), in rock cuts on the Yel-lowhead Highway.

Herbert Lake

As the glaciers of the Wisconsin Glaciation retreated from the major valley bottoms of the Rock-ies 11,000 years ago, they created many lakes. Depressions scoured from the bedrock by the moving ice became natural places for

Mt. Balfour is largely concealed from view in the Bow Valley, and early mountaineers had difficulty discovering a feasible approach. The first ascent in 1898 capped a series of expeditions that greatly increased knowledge of the area north of Lake Louise. Balfour is the highest mountain on the Wapta and Waputik Icefields.

water to collect. Moraines deposited by the retreating ice dammed meltwater, creating other lakes. Lakes formed by these processes are called tarns. Herbert Lake is a fine example.

In other cases, huge masses of rubble-covered ice detached from the shrinking glaciers, and melted into slumps, producing kettle ponds such as Wapta Lake and Kootenay Pond. In all there are thousands of glacially formed lakes in the Rockies. The eye is drawn to the waters of these mountain jewels, as much as it is to the peaks above.

The setting of Herbert Lake gives perfect reflections of Mt. Temple and other mountains near Lake Louise, and provides a promising early morning or late evening haunt for the photographer. For a few weeks in summer when its waters are warm enough, locals use the lake as a swimming hole.

Cirques

Many of the bowl-shaped depressions on mountainsides in the Rockies were created by cirque (SURK) glaciers, which eroded rearwards and downwards into the underlying rock. In many instances the glacial ice has now melted, and all that remains is the sculpted shape that contained it — the cirque.

Cirques and cirque glaciers are

Grizzly Bear

The grizzly bear is the dominant animal in the Rockies. However, popular conception of the habits and disposition of this impressive animal is generally inaccurate. Not a marauding, great hunter, the grizzly's diet is almost 90% vegetarian. Much of the meat it does eat is carrion, or kills strong-armed from other animals. Although the grizzly has no natural enemies, it is largely solitary and reclusive.

The section of the Icefields Parkway between Hector Creek and Bow Pass is the area in the Rockies where grizzlies are most frequently seen at roadside. The upper Bow Valley provides vegetation favoured by the bear in early and late summer, while side valleys to the east offer it quick access to favourite mid-summer habitat above treeline. The grizzly spends almost every waking moment in quest for food, to tide it over the winter months. Berries, roots, herbs and the occasional rodent comprise the bulk of its diet.

The grizzly passes most of the winter in a state of dormancy. It digs a den into a steep hillside on a north-

prominent on north and east aspects of many mountains along the Icefields Parkway. These slopes are the most shaded and hence most prone to glaciation. The Waputik Range south of Hector Lake features a large number of cirques, some of which still contain vestiges of ice. Very small cirque glaciers like these are also known as pocket glaciers.

Combinations of cirque glaciers, eroding different aspects of a mountain, will produce a horn mountain. Mt. Chephren, The White Pyramid, Mt. Athabasca and Mt. Fryatt are good examples to be seen along the Icefields Parkway.

Mt. Hector
3394 m / 11,135 ft

Mt. Hector dominates the east side of the Icefields Parkway just north of Lake Louise. The mountain was first ascended in 1895 by P.S. Abbot, Charles Fay and C.S. Thompson, members of the Appalachian Mountain Club of Boston. This mountaineering party helped pioneer the Bow Valley route north from Lake Louise and, in doing so, enjoyed as their reward one of the finest views in the Rockies from Hector's lofty summit.

Mt. Hector was named in 1884 for James Hector, in recognition of his contribution to the exploration of the Rockies during the

or east-facing slope in the alpine ecoregion, where deep snow provides insulation. No food is cached in the den. Instead, the grizzly lives off the fat gained the previous summer. During denning, the grizzly's body temperature drops a few degrees and respiration subsides to 2-4 breaths a minute. Its intestines are naturally blocked by a plug of coarse food, and the bear neither defecates nor urinates until spring. This dormancy begins late November, and is broken on warmer days when the bear rises to look around or take a bite to eat. Most grizzlies emerge from their dens in April.

Because their behaviour is unpredictable, all bears are dangerous. Typically, a bear will be more concerned with avoiding you than you are with avoiding it. However, when a bear has learned to associate humans with easily obtainable food, perceives a threat to its young or to a nearby food source, or is suddenly surprised on a trail, it may stand its ground and in some cases become aggressive.

Left: The grizzly bear is sometimes seen at roadside along this part of the Icefields Parkway. Please drive carefully.

NO HUMP

BLACK BEAR

HUMP

GRIZZLY BEAR

Palliser Expedition, 1857-60. The members of the first ascent party of Mt. Hector are commemorated in the names of other mountains in the Rockies and Selkirks: Mt. Thompson at Bow Lake, Mt. Fay at Moraine Lake, and Mt. Abbot at Rogers Pass. Abbot died in 1896 during an attempt on Mt. Lefroy near Lake Louise.

Bears and People – Avoiding Problems

Given the number of visitors to the Rockies, bear-human encounters are surprisingly rare. Most of the incidents recorded involve bears becoming habituated to the presence of garbage and unattended food, and some unfortunate occasions when hikers have surprised a bear on the trail or feeding at a kill. By adhering to the following guidelines, you will help minimize the risk. Please remember it is easier for us to modify our behaviour to protect bears than it is for Nature to replace "problem" bears that must be destroyed as a consequence of complications caused by human carelessness.

1. Do not leave food unattended. Keep it locked in the trunk of your car, or in a bear-proof container in campgrounds. Backcountry campers should store food at least five metres off the ground, strung between two trees at least five metres apart. Most backcountry campsites are equipped with bear poles, but carry enough rope for this purpose if you will be random camping.

2. Do not cook or eat in or near your tent. Eat everything you cook. Avoid using aromatic foods. If fishing, do not dump fish cleanings at waterside or at your campsite. Pack them out, or burn them where fires are allowed.

3. Keep pets on leashes or enclosed in vehicles. Do not take pets into the backcountry. A dog will not protect its owner from a grizzly bear, and may provoke a bear to charge.

4. Travel in groups and stay on trails. Make noise (whistle, sing or shout) while hiking. Avoid bear habitat. Make lots of noise on avalanche slopes and along streams. If you encounter fresh bear sign (scrapes, scats, carrion, smell), and have a choice, call it a day and return. If you must continue, detour widely around the area and make even more noise.

5. If you see a bear, remain in your vehicle. Take photographs with a telephoto lens. Never interfere with the relationship between a mother and her cubs, or approach a bear that is feeding. Report your sighting to the nearest Park Warden office or Information Centre.

6. In the backcountry, an encounter with a bear can be a very complex situation. It is a good idea to follow the general rule of *not running*. Climbing a tree sometimes provides a means of escape. Consult a Warden Office or Information Centre for detailed theories on what to do, and what not to do, in a bear encounter.

Are They Ski-Runs?

Although they look like ski-runs, the treeless swaths on mountainsides, such as those on Dolomite Peak, are products of a natural process – the snow avalanche. Accumulations of winter snow on steep slopes can release, and slide downhill en masse. The force generated by the sliding snow and accompanying wind can be enough to snap mature trees at their bases. Once a snow avalanche has cleared a path through vegetation, that path is likely to be avalanched each year.

Snow avalanches are both a destructive and creative force. They contribute to the overall ecology of mountain regions by creating open habitat in the forest. Willows, shrubs, and tall wildflowers thrive on the slide paths, providing sources of food for elk, moose, deer and bear.

In many places in the Rockies, as at Dolomite Peak, the avalanche paths reach the road. In winter and spring, park wardens periodically close roadways, and use explosive charges to trigger avalanches, reducing the possibility of traffic

being caught in a large slide. It is illegal to stop in posted avalanche areas.

Although they appear inaccessible, most of the castellated towers on Dolomite Peak pose little challenge to mountaineers. In fact, many were first climbed in the 1930's by work crews involved in the construction of the Icefields Parkway.

Park wardens periodically close highways in winter and use explosives to trigger avalanches, thereby preventing them from releasing spontaneously and inundating traffic. This avalanche from Mt. Field in Yoho resulted when a hand charge was dropped from a helicopter. The avalanche crossed the Yoho Valley Road and the Trans-Canada Highway.

Since the end of the Little Ice Age in the late 1870's, most glaciers in the Rockies have been in retreat. The extent of this retreat is evident in comparing the contemporary view of Crowfoot Glacier on the opposite page, with the archival photo taken by Byron Harmon in 1917.

Mt. Balfour
3272 m / 10,735 ft

During the first ascents of Mts. Stephen, Hector, Lefroy and Victoria, surveyors and climbers had all noticed an impressive mountain on the Continental Divide, some 20 km north of Lake Louise. This peak, which had been named Mt. Balfour by James Hector, was scarcely visible from the valleys. Only from other summits could it be fully appreciated. Apparently of difficult access, it drew the collective attention of the mountaineering elite, and four attempts to climb it between 1897 and 1898 greatly increased knowledge of the area between Lake Louise and Bow Pass.

It was a party from the Appalachian Mountain Club which finally succeeded in reaching Balfour's summit in August, 1898. Members of these expeditions returned to the Rockies repeatedly during the next two decades, and made forays further north along the present day route of the Icefields Parkway.

Mt. Balfour can be seen briefly from just north of the Hector Lake viewpoint. The mountain retains an air of inaccessibility today, and its ascent is a favourite challenge in winter and spring for local ski mountaineers.

Bow Peak
2868 m / 9410 ft

As mountaineers know, the best views are often provided from mountain summits of only modest elevation. While several thou-

sand mountains in the Rockies are probably higher than Bow Peak, few can match the view from its summit – a fact attributable to its comparative isolation in the Bow Valley.

Bow Peak was first ascended by explorer Walter Wilcox in 1896, and was later occupied as a camera station during the Interprovincial Boundary Survey, which mapped the boundary between the provinces of Alberta and British Columbia.

Crowfoot Glacier

Looking at Crowfoot Glacier, it is easy to see how a glacier forms. The massive upper cliff of Crowfoot Mountain is a natural snow fence, depositing snow on the plateau beneath. In the lee and shade of the mountain, little of the accumulated snow melts, and over time it becomes glacial ice. Under the influence of gravity, the ice flows downhill towards the lower cliff edge.

Glacial retreat has been quite dramatic at Crowfoot Glacier. Photographs taken earlier this century show the ice formerly extended out from the base of the lower cliff, creating the prominent horseshoe-shaped terminal moraine still visible.

If the ice to the observer's right above the lower cliff is considered as one "toe," then the hanging lobes of ice constitute the other two toes of the crow's foot.

It is interesting to compare this contemporary view of Crowfoot Glacier with the historical image on the opposite page. The two photographs were taken more than 70 years apart.

Bow Lake is one of the larger lakes along the Icefields Parkway. It is fed by meltwaters of Bow Glacier and the Wapta Icefield, and is the headwaters of the Bow River.

Bow Lake

When Bow Glacier retreated from the Bow Valley at the end of the Wisconsin Glaciation, it left behind many glacial deposits. Among these were moraines that have subsequently helped create Bow Lake by damming meltwaters. Such moraine-dammed lakes are common in the Rockies.

Sport fishing for various species of trout is popular at the southern end of Bow Lake. A national park fishing licence is required. The swampy area at the lake's outlet is a good place to see moose.

Bow Glacier

Spilling over the cliffs beyond the far shore of Bow Lake, Bow Glacier is literally the tip of an alpine iceberg. This tongue of ice is an outlet valley glacier for the Wapta Icefield, which occupies over 40 sq km of the upland area beyond. As is the case with many glaciers in the Rockies, Bow Glacier has receded greatly during this century. The ice formerly cascaded over the lower cliff as well. In between the two cliffs, and concealed from view, is a small lake which is dotted with icebergs in the summer months.

Capable hikers are encouraged to use the lakeshore trail that departs from the lodge, to make a half-day exploration of the many interesting features in the forefield of Bow Glacier, including a natural bridge across a canyon. The waterfalls on the lower cliff freeze in winter, and are a popular location for the sport of waterfall ice climbing.

By studying this view, one can easily grasp the significance of glacial ice to the earth's freshwater supply. The melting ice of Bow Glacier is the principal source of all the waters in Bow Lake and the upper Bow River. Other icefields along the backbone of the Rockies are the sources of some of the other major rivers of western North America. The overall trend of glacial retreat and reduction of freshwater supply, at a time when demand for freshwater is increasing, is therefore a vital concern to everyone.

Bow Lake and the Icefields Parkway from the summit of Mt. Jimmy Simpson.

Mt. Thompson
3065 m/10,056 ft

The prominent peak to the viewer's right of Bow Glacier is named for American climber C.S. Thompson, who was in the first party to set foot on the Wapta Icefield in 1897. During this party's ascent of Mt. Gordon, Thompson slipped into a crevasse near the summit. Roped to other members of the party, he was eventually rescued when J. N. Collie was lowered into the icy depths to lend assistance.

Recalling the event, Collie named this mountain when he accomplished its first ascent the following year.

Top: Bow Glacier is one of five outlet glaciers of the 40 sq km Wapta Icefield. Its meltwaters are the principal source of the Bow River.

Bottom: Pioneer outfitter and guide Jimmy Simpson began building Num-ti-Jah Lodge at Bow Lake in 1920. Simpson was perhaps the most knowledgeable guide ever to work in the Rockies. The mountain immediately north of the Lodge is named for him.

Jimmy Simpson

The Red Roof at the Blue Lake

Pioneer outfitter and guide Jimmy Simpson began building Num-ti-Jah (numm-TAH-zjaah) Lodge on the shores of Bow Lake in 1920, replacing a camp he had operated since the early 1900's. The octagonal shape of the main lodge resulted from the desire to build a large structure when only short timbers were on hand. Num-ti-Jah is a Native expression for the American marten, a member of the weasel family that once inhabited the surrounding forest in great numbers.

Simpson was known to Natives as "Nashan-essen," which means "wolverine go quick" — a refer-

Glacially fed lakes in the Rockies are renowned for their remarkable colours. Nowhere is the effect as great as in the view of Peyto Lake from the overlook at Bow Summit. The lake's colour is the product of reflection of the blue/green spectrum of light, caused by tiny particles of rock flour suspended in the water.

A Cool Place

If you have noticed the air at this viewpoint seems cool, you're right. Large masses of ice act as giant refrigerators, chilling the air above. Cold air is more dense than warm air, so it flows downhill off the ice as a catabatic wind. Areas influenced by catabatic winds are known as frost hollows. If the cold air happens to settle over the cold waters of a lake, as is often the case in the Rockies, it retains most of its chill, even on a hot summer day. The effect produces a harsh, local micro-climate that stunts vegetation and prolongs winter.

Known for his outrageous garb and off-beat sense of humour, English-born "Wild" Bill Peyto was one of the most colourful characters attracted to trail guiding in the Rockies. He began work with Tom Wilson's company in 1897.

ence to his legendary ability to travel quickly in the mountains. He was one of the more colourful figures of Rockies history, and began his career guiding with Tom Wilson's company in 1899.

Simpson was a great hunter. He claimed that he dreamt about the locations of game, and that he always found the animals where he had dreamt they would be. He is credited with taking a world record bighorn ram in 1920. Interestingly, he poached the animal — he killed it three days after the end of hunting season.

Simpson cultivated an elite and wealthy clientele of hunters from the eastern United States, and brought noted wildlife artist Carl Rungius to the Rockies in 1910. Rungius was so taken by the scenery, the wildlife, and his host, he returned regularly, trading artwork for outfitting. Simpson eventually built a studio for Rungius in Banff, and amassed a valuable collection of his work. At Rungius's suggestion, other wildlife artists and big game hunters sought Simpson's services. Soon he became known as the best big game hunter in western Canada.

In the winters Simpson hunted and trapped alone between Bow Lake and the Alexandra River, an area he probably knew better than anyone else. He became the greatest authority on travel in the Rockies, and like Tom Wilson was something of a living legend. He died in 1972. The mountain immediately north of Num-ti-Jah was named in Simpson's honour two years later.

Glacier Lily

The glacier lily is a true harbinger of spring in the subalpine ecoregion. Two broad, pointed leaves frame a bright yellow, nodding flower. The plant often grows through the edge of receding snow banks. The blossom of the glacier lily is not long-lived, but for a while entire meadows are transformed by dense clusters of this colourful flower. Also called dogtooth violet and avalanche lily, the root of this plant is a favourite food of bears.

Bow Summit

At 2069 m, Bow Pass is the highest point crossed by highway in Canada. A short sideroad takes you to Bow Summit trailhead. This interpretive trail leads through open glades of the upper subalpine forest. Here, just below treeline, and under the chilling influence of the nearby Wapta Icefield, one can observe a micro-ecosite that combines elements of both the subalpine and alpine ecoregions.

The stands of Engelmann spruce and subalpine fir trees are interspersed with small, damp meadows that are home to a variety of wildflowers and small rodents. Higher up the slope to the south, stunted krummholz, the "wind timber," mark treeline. These slopes are a favourite early winter haunt of skiers.

Species of anenome (an-ENN-owe-me — "wind flower") and the glacier lily are the first flowers to emerge from the melting snow in June. The snow lingers in these meadows until July, and the thin soils and fragile vegetation are easily damaged. Please stay on the paved pathway, and dress warmly for a walk in this windy area.

Peyto Lake Overlook
Wild Bill's Lake and Glacier

The vista revealed by following the Bow Summit trail to the Peyto (PEE-toe) Lake overlook is well worth the short walk. In no other place in the Rockies is such an aerial overview of a glacial lake possible with so little effort.

Extremely fine particles of till are known as rock flour. The minute and uniform size of the rock flour particles causes them to reflect the blue/green spectrum of light. This phenomenon is principally responsible for the remarkable colour of Peyto Lake. Shortly after the ice melts from the lake's surface in June, its waters will be largely free of sediment, and will appear blue in colour, much the same as any other lake viewed from above. As the glacier melt season progresses, and the amount of rock flour in the water increases, the colour of the lake will change to one of its famous hues. Mineral content is not a significant factor.

The lake was named after pioneer outfitter, and later park warden, "Wild" Bill Peyto. During an expedition which camped at Bow Lake in 1898, Peyto disappeared from camp one evening to sleep in solitude near this place. Later, on seeing the lake for himself, J.N. Collie, a member of the expedition, christened it "Peyto's Lake." The turreted peak in view from the viewpoint, with the prominent chute descending from its summit, is also named for Peyto.

The Mistaya (miss-TAY-yah) Valley is in view north of the lake.

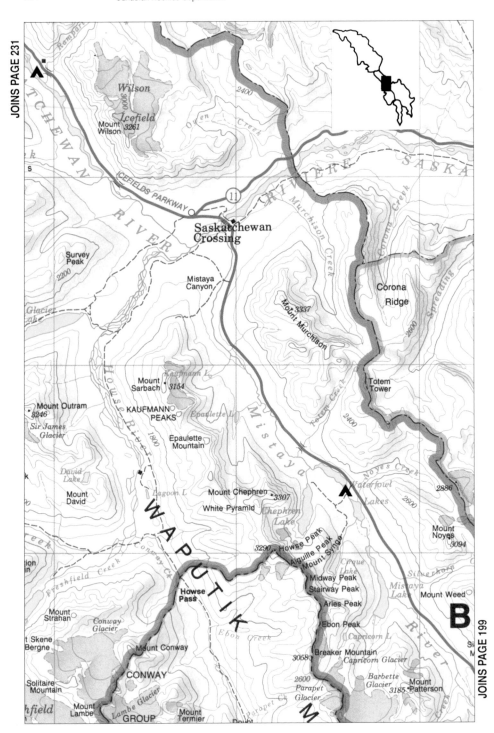

JOINS PAGE 231

JOINS PAGE 199

Snowbird Glacier
A Battle With Gravity

The spectacular, frozen cascade of Snowbird Glacier is one of the best examples of a niche glacier in the Rockies. Clinging to the northeast face of Mt. Patterson, the ice conforms to many indentations, producing the remarkable mile-high, winged shape. As the bonding power of the ice and snow gives way to the relentless pull of gravity, avalanches sweep the mountainside.

A formidable and dangerous test piece for mountaineers, the northeast face of Mt. Patterson was first climbed in 1967 by a route which included the lower tongue of the Snowbird.

The Continental Divide
Backbone of the Continent

The ice-clad ramparts of the Continental Divide are most impressive when seen from the Howse Peak Viewpoint. A nine kilometre ridge, never less than 2,750 m (9,000 ft) in elevation, contains seven mountains, and culminates in the lofty 3290 m / 10,793 ft summit of Howse Peak. The Divide separates waters that flow west to the Pacific via the Blaeberry and Columbia Rivers, from those which flow east to Hudson's Bay and the Atlantic, via the Mistaya and North Saskatchewan Rivers.

This mountain wall intercepts a great deal of the moisture from the prevailing southwest winds, creating a rain shadow to the east.

Howse Peak is the highest mountain on the Continental Divide between Kicking Horse Pass and Saskatchewan River Crossing. The first ascent was accomplished by J.N. Collie in 1902, using a route on the opposite side of the mountain. In recent years mountaineers have climbed difficult routes on the imposing north and east flanks, facing the Parkway.

Little Critters

The smallest of the two most common striped rodents in the Rockies is the least chipmunk – the smallest chipmunk in North America. Four gray stripes with black borders, running from nose to tail, differentiate it from the larger golden-mantled ground squirrel, which has two white stripes with black borders beginning behind the ears. Both species are very animated. As a prized food of many larger predators, they have to keep moving to avoid becoming easy prey.

These critters eat seeds, insects, tender flowers and shoots, and spend the summer stockpiling dry foods in and around their burrows, in which they spend six months of the year in quasi-hibernation.

The Columbian ground squirrel is one of the most frequently seen mammals in the Rockies. Typically, it is observed standing upright at its burrow entrance, emitting an irritating "yeeek." The burrow is one of many in a colony. When alarmed these rodents dive for cover, chattering loudly, only to poke their curious heads above ground a short time later.

The coat is gray on the back, and reddish-orange on the underside and feet. The Columbian ground squirrel eats incessantly: berries, roots, leaves, insects, seeds, flowers and carrion. What it doesn't eat immediately, it stores in its burrow to snack on during the eight months of the year spent in hibernation.

The red squirrel, noisy resident of the forest, is probably the most frequently heard and seen mammal in the Rockies. Its coat is a dark, reddish-brown, with a white underside and white around the eyes. The bushy tail is tipped with black. Unlike the other ground squirrels and chipmunks, the red squirrel is not particularly approachable, and will often greet an intruder with a long-winded array of staccato chattering, a ruckus out of proportion to its diminutive size.

The red squirrel prefers to eat the seeds from spruce and fir cones. Although it is commonly seen leaping from branch to branch, gathering cones, it also spends much of its time on the forest floor creating a midden – a pile of scales discarded from cones during feeding, within which it makes its burrow. The seeds are stashed in and around the midden, and the caches are eaten during the winter. Bark, berries, plant seeds, insects, fungi, and unattended nestlings round out its diet.

Top to bottom: Least chipmunk, Golden mantled ground squirrel, Columbian ground squirrel, red squirrel

The Continental Divide swings west from Howse Peak, and does not approach roadside again until Yellowhead Pass nearly 150 km to the northwest.

A short walk from the viewpoint leads across the old road bed to the marshy shores of Upper Waterfowl Lake. The lake's shallow waters allow for abundant growth of aquatic vegetation preferred by moose. This animal is frequently seen here in the early morning and evening.

Waterfowl Lakes

If you walk to the beginning of the Chephren Lake and Cirque Lake trailhead in the Waterfowl Lake campground, you will find a footbridge over the Mistaya River. The river here is very narrow and is not confined in a canyon. Why have the waters of Upper Waterfowl Lake been constricted into this tiny stream, only to form into another large lake further on?

Lower Waterfowl Lake is a tarn, occupying a glacially sculpted basin. Noyes Creek, emptying into the Mistaya Valley from the east, carries a large amount of rock and debris. When the creek enters the valley, the angle of the streambed and velocity of water flow decrease, causing this material to drop out of the water. Over time, these deposits have created a landform called an alluvial fan. In this case, the fan has spread almost entirely across the valley bottom, nearly damming the Mistaya River and creating Upper Waterfowl Lake.

The Waterfowl Lake campground is built on this alluvial fan.

Lower Waterfowl Lake is another of the many lakes in the Rockies which fill glacially scoured hollows. The Waterfowl Lakes were originally named "Wildfowl Lakes" by mountaineer J.N. Collie in 1902.

Evidence shows a great deal of the material in the alluvial fans in the Rockies was deposited between six and seven thousand years ago, when the last vestiges of ice from the Wisconsin Glaciation melted from the high peaks.

The lakes appear on mountaineer J. N. Collie's 1903 map as the "wildfowl lakes." Geese and ducks will still be seen here in the present day.

Moose

The moose is the largest antlered animal in the world, and the largest free-ranging mammal in the Rockies. Adult males are two metres tall at the shoulder, and specimens have been weighed at over 600 kg. Favourite habitat frequently occurs at roadside along the Icefields Parkway, so motorists have a good chance of seeing this normally reclusive creature.

At first glance, the moose seems homely and, with those long legs, clumsy. However, the moose is agile, and travels easily through dense bush, and snow over a metre deep. It can run 55 km/h, and is also perfectly at home in water, where it swims faster than most other land mammals.

The favourite summer foods of moose are the aquatic plants of marshes and wetlands. It will occasionally obtain this vegetation by diving in deep water. In winter the moose ranges higher onto avalanche slopes, browsing on aspens, willows and poplar. ("Moose" is a translation from a Native word meaning "twig-eater.") Moose frequently strip trees of their branches to a uniform height, or break the tops of willows to bring them down to feeding level.

Antlers begin to grow on the male (bull) moose in April, and are full-size by mating time in early September. Bulls challenge each other during the rut, but no harem is gathered. A single calf is born eight months later, and it remains with the female (cow) for a year. Otherwise the moose is a solitary creature. Life expectancy is up to 20 years. There are approximately 80 moose in Banff National Park.

Moose are not normally approachable, and it is especially dangerous to get close to a cow with calf, or to members of either sex during the rut. People have been killed in attacks by moose.

The banding in Mt. Chephren's steep mountainsides clearly shows the different sedimentary formations of which the mountain is comprised. Relatively undisturbed horizontal layering such as this is typical of mountains in the eastern main ranges. Mt. Chephren is a horn mountain. Its shape is a product of glacial erosion.

Mt. Chephren

Cirque glaciers erode rearwards and downwards into mountainsides, producing bowl-shaped depressions called cirques. When cirques form on opposite sides of a mountain, they produce the classic Matterhorn-style peak: the horn mountain. Mt. Chephren (KEFF-ren) is a good example.

Chephren was son of Cheops, builder of the Great Pyramid in Egypt. Mt. Chephren was originally called Pyramid Mountain by explorer Mary Schäffer, and was also known as The Black Pyramid. (The peak immediately west is still called The White Pyramid.) The name was changed in 1918 to avoid confusion with Pyramid Mountain near Jasper. Mt. Chephren is visible along a great length of the Icefields Parkway, from Bow Pass to the top of the Big Bend Hill. The first ascent was accomplished in 1913.

Mt. Murchison
3333 m / 10,935 ft

In 1858 James Hector reported that Natives considered Mt. Murchison to be the highest mountain in the Rockies. This is understandable, since Murchison pres-

Natives thought massive Mt. Murchison was the highest peak in the Rockies. It isn't, although it rises more than a vertical mile above the North Saskatchewan Valley.

ents an impressive vertical rise of 1920 m/6300 ft when viewed from the North Saskatchewan Valley.

Murchison's principal peak doesn't even place in the top 50 highest of Rocky Mountain summits. But if it's not the highest, Murchison certainly is one of the largest mountains by area. With 10 summits spread over an area of more than 30 sq km, Murchison is an example of a massif — a miniature mountain range.

First ascent of one of the two principal summits of Murchison was claimed in 1902 by a party that included noted Scottish mountaineer J. N. Collie. However, recent evidence indicates the highest summit was probably not reached until 1985.

The mountain was named after R. I. Murchison of the British Geological Survey, the man who recommended Hector to the Palliser Expedition.

Mistaya Canyon

When glaciers receded at the end of the Wisconsin Glaciation, the mouth of the Mistaya Valley was left hanging above the floor of the North Saskatchewan Valley. The waters of the Mistaya River are now carving a canyon through the limestone lip at the mouth of the valley. The short walk down to the footbridge over the canyon is worthwhile for close-up views of potholes, a natural arch, and other interesting effects of erosion by water.

Beyond the canyon, the trail branches, one fork climbing steeply to the old site of the Sarbach fire lookout, and the other contouring around Mt. Sarbach into the Howse Valley and, eventually, Howse Pass. Mt. Sarbach commemorates Peter Sarbach, the first Swiss Guide to visit Canada. He led the mountain's first ascent in 1897.

A Mountain Crossroads

During your descent into the North Saskatchewan Valley, you have probably noticed a change in the character of the vegetation at roadside. Since leaving Bow Pass, the Icefields Parkway has lost over 700 m (2,300 ft) of elevation, and taken you from the upper subalpine ecoregion into the montane ecoregion. Saskatchewan River Crossing is the lowest point on the Icefields Parkway south of Columbia Icefield, and has an elevation similar to Banff townsite.

The North Saskatchewan, Bow and Athabasca Rivers are the main arteries leading from the heart of the Rockies out to the foothills. Warmer and drier air from the east tends to back up these valleys, creating micro-climates not normally found in such proximity to high mountains. Thus, in many ways, the area around Saskatchewan River Crossing is more typical of the foothills than of a valley bottom in a mountainous area. High winds and low precipitation keep the Crossing relatively free of snow, making it favourite winter range for members of the deer family, bighorn sheep and mountain goats.

The North Saskatchewan River is 1,216 km long, and joins the South Saskatchewan River in central Saskatchewan. Over 80% of the water carried by this river system originates in the meltwater and runoff of the Canadian Rockies. The North Saskatchewan River was named a Canadian Heritage River in 1989.

Top: Mistaya Canyon is reached in a short walk from roadside.

Bottom: The North Saskatchewan River's broad valley serves as the principal travel route for the region's abundant wildlife.

The Crossing to Columbia Icefield

"The Crossing"

The Howse Valley is one of the wilder watersheds in the Canadian Rockies. The valley leads southwest from The Crossing towards Howse Pass and the 70 sq km Freshfield Icefield.

There were many obstacles to early travel along The Wonder Trail, but none was greater than the crossing of the North Saskatchewan River at high water. Historical accounts are elaborate in their descriptions of the danger, the techniques, and the antics involved. Many an expedition was cut short because of supplies lost or ruined when pack animals submerged. No human fatalities were recorded, but many times both outfitter and client went for a swim.

When construction of the Icefields Parkway was underway in the late 1930's, the crossing of the North Saskatchewan again posed an immense problem. Over nine kilometres of riverbank were inspected before the site for the bridge was chosen. Racing against freeze-up, the pouring of the bridge footings proved both dangerous and difficult.

Many travellers today cross this bridge unaware of the drama that unfolded in the past at "The Crossing." It is worthwhile to stop at the warden station and walk down to the riverbank, in order to fully appreciate the difficulties faced by the early explorers.

Souvenirs, meals and accom-

Top: In the journey north from Lake Louise, the crossing of the North Saskatchewan River was the principle obstacle facing explorers on horseback. Many expeditions were cut short because of supplies lost in the river when horses were submerged.

Bottom: The Howse River Viewpoint gives an impressive overlook of three major valleys: the Mistaya, the North Saskatchewan, and the Howse. To the west is Mt. Forbes, second highest peak in Banff National Park.

modation are available at The Crossing Resort, on the north side of the river.

Howse River Viewpoint

The Howse River viewpoint offers an expansive panorama of the North Saskatchewan Valley and the valleys of its two main tributaries, the Mistaya and Howse rivers. Mt. Murchison broods over the North Saskatchewan to the east. To the south, glaciers plaster the east faces of the peaks above the Mistaya River. And far to the west Mt. Forbes can be glimpsed, the second highest mountain in Banff National Park. Concealed from view near Mt. Forbes is Glacier Lake, one of the largest lakes in the Rockies. On the western skyline is the Mons Icefield.

The Howse Valley, which lies to the left of Mt. Forbes, leads towards one of the largest masses of glacial ice in the Rockies, the

Freshfield Icefield. First visited by James Hector of the Palliser Expedition in 1859, the icefield was named by mountaineer J. N. Collie in 1897, for the eminent British scientist, explorer and mountaineer, Sir Douglas Freshfield. The icefield occupies an area of some 70 sq km and connects with other icefields and glaciers to form a massive system of ice. It is ringed by 16 summits over 3050 m/

Byron Harmon

By the early 1900's, the Canadian Pacific Railway was doing a more than respectable job of "importing the tourists" to the Rockies. But no one had fully realized that if the physical scenery couldn't be exported, photographic images could. The Rockies were awaiting the first photographer who would take up the considerable challenge of bringing the mountains to the world. Just such a person stepped off the train in Banff one day in 1903. Byron Harmon, an itinerant, energetic, imaginative photographer from Tacoma, Washington, had found his niche.

Harmon quickly moved away from portraiture, the standard fare of the day, and took a photographic interest in the mountain landscape about him. Having developed a love of hiking and mountaineering, he was a natural to be amongst the founding members of the Alpine Club of Canada in 1906, and was named official club photographer at the outset. In this capacity Harmon travelled to the annual summer mountaineering camps, and broadened his familiarity with the Rockies and Selkirks. His direct involvement with those doing exploration gave his images an authenticity and impact that could not be matched. The public gobbled them up. Seeing more and more of the range each year, it became Harmon's goal to photograph every mountain and glacier in the Rockies.

Harmon's business in Banff enjoyed great success, too. He developed a popular series of postcards and calendars, featuring views "Along the Line of the C.P.R.," and these were marketed at home and abroad. His photographs were circulated widely in newspapers and mountaineering journals, and his movie footage was sought for international distribution. By 1920 Harmon's name was globally recognized as synonymous with the Rockies. The *Banff Crag and Canyon* wrote: "Byron Harmon is the best asset Banff has in the line of advertising the village to the outside world."

Harmon eventually rambled further afield in the world, on trips of personal exploration, but he always held the Rockies as his favourite landscape. He died at Banff in 1942. A collection of over 6,500 of Harmon's images is housed in the Whyte Museum of the Canadian Rockies. Byron's son Don and granddaughter Carole have carried on the Harmon tradition of photographing the Rockies. Carole, and her husband Stephen Hutchings, operate Altitude Publishing, which publishes the *SuperGuide*.

10,000 ft in elevation. Freshfield Glacier, flowing north from this icefield, was the first glacier draining into the North Saskatchewan River to be studied by scientific survey.

The David Thompson Highway

In autumn of 1940, five enthusiastic trailblazers drove two trucks west from Red Deer to the new Icefields Parkway. The *Banff Crag and Canyon* proposed this route be called the David Thompson Highway, foreshadowing by decades the construction of the road which now bears that name.

The David Thompson Highway (Highway 11) makes a worthwhile sidetrip from the Icefields Parkway. The road soon takes you out of Banff National Park, following the North Saskatchewan River through the front ranges and foothills, to the plains beyond.

Much of the area between the park and Rocky Mountain House is provincial forest land. There are many excellent campgrounds, and services are available in summer at the David Thompson Resort near Abraham Lake, and year-round at Rocky Mountain House. The Kootenay Plains Ecological Reserve, downstream from the Big Horn Dam, is prime habitat for deer, moose, elk and sheep. Large stands of tamarack and black spruce occur at roadside. The needles of the tamarack turn gold in late September. Rocky Mountain House National Historic Site details the history of the fur trade in this area.

Motorists travelling into Banff National Park along the David Thompson Highway require a park motor vehicle permit.

Mt. Wilson
3261 m/10,700 ft

The ramparts of Mt. Wilson form the northern backdrop at The Crossing. The impressive yellowish cliffs high on Mt. Wilson are composed of the erosion resistant Mt. Wilson Quartzite. The dark streaks are caused by water and rock lichen. Mountain goats are frequently seen on the grassy benches at mid-height on the mountain, especially as you drive north from the Crossing. Several flash flood stream courses cross The Parkway in this area.

The mountain was named in 1898 by mountaineer J. N. Collie for Tom Wilson of Banff — trail blazer and outfitter.

In 1903, pioneer outfitter and guide Tom Wilson built a homestead and ranch on Kootenay Plains along the North Saskatchewan river, slightly east of the area which is now Banff National Park. Wilson's cabins were removed when the Big Horn Dam was completed in 1972. Most of Kootenay Plains was subsequently flooded by the reservoir of Abraham Lake.

with his own climbs, tallying 52 first ascents in the range.

Thorington led the "second wave" of mountaineering in the Rockies, arriving on the scene two decades after Collie, Fay, Outram and company. In the interim many of the areas that attracted those mountaineers had plunged into obscurity. Prominent mountains in plain sight of the trails were still unclimbed, as were many less accessible mountains.

To illustrate this point, in a five day period in 1923, Thorington, W.S. Ladd and guide Conrad Kain accomplished a tour de force in the vicinity of Columbia Icefield, making the first ascent of North Twin (third highest in the Rockies), the first ascent of Mt. Saskatchewan, and the second ascent of Mt. Columbia — 123 km of travel in an area that had scarcely seen footprints in 20 years. A few days later they made the third ascent of Mt. Athabasca.

Thorington's book is one of the classics of Rockies history. He later became heavily involved with publications of the American Alpine Club. He edited its journal, and contributed his extensive knowledge to Rocky Mountain guidebooks. In the 1940's he served as the club president. Thorington died in 1989.

Saskatchewan is a Cree Native word meaning "swift current." Although prominent in the view from this section of the Parkway, Mt. Saskatchewan (3341 m/ 10,964 ft) is not easy to access, and has been climbed infre-

The prominent mountain northeast of The Crossing commemorates a key figure in Rockies' history — outfitter Tom Wilson. Wilson's guides led many mountaineers through the Rockies in quest of first ascents. One of these mountaineers, J. N. Collie, named the mountain for him in 1902.

James Monroe Thorington

James Monroe "Roy" Thorington, an opthamologist from Philadelphia, made his first trip to the Rockies in the early 1920's. It was the beginning of a life-long love affair with "The Glittering Mountains of Canada," as he titled a book in 1925. Thorington was a mountaineering scholar. No other climber and author made such an extensive analysis of the history of mountaineering in the Rockies. And his contribution was not strictly literary. Thorington wrote a great deal of the history

Rick Kunelius
Senior Wildlife Warden,
Banff National Park

While I was studying at the University of Calgary, I climbed and skied in the mountains whenever I could. After university I decided what I really wanted to be was a documentary cameraman, so I went to Toronto to take some courses. When summer came, a friend who worked for the Parks in Yoho called to say they were looking for someone with a science background who could climb, and that's how I got started. Come September, we were sitting around, watching the snow come down, the larches were golden, and I remember distinctly sitting by the fire and thinking, "I could go back to Toronto next week, back into that mad rat race, or I could stay here and really enjoy life" — and I never even went back to pick up my clothes!

***

Wardens work in three main areas — public safety, general warden work, and law enforcement. Public safety includes everything from avalanche control, to sprained ankles at Johnston Canyon, to what we call mountain rescue work, where we often have to use a helicopter to assist us in getting to the victim. General warden work includes patrolling the backcountry, checking the trails, checking fishing licenses and camping permits, continuous random wildlife observation, and so on. When it comes to law enforcement, wardens have the powers of the RCMP within the parks, and so they can be responsible for all the National Park Act camping and fire regulations, poaching regulations, and of course the rules of the Highway Traffic Act.

***

As Senior Wildlife Warden, I'm involved in monitoring wildlife and responding to problem animals. Right now, wildlife numbers are high, and it's a very exciting place to be. Since we containerized the garbage system here, we're down to two or three problem bears a year, but we also keep a series of research bears with radio collars on, which have to be changed every couple of years. That's probably my greatest moment in the summertime, working with an animal that's essentially unconscious but never totally — having to draw blood, take measurements, pull teeth and just generally be around a big bear like a grizzly gives you a lot of thrill, it's just that little adrenalin rush you need once in a while.

***

It's just exciting to be in a place where there are seven different languages being spoken, there are international restaurants of all kinds, the Banff Springs Hotel is just up the way — the mix of people, outdoor activities and cultural opportunities really makes Banff a special place. I can't think of a nicer small town to live in anywhere in Canada.

James Monroe Thorington made 52 first ascents in the Canadian Rockies during the 1920's and 30's. This photograph shows him with guide Conrad Kain (left), atop Trapper Peak on the Wapta Icefield in 1933.

quently since James Monroe Thorington's ascent.

Graveyard Flats

This gravelly plain beside the Icefields Parkway, where the Alexandra and North Saskatchewan Rivers join, was also a rendezvous place and natural campsite for Natives and early explorers. Although one might think the name "Graveyard" comes from the skeletal appearance of the abundant driftwood, it actually refers to when explorer Mary Schäffer camped here in 1907 and found animal skeletons left by Native hunters. The Graveyard Flats allowed easy travel on horseback, and were a welcome relief to travellers after the exasperating trail through the Bow and Mistaya valleys.

The Alexandra River was named in 1902 by mountaineer J. N. Collie, after Queen Alexandra, wife of King Edward VII.

Mt. Amery

With Mt. Amery we have the very unusual situation of a mountain being named for a person *before* that person participated in what was claimed as the first ascent. L. S. Amery was a British statesman, mountaineer, and editor of the *Times of London* in the early part

Rock and Roll!

As with Waterfowl Lake campground, the campground at Rampart Creek is built on an alluvial fan where a tributary stream enters the main valley. The night of August 1st, 1989 will long be remembered by those who were camped here. Heavy rains saturated the slopes on the east side of the Parkway between Mt. Murchison and Mt. Coleman. Flash floods containing a slurry of mud, rocks and vegetation swept down to the road, blocking it in several places.

In the narrow canyon upstream from the campground, some of this material built a natural dam, which eventually broke, releasing an enormous torrent of water and rocks. An estimated 4,000 cubic metres of this material surged onto the alluvial fan and inundated part of the campground, destroying one cook shelter and forcing evacuation. Fortunately no one was injured. The campground was closed for the remainder of the summer.

The impressive Rampart Creek canyon, source of the deluge, can be reached during low water in a few minutes walk from the hostel.

of this century. Amery had visited the Mt. Robson area in 1909. In 1929 he returned to Canada to make the first attempt on the mountain which had been named for him by surveyor A. O. Wheeler.

In wretched weather, Swiss guide Edward Feuz Jr. led Amery and his partner to the summit – or so they thought. In the summit photograph, Feuz and Amery stand together beside a huge cairn that Feuz had built. A good-weather ascent of the highest point of Mt. Amery by a Calgary mountaineer in 1985 revealed no

Black Bear

The vicinity of Rampart Creek campground is one of the best places in the Rockies to see black bears. The black bear is principally nocturnal, and eats berries, leaves, insects and carrion. It is solitary, except when with cubs, and dormant for much of the winter, when it dens in natural shelters on lower mountainsides. The black bear is a more adept tree climber than the grizzly, and will use this tactic to avoid danger. Although its coat is generally black in colour, sometimes with a white patch on the chest, cinnamon coloured bears also occur in the Rockies.

Our society attributes to bears a cuddly, loveable nature. In reality bears are dangerous, unpredictable, and best avoided. Unfortunately, the black bear readily comes to associate humans with easily obtainable food, particularly at campgrounds and in townsites. As recently as the 1970's, bears were encouraged to eat garbage at open dumps in the parks. Many old postcards and newsreels show bears being fed by hand at roadside, and otherwise being treated without the respect they deserve. Gone are the open garbage pits, and the toleration of feeding bears. Food garbage is now stored in bear-proof containers and trucked out of the parks to landfill sites. However, some bear/human problems remain.

Unattended or improperly stored food and garbage baits bears into situations that may ultimately be both dangerous and destructive. Except for rare cases, when a bear actually shows a mean or evil temperament towards humans, conflicts with people generally arise because the animals are simply trying to get enough food to endure the winter. And the easier the calories come, the better.

Studies of bear-human encounters have shown that while the grizzly is the more formidable animal, the black bear is highly unpredictable and therefore probably more dangerous to humans.

Swiss Guide Edward
Feuz Jr. led British
statesman L. S.
Amery to the summit
of Mt. Amery in 1929
— or did he? Recent
evidence indicates
that they may not
have quite reached
their goal.

such cairn, and no suitable rocks with which to build one. So it is possible Amery did not quite reach the true summit, and 56 years intervened before anyone succeeded.

The Weeping Wall

The waterfalls for which The Weeping Wall is named are mostly the product of melting snow and small seeps high up on Cirrus Mountain, and are at their best on hot days in late spring and early summer. In winter, the seep water freezes into sheets and pillars of ice, draping the cliffs in ice. The result is a playground for waterfall ice climbers.

Climbing ice has long been one of the most demanding facets of mountaineering. In the late 1950's, Scottish mountaineers began to attempt icy routes in the most difficult gullies on their homeland cliffs in winter, and the pursuit of waterfall ice climbing was born.

Most waterfalls in the Rockies are frozen for 5-6 months of the year. In addition, seeps which appear as mere trickles in summer create huge sheets and pillars of ice in winter. By the early 1970's, Canadian mountaineers were beginning to contemplate climbing the many frozen water-

Mountain Avens

The evergreen wildflower, mountain avens, forms dense mats on river gravels, glacial deposits and disturbed land from montane valley bottom to mountain top. Avens are one of the first plants to colonize riverbeds, stabilizing the soil to the benefit of larger plants, which can then take hold. There are two species: yellow, found in the montane and lower subalpine, and white, of the upper subalpine and glacial areas. The yellow species has a nodding flower that never fully opens. When gone to seed, the twisted flower pod releases a dandelion-like fluff. The Latin name is "dryas," and botanists refer to these gravels as dryas flats.

JOINS PAGE 259

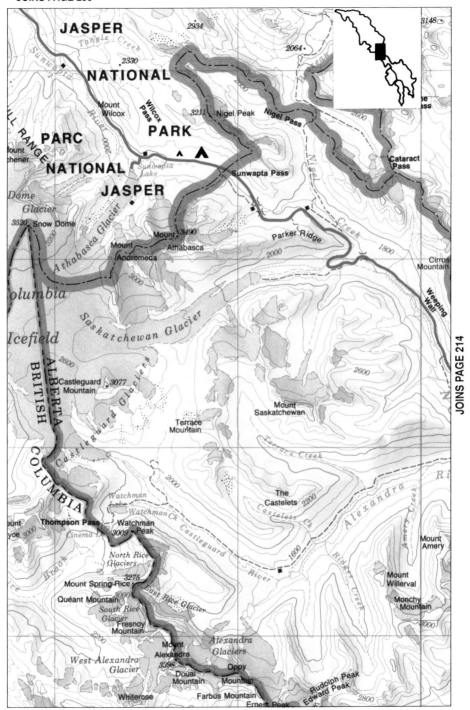

JASPER

Tangle Creek

2934

2064 ·

3148

NATIONAL

PARK

2330

Mount
Wilcox

Wilcox
Pass

3211

Nigel Peak

Nigel Pass

2600

Cataract
Pass

PARC

NATIONAL

JASPER

Sunwapta Lake

Sunwapta Pass

Parker Ridge

Cirrus
Mountain

*Dome
Glacier*

3520 · Snow Dome

Athabasca Glacier

Mount 3490
Athabasca

Mount
Andromeda

2000

1800

olumbia

3000

Saskatchewan Glacier

2600

Weeping Wall

Icefield

ALBERTA
BRITISH

Castleguard
Mountain

3077

Castleguard Glaciers

Terrace
Mountain

Mount
Saskatchewan

2600

COLUMBIA

Castleguard River

2000

Watchman Lake

Watchman Ck

Terrace Creek

The
Castelets

Castelets Ck

2200

Alexandra R

2000

Thompson Pass

Watchman
Peak

3009

Cinema Dr

North Rice
Glaciers

3275

Mount Spring-Rice

Quéant Mountain

3000

South Rice
Glacier

Fresnoy
Mountain

East Rice Glacier

1600

River

Ridge Creek

Amery Creek

Mount
Amery

Mount
Willerval

Monchy
Mountain

3000

2200

West Alexandra
Glacier

Mount
Alexandra

3398

Douai
Mountain

*Alexandra
Glaciers*

Oppy
Mountain

Whiterose

Farbus Mountain

Ernest Peak

Rudolph Peak
Edward Peak

2800

JOINS PAGE 214

Top: Melting snow and seeps of water are sources of the many cascades on The Weeping Wall. The flow of water is greatest on a hot afternoon in late spring or early summer.

Right: In winter, the seeps on The Weeping Wall freeze into sheets and pillars of ice, and become a waterfall ice climbing playground.

falls in the central Rockies. Equipment lagged behind determination and courage, and the early ascents of long routes on The Weeping Wall, Takakkaw Falls

and Snow Dome were tremendous achievements.

Typical of many pursuits, equipment and skill have recently advanced to the point where routes formerly considered extreme are now climbed solo by unroped climbers, in a fraction of the time required for the first ascent. Vertical and overhanging ice is routinely ascended. In pushing the limits of their sport, some ice climbers have established routes combining a high degree of difficulty and danger, in remote settings.

The Canadian Rockies are the ice climbing mecca of the world. If you're visiting in winter, look for climbers on the many waterfalls along the Icefields Parkway, and near the town of Field.

The Big Bend

To the frustration of cyclists, the Icefields Parkway now loses 100 m of elevation, before beginning the long, 360 m climb to Sunwapta Pass. If The Big Bend seems an unusual feature to incorporate into a road, consider the dilemma facing the road builders. At this point, the North Saskatchewan Valley swings west to Columbia Icefield. In order for the road to continue north, the builders had to find a line with an acceptable grade, while contouring around the east end of Parker Ridge and staying above the canyon of Nigel Creek. Not an easy task! The Big Bend helps lessen the steepness of the grade by taking the lower part of the climb along Parker Ridge as a sideslope.

In 1896, one of the first explorers in the area, Walter Wilcox, made a foray west through the small canyon opposite the middle of The Big Bend. It proved to be a wrong turn, but his party was the first to see Saskatchewan Glacier, which lies just beyond.

It was on the Big Bend Hill in 1939 that road crews working from Jasper and Lake Louise met and completed the Icefields Parkway.

Cirrus Mountain

During mountain building, the sedimentary formations of which the Rockies are comprised were subjected to enormous stresses. Sometimes the rock was bowed upwards or downwards into folds. Whenever you see layers of sedi-

mentary formations that are U-shaped, you are looking at a type of fold known as a syncline. On either side of a syncline there was usually a corresponding upward, arching fold called an anticline.

At Cirrus Mountain, the great Castle Mountain Syncline is revealed by the U-shaped fold of the sedimentary layers in the middle of the mountain. This syncline runs from Castle Mountain in Banff to Mt. Kerkeslin in Jasper.

The overview of the North Saskatchewan Valley from this viewpoint clearly shows the U-shaped, glacial trough, and gives an impressive indication of the thickness of the ancestral Saskatchewan Glacier which once carved and filled this valley. The steep, slabby slopes south of The Big

Ice climbers use specialized tools — ice axes and hammers, and sharp, pointed crampons for the boots — to enable them to climb steep and overhanging ice. The Icefields Parkway is one of the most popular areas in the world with ice climbers.

The North Saskatchewan Valley clearly shows the U-shape produced by glacial erosion. The downwards fold in the sedimentary formations of Cirrus Mountain is the Castle Mountain Sycline, which runs for a great distance through Banff and Jasper National Parks.

Bend were undercut by the glacial ice, and now massive rockslides are triggered when sheets of rock split away along weak layers.

Coleman's Country

Native peoples knew better than to tackle the difficult terrain of the Bow, Mistaya and North Saskatchewan Valleys when travelling from south to north in the Rockies. They developed an easier route through valleys in the front ranges to the east.

In 1892 and 1893, A. P. Coleman, a geology professor from Toronto, used these valleys to head north in his search for the fabled giant summits of the Rockies, Mts. Hooker and Brown. He obtained information on the route from Chief Jonas of the Stoney tribe, and named a pass and creek in the high country northeast of here in honour of the chief.

Coleman made repeated visits to the Rockies, and published accounts of his travels in *The Canadian Rockies: New and Old Trails*. Unfortunately for other early explorers, the book and its wealth of information did not appear until 1911. Explorer Mary Schäffer had a chance meeting with Coleman on the trail at Wilcox Pass in 1907 and, with the information garnered, she set out across Nigel Pass in quest for Maligne Lake. At that time Coleman was in the process of making the second recorded journey from Lake Louise to Jasper, using the main range valleys he had previously avoided!

In the present day, the trail to Nigel Pass gives backpackers quick access to Coleman's front range valleys, where some of the most exquisite alpine and sub-alpine scenery in all the Rockies is found. "Nigel" was the camp cook on J. N. Collie's 1898 mountain-eering expedition.

Parker Ridge
A Walk on the Wild Side

If you're going to get out of your vehicle only once along the Icefields Parkway to go for a walk, Parker Ridge is the place to do it. A short but steep excursion to the ridge crest takes you into the barren world of the alpine ecoregion, and gives a splendid panorama of Saskatchewan Glacier and the southeast fringe of Columbia Icefield.

Since leaving The Weeping Wall, the Icefields Parkway has gained over 450 m of elevation This fact alone will produce a temperature some 3°C lower at Parker Ridge trailhead. However, proximity to the chilling mass of Columbia Icefield may lower the temperature as much as 10°C from that you experienced on the floor of the North Saskatchewan Valley a short while ago. Parker Ridge is a windy place too, so bundle up. Take extra clothing, a snack and some water with you on your hike, and allow 2-4 hours for the round trip.

The trailhead is near treeline, where the upper subalpine and alpine ecoregions meet. The for-est is thin, and comprised solely

of scattered tree islands of Engelmann spruce and subalpine fir, some of them in the stunted krummholz form. The trees lean away from the prevailing north-west wind of this locality, and some develop branches only on their southeast side. The slopes to the right and left of the trailhead are denuded of vegetation by fre-quent winter snow avalanches.

When it comes to sustaining plant and animal life, Parker Ridge has everything going against it. Thin soils, near constant catabatic winds, heavy snowfall, high ele-vation and north-facing slopes

On a quest to find the highest mountains in the Rockies, geology professor A. P. Coleman made journeys through the front range valleys east of here in 1892-93. Coleman named one valley and pass, Jonas, after a Stoney chieftain. Another was named Poboktan — the Stoney word for "owl."

combine to create an extremely short growing season which eliminates all but the hardiest species. Some snow patches may linger year-round. It is not uncommon to see die-hard skiers here in August.

As you begin your ascent of the trail, the trees quickly give way to stunted alpine vegetation. The tiny white, pink and yellow bell-shaped flowers of the minuscule evergreen, mountain heather, are common. Snow willow and alpine willow often grow amongst them.

David Day
Former Superintendent,
Banff National Park

We have about six hundred staff, so it's a big organization. And people say to me, this must be a great job, you get to sit on your horse, ride around, and look after this huge park. And it's true, if I really get totally bezonkers here, I do have a horse and a saddle, so I can go for a ride, but I can never find the time to get more than ten feet from the barn. It's a real killer on family life, unless your family is as supportive as mine is.
***
When you're a superintendent, you're pretty well in charge of all the federal parks facilities inside the national park. And it runs from maintaining roads to looking after all of the leases. You're also responsible for all the wildlife protection, public safety, law enforcement on the national park side — not criminal code, the police look after that. Right through to collecting fees, fire management and so on. Everything that the park offers by way of its visitor welcoming,

reception programs through its resource management protection programs. It's an all-encompassing sort of job.
***
It's important that we maintain the quality of experience because if that's there, then people will support our being pretty particular about how we manage the park. This park has the capacity to accept a lot more visitors, but not all at the same time. I mean, in the summertime now our infrastructure is pretty full — you can keep pumping people onto the shore of Lake Louise, but eventually they can't stay five minutes, they can't enjoy it. And right now the challenge is how do we stop everybody from going there between 11 am and 1 pm. The place is empty from 9 am to 11 am and from 1:30 to 5 pm.
***
A national park can't be everything to everybody or it's going to be nothing for most people. And that's the vision that the park management plan has — my job is to propel us that way.

Top: The panoramic view from the crest of Parker Ridge reveals Saskatchewan Glacier and the southeast fringe of Columbia Icefield.

Left: This view of Mt. Athabasca is from Wilcox Pass on the east side of the highway. Athabasca Glacier can be seen on the right.

The blue gentian and alpine forget-me-not contrast with one of the most striking plants of the alpine, moss campion. This cushion plant of tiny green leaves is dotted with a multitude of pink flowers.

If many of the other wildflowers you see look like scaled-down versions of ones familiar at lower

White-tailed Ptarmigan

The white-tailed ptarmigan (TAR-mih-gun) is a common resident of rocky slopes in the upper subalpine and alpine ecoregions. It molts – shedding and changing its feathers to match the white of winter snow, and the mottled grays, blacks and browns of summer boulderfields. There is a red comb over each eye.

The ptarmigan's camouflage is so good, you'd expect to have trouble seeing them. But these birds have the habit of giving themselves away by unnecessarily flapping their wings, clucking, cooing and otherwise making a fuss, even though you were about to walk by oblivious. This behaviour earned them the nickname "fool hen," and during the early days of exploration in the Rockies many an unwary ptarmigan ended up in the pot for supper.

Ptarmigan are social birds, and where there's one there may often be as many as a dozen. The young are most entertaining, running circles round mother hen. Ptarmigan eat plants, seeds and insects. Major predators are hawks and owls. Ptarmigan nest on the ground, seldom fly, and generally stay in the mountains year-round.

elevations, you're right. Larger stems, leaves and flowers need more nutrients than are available here, and they would lose too much moisture to the harsh effects of wind and sunlight at this elevation. Large plants simply cannot survive in the alpine.

On your way to the ridge crest, keep an eye out for white-tailed ptarmigan, pika, golden eagle, raven and mountain goat. Parker Ridge is one of the best places to get close to mountain goats in the Rockies. And if you don't see the animals themselves, you will most certainly see their pellet-like droppings and cloven tracks.

On the ridge crest itself, a few hardy grasses and rock lichens are about all that grow in the thin, shaly soil. The lichen colonies may be as much as 11,000 years old! To avoid damaging this incredibly sensitive, ancient and fragile environment, please keep to the beaten path, and avoid making shortcuts. The winding trail has been built with a purpose in mind – it skirts around the lingering snow patches of early summer.

The trail crosses a saddle over the ridge at an elevation of 2260 m/7450 ft, and descends slightly to reveal an overview of the nine kilometre-long Saskatchewan Glacier, the longest outlet valley glacier of Columbia Icefield. From the icefield rim to its terminus, this mighty river of ice drops over 750 m. Apart from its size, the Saskatchewan Glacier is a relatively unspectacular one, having no icefalls and very few crevasses.

Castleguard Mountain stands in isolation at the head of Saskatchewan Glacier. South of this mountain is the entrance to Castleguard Cave, one of the largest cave systems in Canada. Over 20 km of passages have been explored, some leading out under Columbia Icefield. To the left of Castleguard Mountain, in the distance, is the magnificent 3487 m/11,507 ft summit of Mt. Bryce, which lies entirely in British Columbia. To your right from this vantage point are the southern flanks of Mt. Athabasca and Mt. Andromeda (with a spectacular icefall). On the north side of these mountains lies Athabasca Glacier.

The view is breathtaking, and so is the chill in the air. If the day is typical, you will not want to linger long on your foray into the alpine ecoregion before returning to the warmth of your vehicle.

Sunwapta Pass

At 2023 m/6676 ft, Sunwapta Pass is the second highest point on the Icefields Parkway. Apart from the climb of the Tangle Creek Hill ahead, the Icefields Parkway loses one kilometre of elevation in the 110 km between here and Jasper townsite.

Sunwapta Pass marks the boundary between Banff and Jasper National Parks, and the watershed divide between North Saskatchewan River, which drains to Lake Winnipeg, Hudson Bay and the Atlantic Ocean, and the Sunwapta River, which eventually drains to the Arctic Ocean.

The name Sunwapta was given by A. P. Coleman in 1892. It is applied to five features along the Icefields Parkway, and means "turbulent river" in the Native Stoney language.

Road Blocks

When Walter Wilcox passed this way in 1896, Athabasca Glacier blocked the Sunwapta Valley ahead. To detour around the ice, Wilcox's party climbed over the pass now bearing his name, and dropped down a rough track beside Tangle Creek to re-enter the Sunwapta Valley. This detour also by-passed the constriction of the Sunwapta Canyon and the terrific jumble of the Mt. Kitchener Slide, just north of Athabasca Glacier.

By the time the Icefields Parkway was completed in 1939, Athabasca Glacier had receded so much that the road could easily pass through on the floor of the Sunwapta Valley. However, extensive rock cuts were still necessary to by-pass the Sunwapta Canyon. If Athabasca Glacier ever re-advances, the present day route of the Parkway will be in jeopardy.

You can hike the Wilcox Pass trail today, just as the explorers did, to make a day trip to Tangle Creek. The trail traverses alpine tundra – the haunt of bighorn sheep and grizzly bear. Significant karst features – underground drainage in limestone – occur in the region.

Columbia Icefield

Above: Athabasca Glacier, in Jasper National Park, is the best-known glacier in the Rockies.

Opposite: This aerial view shows Athabasca Glacier flowing from the Columbia Icefield (bottom) to a position 1.5 km from the highway (top). Dome Glacier can be seen on the left.

Icy Crown of the Continent

Columbia Icefield is the largest sheet of glacial ice in the interior of North America. Its meltwaters feed three of Canada's largest river systems and, eventually, three oceans: the Pacific via the Columbia River, the Arctic via the Athabasca and Mackenzie Rivers, and the Atlantic via the North Saskatchewan River and Hudson Bay. The summit of Snow Dome, one of the mountains on the icefield, is the apex of this tri-oceanic watershed.

Columbia Icefield is part of a chain of icefields which cloak the Continental Divide between Kicking Horse and Athabasca Passes. Seventeen other ice sheets in the Rockies are officially called icefields. There are many other large, upland glaciers to which this term could be applied.

The Ice Factory

Glaciers form in areas where more snow accumulates annually than melts. This is usually a gently rolling, alpine area, ringed by high mountains, and subject to a moist air flow. The mountains cause the air to rise, cool, and release precipitation. Because of the effects of elevation on temperature, most

Glacial ice is formed from compacted snow. Air and other impurities in the ice on a glacier's surface reflect all wavelengths of light, making the ice appear white. The compressed ice crystals deep within a glacier have most of the air squeezed out of them, and reflect only the blue spectrum of light.

of this precipitation falls as snow and little of it melts.

Columbia Icefield has an average elevation of 3000 m/9845 ft. More than 10 m of snow falls on the icefield every year, and the gentle slopes prevent loss of this snow to avalanche, as often occurs on steeper terrain at lower elevations.

As the fallen snow crystals age, they change shape from flakes to grains. Over time, these grains compact under the weight of successive annual accumulations. This process is helped along by saturation of the snowpack with meltwater which trickles down from the surface in summer. Finally, when a thickness of 30 m of compacted snow has accumulated, the lower layers will begin to transform into glacial ice.

Once a mass of glacial ice has developed, it must move in order to be considered a glacier. Because it is heavy, glacial ice will follow inclines, and seek natural breaks through which to flow downhill.

Athabasca Glacier
A River of Ice

The surface of Athabasca Glacier contains many features common to glacial ice. By studying its surface in detail, we can better understand the dynamics of glacial motion, and the effects of moving ice on the landscape.

From the icefield rim (on the skyline) to its terminus, Athabasca Glacier drops 600 m in 5.3 km. The steepest drop occurs about one kilometre from the rim, and is marked by a prominent icefall. Here the ice attempts to conform to a cliff in the bedrock beneath. The surface of the glacier is moving faster, and is under less pressure than the ice in contact with the bedrock. It therefore accelerates over the drop, and becomes heavily fissured. These fissures are known as crevasses (creh-VASS-es). Crevasses are of several varieties: transverse, which run from side to side; marginal, which form at the sides and parallel the glacier's flow; and radial, where the ice splays out near the terminus. It is estimated there are over 30,000 crevasses on Athabasca Glacier.

Towers of ice that form in icefalls or on the cliff edges of hanging glaciers are called seracs (sir-RACKS). A serac wall clings to the east face of Snow Dome just to the right of the upper icefall. Avalanches of ice from this cliff frequently crash down onto the glacier surface. If you think you hear thunder on a clear day, look to this serac wall and you might see the end of an avalanche.

In August, look for the annual snowline in the vicinity of the uppermost icefall. Snow towards the icefield rim from that point is in the accumulation zone, and will likely endure the summer, on its way to becoming glacial ice. Between the annual snowline and the terminus is the ablation zone, where the glacier surface is free from snow, and the ice mass of the glacier is melting.

To the viewer's left of the lower of the three icefalls, several glaciers tumble from the steep slopes of Mt. Andromeda, and avalanche their ice onto the surface of Athabasca Glacier.

The sides and base of a glacier lose momentum to friction with the surrounding rock, so the surface ice in the centre of the glacier moves the fastest — in this case, about 125 m a year at the icefalls, 80 m a year at the halfway point, and 15 m a year at the terminus.

There are many meltwater streams on the surface of Athabasca Glacier. The water sculpts runnels in the ice, sometimes disappearing into crevasses or chutes known as moulin (moo-LANN) or millwells. The water emerges later from the terminus, after flowing within or beneath the ice. It is thought this meltwa-

Icefields of the Canadian Rockies

Name	Approximate Area/sq km	Visible from road?	Location/Where Visible
Washmawapta	6	no	northern Rockwall, 10 km w. of Marble Canyon
Waputik	32	yes	Hector Lake viewpoint
Wapta	40	yes	Hector Lake, Bow and Peyto Glacier vpts.
Freshfield	60	no	25 km southwest of Saskatchewan Crossing
Campbell	10	no	west of Freshfield Icefield
Mons	16	yes	20 km west of Howse River viewpoint
Lyell	35	no	slightly north of Mons Icefield
Wilson	20	yes	Mt. Wilson viewpoint
Columbia	325	yes	Parker Ridge crest to Sunwapta Flats
Clemenceau	200	no	west of Columbia Icefield
Chaba	20	no	west of Columbia Icefield
Hooker	60	no	east side of Athabasca Pass
Mt. Brown	8	no	west side of Athabasca Pass
Brazeau	25	no	10 km southeast of Maligne Lake
Reef	25	no	15 km east of Mt. Robson
Swiftcurrent	30	no	15 km northwest of Mt. Robson
Resthaven	40	no	35 km northwest of Mt. Robson
Lloyd George	70	no	600 km northwest of Jasper

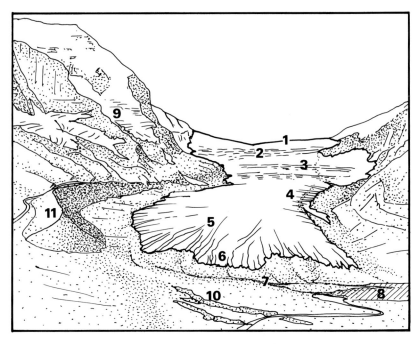

This drawing of Athabasca Glacier shows the following glacial features: 1. The Columbia Icefield, 2. icefalls, 3. transverse crevasses, 4. marginal crevasses, 5. terminal crevasses, 6. the "toe" of the glacier, 7. meltwater stream, 8. meltwater lake (Sunwapta), 9. tributary glacier, 10. terminal moraine, and 11. lateral moraine.

ter helps lubricate the base of the glacier, allowing the ice to flow more easily. A major sub-surface stream network on the Athabasca Glacier empties on the viewer's right of the terminus. From year to year this point is marked by an ice cave of varying dimensions.

The Rubble-Strewn Path

Moraines are the most common landforms created by glaciers. Ground moraine is till (glacial debris) that blanketed the surface or underside of a glacier, and was left in place when the ice melted. Ground moraine covers most of the valley bottoms in the Rockies. Thus till, not bedrock, is the most common element in riverbeds and streambanks.

The most easily recognized moraine type is the end moraine, which forms where till is deposited at the terminus of a glacier. End moraines include terminal moraines, which are deposited at the maximum extent of a glacial advance, and annual or recessional moraines, which show positions of the terminus during glacial retreat. The road to Athabasca Glacier cuts through a series of recessional moraines, with signs indicating the years in which they were formed. The most recent terminal moraine of Athabasca Glacier abutted the slopes of Mt. Wilcox behind the Information Centre and is not readily discernible. Easily recognized terminal moraines can be seen at Mt. Edith Cavell, Snowbird Glacier and Crowfoot Glacier.

A lateral moraine is composed of till deposited by the glacier against the valley walls. The most impressive moraine in the vicinity of Athabasca Glacier is the lateral moraine on the viewer's left. This feature towers over 120 m above the surface of the terminus. The Snocoach ride to Athabasca Glacier takes you down the steep slope of this moraine. Other good examples of lateral moraines can be seen nearby at Dome Glacier, and elsewhere at Cavell, Peyto, Victoria and Wenkchemna Glaciers.

Often the interior of a lateral moraine has an ice core. Ice-cored moraines are highly unstable, and may avalanche debris back onto the surface of the ice. This is one way in which surface moraine is formed. Rockfall from cliffs above is another. As surface moraine is carried down the glacier it spreads out, uniformly covering and insulating the ice. Dome, Cavell, Stutfield and Victoria Glaciers show extensive surface moraine.

An unusual feature that can result from surface moraine is the glacier table. These are rocks whose large size prevents the melting of ice directly beneath them, leaving them balanced on the resulting pedestals.

Extremely large boulders of surface moraine were sometimes transported great distances from their places of origin by the ancestral glaciers of past ice ages. Known as glacial erratics, these rocks give glaciologists an indication of the former extent of the

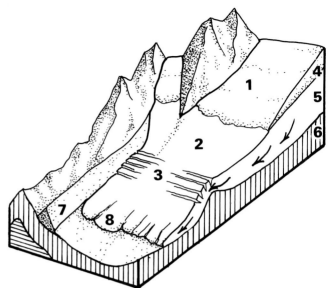

This cross-section diagram of a glacier shows: 1. the accumulation zone (where new snow is converted into glacial ice) and 2. ablation zone, where glacial ice melts into water.

Other features include: 3. crevasses, 4. new ice, 5. the movement of glacial ice, 6. the underlying bedrock, 7. a lateral moraine, and 8. the toe of the glacier.

Left: Glacial meltwater sculpts deep channels into the surface of glacial ice. Sometimes the water disappears into the glacier to flow in sub-surface streams. Glacial meltwater is the principal source of all major rivers in the Rockies. Meltwater from Athabasca Glacier feeds the Sunwapta, River and eventually reaches the Arctic Ocean.

Glaciers are accurate indicators of long-term trends in climate. When the earth's climate cools and more snow accumulates, the mass of glaciers builds and the rivers of ice advance into the surrounding valleys. If the climate warms, as presently, the glaciers retreat. Athabasca Glacier has retreated 1.6 km since 1870. Signs along the road on the way to the glacier indicate the various positions of the glacier terminus during the last 100 years.

glaciers of the Rockies. Any time you see a large boulder in a valley bottom in an area not prone to rockslides, it is probably a glacial erratic. There is a prominent "bear-shaped" erratic deposited by Athabasca Glacier opposite the Columbia Icefield Chalet.

The last feature of glacial deposition will make the greatest impression on those who stray from the trail to the terminus of Athabasca Glacier. A thick, finely grained black mud known as glacier goo claims many a running shoe here every summer. The goo is difficult to spot until you've taken one step too many, so it's a good idea to keep to the beaten path.

Glacial Advance and Retreat

If more snow is accumulating in the accumulation zone than is melting in the ablation zone, a glacier is in advance. If the reverse is true, a glacier is in retreat.

Generally, the earth's climate has been warming since the Little Ice Age ended in the late 1800's. Although some glaciers in the Rockies have experienced periods of minor advance since that time, the current state of glacial affairs is one of overall retreat. A few consecutive dry winters and unusually hot summers in the Rockies can greatly influence the well-being of its glaciers.

Sunwapta Lake

Sunwapta Lake, adjacent to Athabasca Glacier, is a glacial tarn whose days are numbered. The lake began to form in 1938 when the retreating ice uncovered a depression it had scoured in the bedrock. The lake reached maximum size in 1966, and is now decreasing in size and depth, as four different tributary streams build four gravelly deltas into its waters. Five hundred and seventy tonnes of mud, gravel and rock is deposited into the lake by meltwater, each warm day in the summer months.

Eventually, the depression in which Sunwapta Lake lies will either be completely filled, or buried by the ice of a re-advancing Athabasca Glacier. A similar fate awaits many other lakes in the Rockies.

Watermelon Snow

If you're visiting the Rockies in mid-summer, you've probably noticed that many of the lingering snowbanks are tinged with pink. The colour of watermelon snow is caused by a one-celled algae that actually lives in the snow. This algae provides food for species of tiny snow worms, so it's not recommended that you attempt to verify the watermelon flavour, but you may want to take a sniff — some people claim watermelon snow *smells* like watermelons, too.

A Frozen New World

Native peoples undoubtedly knew the location of Columbia Icefield, but it was not until 1898 that it was first seen by Europeans. The story of its discovery is connected with the search for the two fabled mountains — Mts. Hooker and Brown.

In 1827, Scottish botanist David Douglas crossed Athabasca Pass. En route, he paused long enough to climb a mountain to the west, which he named Mt. Brown. This was the earliest recorded mountaineering ascent in the Rockies. But more importantly, Douglas assigned elevations to Mt. Brown, and another peak he named Mt. Hooker, of almost 4900 m/16,000 ft, and re-

An Ancient Forest

The Little Ice Age advance of the Athabasca Glacier reached its maximum in 1714. During this advance, the glacier encroached into upper subalpine forest. The terminal moraine of the advance is against the lower slopes of Mount Wilcox. This moraine also marks the trimline: trees between this moraine and the glacier were destroyed by the ice, while those outside the moraine survived.

In 1982, an Engelmann spruce in the grove outside the moraine was cored by glaciologists. The core sample showed 680 rings. As each ring records a year's growth, this tree is now at least 690 year's old — the oldest known tree in Jasper National Park. The "inception period" of the tree — a time when rings are not created — may add 20 - 50 years to this age.

ported that they towered some 1800 m over Athabasca Pass.

With the completion of the Canadian Pacific Railway through the Rockies in 1884, climbers and explorers flocked to Banff, Lake Louise and Field. The highest mountains known around Lake Louise also rose some 1800 m above the valley floor, but only to 3500 m/11,600 ft. Mt. Hooker and Mt. Brown must be truly giants! The race was on to be first to climb Mt. Hooker.

A. P. Coleman made three attempts to find the mountains between 1888-93. On the last trip, Coleman's party located Athabasca Pass and ascended Mt. Brown, which turned out to be a peak of less than average stature for the Rockies. Coleman gruffly stated, "We had been humbugged," and let the mountaineering world know he felt Douglas' famed peaks to be frauds. Although Coleman's party ascended several peaks to the east

Common Raven

The common raven is one of nature's most adaptable creatures. At home in deserts, cities, and on mountain tops, ravens are quite capable of coming to terms with the harsh conditions in the vicinity of Athabasca Glacier. The raven's diet is the key to its adaptability. These birds are opportunistic scavengers, and eat virtually anything.

Ravens are normally seen alone or in pairs, picking over the gravels at roadside, or rummaging through garbage. Carrion is a favourite part of the raven's diet, and a congregation of ravens usually indicates that an unfortunate deer or elk has met its end. Recent research suggests ravens may be able to communicate to their fellows the whereabouts of such a feast – for when a good feeding opportunity exists, large numbers of these birds quickly descend on the scene.

Throughout history, we have tended to regard ravens as evil and unintelligent. In

reality, they occupy a prominent niche in the ecology, and with their keen eye-sight, inquisitive nature, varied vocabulary and structured social order, it would be appropriate for us to reverse our impressions.

The raven stays in the Rockies year-round, while its smaller, look-alike cousin, the American crow, migrates a short distance south. In flight, the two can be easily differentiated: the raven has a wedge-shaped tail, while the crow's is squarish.

of Columbia Icefield, the explorers made no claim to have noticed the true giants in this part of the Rockies, Mt. Columbia, Mt. Alberta and North Twin, which would have been in view to the west.

Coleman's announcement was not accepted universally. Some thought he had climbed the wrong mountain from the wrong pass. Others wondered how Douglas, a first rate scholar, could have made such a blunder. In 1896, Walter Wilcox came into the fray. Forging the route now used by the Icefields Parkway, Wilcox got close enough to Athabasca Pass to take a measurement of Mt. Brown's height, but his observations were inconclusive. Twice on this trip, at Saskatchewan Glacier, and from the summit of his namesake peak, Wilcox glimpsed the fringe of Columbia Icefield, but the claim for its "discovery" was not to be his either.

Enter J. N. Collie. In 1897, while returning from a climbing expedition which had focussed on peaks in the vicinity of Saskatchewan River Crossing, Collie became intrigued with the view of the high, snowy mountains further north. Surely the real Mts. Hooker and Brown dwelled there yet? In 1898 he returned and followed Wilcox's route to Sunwapta Pass, ascended Mt. Athabasca and discovered Columbia Icefield.

Collie was adept at matters concerned with topography, and surmised the high mountains on Columbia Icefield did not match those described by Douglas. Upon his return to England, he set out solve the mystery of Mts. Hooker and Brown once and for all. For the first time he looked up Douglas' original account, and in an instant had the solution. Douglas had thought the elevation of Athabasca Pass to be 3350 m/11,000 ft, and had based his estimate of the height of Mt. Brown on that number. The true height of the pass is 1,748 m, of Mt. Brown is 2,799 m and of the shoulder of Mt. Hooker above the pass, 2,600 m.

Douglas had obtained his elevations from a map made by David Thompson. So it was Thompson, a man who in his travels single-handedly mapped a vast area of western Canada, made one of his greatest contributions to the exploration of the Rockies by way of an uncharacteristic blunder. For those who had come in search of the two elusive mountains had reopened travel in areas that had been unvisited for decades. And by way of their literate and artistic renderings of their journeys, these explorers kindled a global interest in the wild peaks and valleys of the Rockies.

Mountaineering

To the general public, the equipment and know-how required for mountaineering is wrapped in mystique. In a nutshell, climbing mountains is a pursuit in which the natural hazards are weighed against the rewards. There are many routes to summits in the Rockies that involve very little difficulty and danger, and there are others to the very same summits that involve difficulty and danger in the extreme. Individual mountaineers choose from these routes according to their ability and the type of experience they desire. The high-tech equipment employed is no guarantee of safe passage, unless sound judgement and preparedness govern its use.

In the Rockies, as with most alpine ranges, it is the shaded,

John Norman Collie

In appraising the history of early exploration in the Canadian Rockies, there are a half dozen people who figure prominently. Of these, J. N. Collie is foremost, and one of the most adept at piecing together the Rockies' varied topography.

Collie was an erudite man: a professor of chemistry, the discoverer of neon gas, a talented artist, a pioneer in the fields of colour and x-ray photography, and one of Britain's best mountaineers, with experience in Scotland, Norway and the Himalaya.

Collie's first visit to the Rockies was at the invitation of Charles Fay in 1897. He participated in the first ascents of Mts. Lefroy and Victoria at Lake Louise, and the first attempt on Mt. Balfour. Later in the summer Collie explored in the vicinity of Mt. Forbes and the Freshfield Icefield. The following year he made first ascents of Mt. Athabasca, Snow Dome and Diadem Peak, and claimed discovery of Columbia Icefield.

Collie returned to the Rockies in earnest in 1902, with companion Hugh Stutfield. They had an ambitious mountaineering plan that included the ascent of Mt. Columbia. James Outram had similar designs, and contacted Collie to suggest a combination of forces. Collie, protective of his discovery of Columbia Icefield, reluctantly agreed, labelling Outram an "interloper." Probably he was jealous of Outram's burgeoning list of Rockies' first ascents, which included Mt. Assiniboine and Collie's namesake peak.

The label proved correct. Outram climbed Mt. Columbia and Mt. Lyell (LIE-ell) before meeting Collie at the prearranged place. Collie's contempt for Outram's actions was barely concealed during the following 11 days, when the combined party made the first ascents of Mt. Freshfield and Mt. Forbes. After Outram departed, Collie added Howse Peak, Mt. Murchison and Mt. Noyes to the expedition's first ascent tally. In 1910 and 1911 he made several first ascents in the remote country north of Mt. Robson.

Collie and Stutfield recorded their 1902 exploits in *Climbs and Explorations in the Canadian Rockies*, published in 1903. The book included Collie's map of the Rockies, a document other explorers relied on heavily for the next 20 years. Collie's name is commemorated in Mt. Collie, on the Wapta Icefield. He died in Scotland in 1942, at the age of 83.

steep and icy north face routes which generally offer the greatest challenge — and risk. Those in view on Mts. Athabasca and Andromeda are moderate in difficulty by today's standards. But those on North Twin, Mt. Alberta, Mt. Columbia and Mt. Kitchener are among the test pieces of the mountaineering world. In addition, some of the winter waterfall ice climbing routes in alpine settings on Snow Dome, Mt. Patterson and The White Pyramid are extreme routes to which few climbers in the world aspire.

There are many routes to the summit of Mt. Athabasca, one of the most frequently ascended peaks exceeding 3353 m/11,000 ft in the Rockies. The ascent and descent of one of these routes will take a competent party 10-15 hours in good weather and climbing conditions.

The remote peaks of Columbia Icefield (North and South Twin, and Mt. Columbia) are best approached on skis in spring. The effort necessitates a form of mountaineering verging on the mini-expedition. Usually it requires a day to approach within striking range, a day to climb the peak and return to camp, and a day to ski out. Add additional objectives, or days allowed for poor weather, and the packs get very heavy with the tent, equipment, food and clothing required. Weather, especially the ground-hugging cloud and blowing snow of the whiteout, often makes the summit day no more than an ex-

ercise in tent-sitting. Travel in such conditions is jokingly referred to as "radar skiing."

So with all that can go wrong and cause discomfort, why bother? The mountains of the Rockies are unforgiving in many ways, and care not the least for the passing of human feet. However, every once in a while they relent to make a summit view, or the alpenglow of a high alpine sunrise or sunset, well worth the price of admission. Being in the heart of wild and remote places at those special times is part of what mountaineering is all about.

Clinging to the steep north face of Mt. Bryce, one of the prominent mountains near the Columbia Icefield, a climber prepares for the final ascent to the summit.

The Silver Ice Axe

Mt. Alberta, the fifth-highest summit in the Rockies, is considered by many mountaineers to be the most difficult peak in the range to climb. A photograph of the mountain was featured on the first climbing guide to the Rockies, published in 1921, and Mt. Alberta came to the attention of mountaineers throughout the world. In 1925, a large mountaineering party from Japan succeeded in making the first ascent. It was rumoured they left a silver ice axe on the summit.

The rumour inspired attempts, but Mt. Alberta is so difficult that it was 23 years before the second ascent was accomplished. The ice axe turned out to be of the ordinary variety, with a steel head and wooden shaft. Much to the chagrin of Canadian mountaineers, it was taken by the second summit party to the archives of the American Alpine Club in New York City.

Pat Morrow
Adventure Journalist,
Second Canadian on
Everest

My wife and I both make our living by writing about and photographing climbing and skiing expeditions around the world — adventure journalism. Mostly we come up with the ideas, and then propose them to magazines and try to put together a trip. For instance, in 1987 my wife and I and another couple did a seven month, 10,000 km overland journey around the Himalayas, and we had mountain bikes and we hiked and climbed in Tibet, Pakistan, India and Nepal. There's a book coming out on it next year, and we did two magazine articles in China on the way to help pay for the trip.
***
Typically we'll work half a day or so, in our office in the basement here, then we'll go for a mountain bike ride or a rock climb. There are 400 established rock routes within a 10 mile radius of Canmore — you can just go out and spend a couple of hours in the afternoon, and stay in good shape, so you don't have to go into an intense training routine for the big trips.
***
I went to photography school at Banff in the early '70s, so I spent a couple of years around here then, and didn't realize at the time just how fantastic it is here. Since then I've travelled extensively around the world and it's confirmed for me that this really is one of the special places on the planet. You can live in a mountain environment, and also be close to an urban centre — Calgary — and take advantage of the cultural things that Banff and Canmore have to offer. And also tap into the great climbing and outdoors community that lives here.

The Snocoach

The Space Age Meets the Ice Age

Vehicle rides on the Athabasca Glacier date to 1952, when operator Bill Ruddy began developing a fleet of 14 Bombardier snowmobiles. Brewster Transportation acquired the operation in 1969 and replaced the snowmobiles with various hybrid vehicles, culminating in the Snocoach, a 56 passenger, all-terrain vehicle which has been in use since 1981.

Today Brewster operates a fleet of twelve Snocoaches built by Canadian Foremost Ltd. of Calgary — a specialist in developing transportation for the oil industry. Each vehicle weighs 19,500 kilograms, is 13 metres long, and is powered by a 210 horse power Detroit diesel engine. Top speed is 42 km/h, although this is never approached during the Snocoach tours. Fully loaded, a Snocoach is capable of climbing a 32 degree slope — the equivalent of a double black diamond ski run.

Snocoach rides can be booked from the building adjacent to the Columbia Icefield Information Centre. A shuttle bus provides transportation along a restricted access road to the loading area on the east lateral moraine of Athabasca Glacier. From there, the Snocoach descends steeply to the glacier, and travels several kilometres along the ice towards the lower icefall. At the turnaround point, passengers may disembark (at their own risk) to walk around on the ice.

The entire round-trip takes less than 90 minutes. There may be a short wait for an available tour.

Brewster Transportation operates a fleet of twelve Snocoaches which trasport visitors several kilometres out onto the surface of Athabasca Glacier.

Glaciers store over 75% of the world's fresh water in frozen form. As they shrink, so does the earth's freshwater reservoir.

The Snocoach rides generally begin operation in early May, and continue until late September.

At the Columbia Icefield Information Centre, displays and audio-visual presentations explain the various human and natural history themes connected with Columbia Icefield. Services, accommodation, souvenirs and meals are available nearby at Brewster's Columbia Icefield Chalet.

The Frozen Well-spring

Almost everyone will agree that glaciers are interesting features that have considerable effect on local topography, climate and vegetation. But why are they so important to the total ecology of the planet?

The answer is: fresh water. Including the glacial ice of polar regions, glaciers store over 75% of the world's fresh water in frozen form. The presence and absence of fresh water greatly influences the distribution of life on earth.

There are many places in the world where formerly fertile farm land has been overworked and overwatered, and is becoming nothing more than nutrient-deficient sand. This process of desertification seriously threatens the future of agriculture and our ability to feed ourselves. Unless humankind develops a truly effective and economical means of de-salinating ocean water, the viability of our future hinges critically on the continued existence of locally available fresh water.

In the past, researchers studied the behaviour of glaciers as a curiosity, attempting to understand the dynamics of glacial ice. The recession of many of the major outlet valley glaciers in the Rockies has been plotted during the last century. While we marvel at the horizontal distances the ice has retreated during this time, what is more impressive is the loss in vertical mass. Some glaciers are 200 m thinner at the terminus than 80 years ago. Athabasca Glacier decreased 57% in area, and 32% in volume, between 1870 and 1971. Earlier this century, it was estimated Columbia Glacier, on the far side of Columbia Icefield, was shrinking at the astonishing rate of 13 million cubic metres a year.

Today, scientists study glaciers out of necessity, looking for changes attributable to the Greenhouse Effect and depletion of the ozone layer. Most glaciers in the Rockies are currently in a state of retreat, and global warming can only accelerate this trend. As the ice of many glaciers worldwide dwindles at an alarming rate, with much of the resulting meltwater polluted or turned to salt water, the condition of the world's glaciers becomes a concern for everyone.

A Landscape of Superlatives

Here are the answers to some of the questions most often asked about Columbia Icefield.

What is the area of Columbia Icefield?
325 sq km. This one icefield accounts for over 30% of the glaciated area in Jasper National Park.

Why is Columbia Icefield the largest icefield in the Rockies?
It occupies a large alpine area ringed by many high mountains. There is a major valley opening towards the southwest that channels the moisture-laden prevailing winds through a vertical rise of 2200 m/ 7500 ft, directly into the heart of the icefield. This elevation change causes the release of a great deal of precipitation – principally snow – and, because of the high elevation at which it falls, little of it melts.

What is the average elevation of Columbia Icefield?
Approximately 3,000 m above sea level.

What is the highest point on Columbia Icefield?
The summit of Mt. Columbia, 3747 m/ 12,294 ft. Mt. Columbia is on the Continental Divide, and is the second highest mountain in the Canadian Rockies. By the most direct line of travel feasible for mountaineers, its summit is 23 km from the Icefields Parkway. The mountain is not visible from the road. The highest summit entirely within both Alberta and Jasper National Park is also found on Columbia Icefield – North Twin is 3683 m/12,085 ft high. It too is concealed from the road.

How thick is the ice?
The maximum known thickness on the Icefield is 365 m. The ice cliffs visible on Snow Dome are over 100 m thick. Athabasca Glacier is about 100 m thick at the upper icefall, and 300 m thick just below the lower icefall.

Why is some of the ice blue?
Air and other impurities of non-uniform size tend to reflect all wavelengths of light, making ice appear white. Ice which has most of the air squeezed out of it reflects the blue wavelength. Ice on the surface of the glacier is therefore gray or white, while that within is often blue.

How long is Athabasca Glacier?
5.3 km from the icefield rim to the terminus. It drops 600 m in that distance. The average width is one kilometre.

Is Athabasca Glacier the longest glacier in the Rockies?
Long, but not the longest. Saskatchewan Glacier is nine kilometres long. Others in the Rockies are even longer.

How fast do glaciers move?
On average in the Rockies, about 15 metres a year. They move faster at icefalls (125 metres a year on the Athabasca), and faster in the centre on the surface than at the sides or the base.

How long does it take for ice to flow from the Columbia Icefield rim to the terminus of Athabasca Glacier?

Approximately 150 years. Some of the ice melting at the terminus may have formed on the icefield over 800 years ago.

How deep are crevasses?

Large crevasses can be over 30 m deep.

How far has the Athabasca Glacier retreated since the Little Ice Age?

About 1.6 km since 1870.

What has been the average annual rate of glacial retreat during that time?

Thirteen metres, but in recent years this has dropped to one to three metres. Global warming may see this figure increase again.

How much does it snow here each year?

At roadside, the average annual snowfall is 6.4 m. On the icefield itself, it is over 10 m.

How many glaciers flow from Columbia Icefield?

There are eight named outlet valley glaciers: Athabasca, Dome, Kitchener and Stutfield (visible from the Parkway); Columbia, Castleguard, and Bryce (hidden from view on the south and west sides of the icefield); and Saskatchewan (visible from Parker Ridge). In addition there are dozens of other alpine valley, cirque and niche glaciers in the vicinity of Columbia Icefield.

Is it safe to drink glacier melt?

In most cases, yes. But glacier melt is cold and full of sediments; guzzled on a hot summer day, it may produce stomach upset.

Will Athabasca Glacier disappear?

Eventually yes, if conditions favouring glacial retreat persist. But not if a colder climate favouring glacial advance prevails. The current trend of global warming may contribute towards a period of accelerated glacial retreat.

How high is Mt. Athabasca?

Its summit is 3470 m/11,452 ft above sea level – nearly a vertical mile above the Icefield Information Centre. Of the 30 highest peaks in the Rockies (all over 3353 m/ 11,000 ft), 13 adjoin Columbia Icefield.

How much does a Snocoach weigh?

19,500 kilograms empty; 25,000 kilograms with 56 passengers and driver.

Columbia Icefield to Jasper

Tangle Creek Hill

The Icefields Parkway now climbs steeply above the Sunwapta Valley, on a road bed cut into the slopes of Mt. Wilcox. A road sign warns: "Watch for sheep on road" and, more often than not, that's exactly where the local band of bighorn sheep will be found.

When driving along this section of the Parkway, please reduce speed, and remember several things: the sheep won't be overly concerned about getting out of your vehicle's way; the drivers behind you may not be aware you will have to stop in the middle of the road; and, it is illegal to feed wildlife in the national parks. If you would like to spend some time in the company of the sheep, pull safely off the road into one of the paved viewpoints.

Sunwapta Canyon

A rockslide from the slopes of Mt. Kitchener blocked the Sunwapta River at this point, with debris piled 50 m deep. The river is eroding through this slide, forming a narrow canyon typical of erosion of limestone rock by water. It's an impressive sight, best seen by peeking over the guardrail at the viewpoint atop Tangle Creek Hill.

Endless Chain Ridge parallels the Icefields Parkway for some 20 km between Poboktan Creek and Sunwapta Falls.

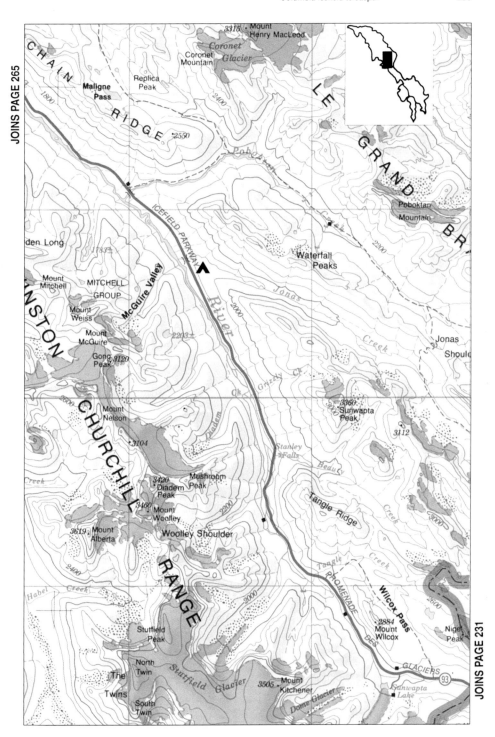

JOINS PAGE 265

JOINS PAGE 231

Top: Bighorn sheep frequent roadside (and middle!) on Tangle Creek Hill, immediately north of Columbia Icefield.

Bottom: Tangle Falls.

Maligne — are formed in bedrock, not in rockslide debris.

Tangle Falls

Mary Schäffer's 1907 expedition to the upper Athabasca Valley used Wilcox Pass to detour around the terminus of Athabasca Glacier and the Mt. Kitchener Slide. The steep descent from the pass was made on a very rough trail alongside this creek. Untracked bush is known to outfitters as "shin tangle." Thus were named the creek and picturesque falls.

Stutfield Glacier

The 1100 m/3500 ft-high cliff between Mt. Kitchener (on the left) and the Stutfield Peaks is the backdrop for an age-old battle — the erosion of rock by glacial ice. The glaciers cascading from the rim of Columbia Icefield above are some of the most contorted and spectacular to be seen from the Icefields Parkway. Unfortunately, Stutfield Glacier is also one of the most difficult views to photograph. The northeast aspect and resultant shading of this scene precludes good lighting, except shortly after sunrise in mid-summer months.

Hugh Stutfield was a companion of J. N. Collie on mountaineering expeditions in 1898 and 1902, during which a number of important first ascents were made. In 1903, he and Collie co-authored one of the standard works of Rockies history, *Climbs and Explorations in the Canadian Rockies*, now a collector's item.

The Mt. Kitchener Slide is the third largest measured rockslide in this part of the Rockies. The better known limestone canyons — Stewart, Marble, Sunwapta, Johnston, Mistaya, Sinclair and

Exit From the Icefield

After the confined and harsh landscape in the immediate vicinity of Columbia Icefield, the open valley bottom of the Sunwapta River Flats comes as a welcome relief. For the next 14 km, the Icefields Parkway travels beside this, one of the largest glacial outwash plains in the Rockies. The old road bed is visible at many places along the east side of this stretch, and from it can be gained a rough hiking trail that leads to Stanley Falls on Beauty Creek.

Looking south from near the Beauty Creek Hostel, the austere form of Mt. Kitchener rises some 1900 m/6200 ft above the valley floor. The ice cliffs on its summit are the fringe of Columbia Icefield. The Earl of Kitchener was a First World War hero and Mt. Kitchener was named for him by surveyor A. O. Wheeler in 1916.

Towards the north end of the flats, the Sunwapta River has created backwaters that are excellent habitat for moose and waterfowl.

Jonas Slide

When the ice of the ancestral Athabasca Glacier scoured the Sunwapta Valley, it undercut the tilted formations of rock in the mountainsides. After the ice receded, some of these formations split away along weaknesses, and tumbled to the valley floor in rockslides. The Icefields Parkway passes through the debris left by one such event, the Jonas Slide. There were actually two rockslides here. The more northerly one

The glacially carved amphitheatre containing Stutfield Glacier is one of the most impressive scenes along the Icefields Parkway. Stutfield is one of eight outlet valley glaciers of Columbia Icefield.

one swept a path almost four kilometres long.

Endless Chain Ridge

The compression that forced thrust sheets to pile over each other during mountain building created steeply tilted formations in the mountains of the front ranges. The resulting mountain shape is a "writing desk peak," or overthrust mountain – one with a uniformly inclined southwest facing slope, and a sheer northeast facing cliff. Endless Chain Ridge is one of the best examples in the

Woodland or Mountain Caribou

Recent estimates give a population of 350 - 400 caribou in Jasper and Banff parks, so you will be extremely fortunate to see this member of the deer family at roadside. There are six caribou herds in Banff and Jasper. One of these dwells in the front range valleys immediately east of here; another in the Winston Churchill Range to the west. Some of these caribou visit the Sunwapta Valley in winter and spring, to take a break from the rigours of life in the upper subalpine and alpine ecoregions.

To quickly distinguish caribou from moose, which also frequent this area, look at the neck, lower legs and tail. If all these are lighter in colour than the rest of the coat, and the neck is fringed on the underside, then you're in luck - it's a caribou! If it's wearing a necklace, don't be alarmed. Some of Jasper's caribou have been fitted with radio collars as part of a study to determine their range and habits.

Both male and female caribou grow antlers that feature a forward-reaching "shovel" over the muzzle (like the barren-ground caribou on the Canadian quarter). When running, caribou carry their heads high and tilted back. They have large, circular hooves that help support them in deep snow. The wolf is the principal predator.

Most caribou eat tree lichens found in old-growth forests. Caribou in the Rockies also eat lichens that grow on the ground and on rocks, seasonally migrating between the mountains and foothills to avoid over-use of food sources in a single area. This different behaviour has earned these animals the unofficial designation "mountain caribou."

The seasonal migrations take most mountain caribou out of the national parks into areas where their habitat and lives are not protected. Between 1960 and 1990, Alberta's caribou population dropped from 9000 to 3000 in the face of habitat loss and hunting. Officially classified as a "vulnerable" species, the small populations of caribou in the Rockies are actually in a more precarious state. In light of indifference by the Alberta government towards the plight of the caribou, the sanctuary offered in Banff and Jasper may not guarantee the animal's local survival.

Rockies. Other overthrust mountains occur near Banff townsite (Mt. Rundle), and along the Yellowhead Highway east of Jasper. Mary Schäffer named Endless Chain Ridge during her explorations of 1907. Although not endless, the ridge is a prominent feature for some 20 km along the Icefields Parkway, and would have been in the view of the early explorers for several days.

Sunwapta Falls

For the last 20 km the Sunwapta River has been flowing to the northwest. At Sunwapta Falls the river makes a 90° dogleg to the southwest, before continuing its former course to join the Athabasca River.

This abrupt change in course is a diversion around a lateral moraine, deposited by the ancestral Columbia Glacier. While making the diversion, the river took advantage of a crack in the limestone bedrock, to create the straight, steeply walled canyon immediately downstream from the footbridge.

A side trail gives access to other waterfalls in a lower canyon. The trail on the opposite side of the bridge is the beginning of a day-long backpacker's route to Fortress Lake in British Columbia's Hamber Provincial Park.

Services and accomodation are available in season at the Lodge and Bungalows on the Icefields Parkway.

Just north of Jonas Creek campground, the Icefields Parkway passes through the rubble of the Jonas Slide - a massive rockslide from the east, caused by the undermining of steep mountainsides by glacial ice. The boulders are Gog quartzite, one of the oldest, hardest and most common rock types in the Rockies.

With its former course blocked by glacial moraine, the Sunwapta River has eroded Sunwapta Falls through a crack system in the underlying limestone. Downstream from the main falls, a trail leads to other falls in a lower canyon.

Athabasca Valley

The Icefields Parkway now descends into the Athabasca Valley. Revealed is the full breadth of the valley, giving an idea of how massive the glaciers of the Wisconsin Glaciation were when they filled it, nearly to the brim.

South from here, the Athabasca Valley extends into the heartland of glacial ice along the Continental Divide. This is one of the few remaining wild watersheds in the Rockies. It was first

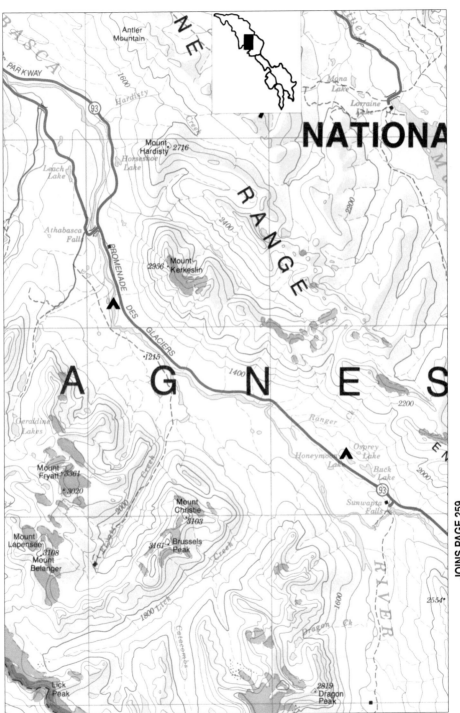

Antler
Mountain

NE

NATIONA

RANGE

AGNES

1600

Hardisty Creek

Mount
Hardisty · 2716

Horseshoe
Lake

Leach
Lake

PARKWAY

93

BASCA

2400

2200

Mona
Lake

Lorraine
Lake

Athabasca
Falls

Geraldine
Lakes

PROMENADE

DES

GLACIERS

·1215

1400

2956

Mount
Kerkeslin

Mount
Fryatt ·3361

·3020

2200

Ranger Ck

Osprey
Lake

Honeymoon
Lake

Back
Lake

2000

93

Sunwapta
Falls

Mount
Lapensee

·3108

Mount
Belanger

2200

3161

Mount
Christie
·3103

Brussels
Peak

RIVER

2554·

1800 Lick

Cascomb

Creek

Lick
Peak

1600

Dragon Ck

2819
Dragon
Peak

Although few glaciers are visible from Goats and Glaciers viewpoint, the hanging valleys across the Athabasca River, and the silty waters of the river itself, give evidence of past and present glaciation in the area.

visited by German explorer Jean Habel (AHH-bull) in 1901, and by Mary Schäffer in 1907.

North from here, the montane ecoregion occupies the valley bottom, providing excellent habitat for both black and grizzly bears, as well as elk and deer.

Mt. Fryatt
3361 m/11,026 ft
Captain Fryatt evacuated many Allied troops from France in his boat, *The Brussels*, during the First World War. He was captured and executed in 1916. Surveyor A. O. Wheeler named the peak for him. Mt. Fryatt is the second lowest of the 53 summits in the Rockies that exceed 3353 m/11,000 ft, and was first climbed in 1926. The name of Fryatt's boat is celebrated in the striking, turreted form of

nearby Brussels Peak, which is visible further north along the Parkway.

Goats and Glaciers Viewpoint
Although its view of glaciers does not compare with others to be had further south along the Parkway, the prospect from Goats and Glaciers Viewpoint gives an impressive panorama of the Athabasca Valley. It is also one of the best places in the Rockies to see mountain goats at close range.

The Athabasca is now a major river, containing meltwaters from two large icefields and many glaciers. On a hot summer day it will have the milky colour characteristic of glacially fed rivers. The Athabasca and its tributaries drain over 75% of the the area of Jasper National Park.

In the dense forest west of the river, the older stands of trees that survived the most recent forest fires in this valley can be seen. The canopy of the younger pine forest is light green, while that of the older spruce/fir forest is darker.

South of the viewpoint, the unmistakable turret of Brussels Peak is prominent in the view. The difficult first ascent of this seldom-climbed mountain was not accomplished until 1948, after at least three previous attempts had failed.

Mountain Goat

The adult mountain goat is easily distinguished from the brown, bighorn sheep by its thick white or cream-coloured coat. A shaggy tuft of hair hangs from the throat. Both sexes have permanent thin, black horns that curve rearwards. The hooves are black. Not a true goat, this animal is more closely related to the mountain antelopes of Asia. The bottom of its hoof is comprised of a soft pad surrounded by a hard shell. This allows the hoof to be used in two ways on steep terrain: to stick on steep slabs, and to lever upwards on small ledges. Mountaineers marvel at the mountain goat's agility in steep places. The animal has even learned to turn around on narrow ledges, by standing on its front legs and walking its rear legs around on the cliff face above!

Because of its agility and fondness for inaccessible places, the mountain goat has few enemies and is accustomed to only looking for danger from below. Cougar and eagle will take advantage of this trait by hunting the goat from above. As with sheep, the young can be knocked from ledges by diving eagles, and the protective pose of mother standing over its young is common. The most frequent causes of death amongst goats are rockfall and snow avalanche. Given that goats spend so much time in areas where these hazards exist, they are surprisingly oblivious to the dangers. It is not uncommon to observe lame goats, or those missing horns as a result of a close call.

Banks of mineral-rich clay and gravel lure mountain goats from their safe haven on Mt. Kerkeslin, to roadside on the Icefields Parkway. The goats lick the clay to supplement their diet. Goats appear to be tolerant of humans when at these licks, but in reality are probably very nervous about having so many people close by. If you are fortunate enough to see goats at a lick, use a telephoto lens to take photographs, and do not, under any circumstances, attempt to get close to the young.

The airborne spray produced by the falls keeps the local area moist and cool, and allows the growth of a canyon forest. Feather mosses and lichens, along with shade-tolerant shrubs and wildflowers, thrive in this area.

Looking east from Athabasca Falls, Mt. Kerkeslin is visible in the distance. The mountain was named by James Hector of the Palliser Expedition in 1859. The name is a Stoney Native word for "wolverine."

Athabasca River

Slightly downstream from the bridge over the Athabasca, the river begins to cut across the southeast/northwest grain of the Rockies, flowing to the plains beyond. It is thought that the Athabasca is as old as the mountains, and was able to erode downwards through them as they were being uplifted, hence taking this unlikely course. The Athabasca River was designated a Canadian Heritage River in 1990. As with the two other Heritage Rivers in the Rockies, the designation for the Athabasca ends at the national park boundary.

The unmistakeable shape of Pyramid Mountain forms the backdrop for the townsite of Jasper in the view north.

When glaciers advance through a valley, they often produce a series of steps in the underlying bedrock. Athabasca Falls cascades over a glacial rock step. The interpretive walk offers close-up views of the falls, the rock step, potholes and abandoned river courses.

Athabasca Falls

The rock step underlying Athabasca Falls is comprised of Gog quartzite, one of the toughest rocks in the Rockies. The ancestral Athabasca Glacier had trouble eroding this rock, as do the waters of the Athabasca River in the present day. Many potholes and abandoned channels can be seen — a legacy of the water seeking the easiest course.

Below the falls, the rock step extends for several hundred metres before dropping abruptly to the water level. The river has eroded a narrow canyon through this part of the step. Interesting views may be obtained by following the interpretive walkway. Please stay behind the guardrails. Fatal slips into the canyon have occurred.

JOINS PAGE 303

JOINS PAGE 285

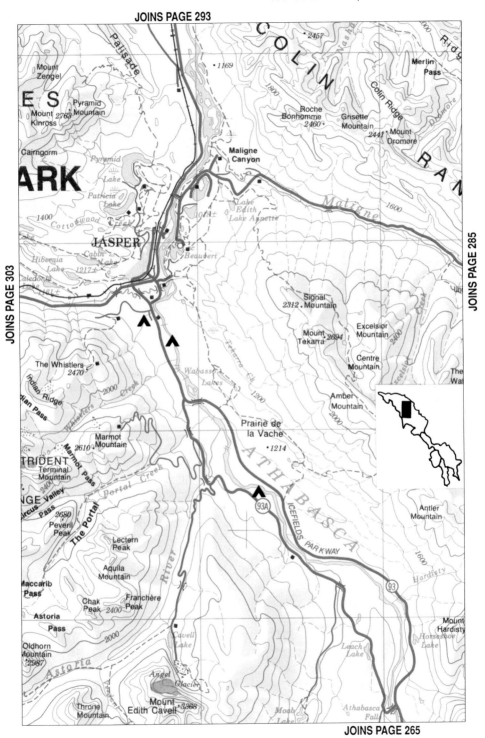

Jasper

Jasper National Park is a land of lakes. The many lakes in the vicinity of Jasper townsite are popular with boaters, swimmers, fishermen, birdwatchers and photographers. This photo shows Lac Beauvert.

Jasper National Park

It was a proposal to build a second transcontinental railway in Canada that led to the founding of Jasper, Canada's seventh national park. In 1902, the Grand Trunk Pacific Railway approached the federal government to form a partnership and build a more northerly line, linking New Brunswick with British Columbia, and crossing the Rockies via Yellowhead Pass.

While boom times had come to the Bow and Kicking Horse Valleys with the completion of the Canadian Pacific Railway in 1885, the Athabasca and Miette valleys were still the domain of trappers, outfitters, mountaineers and a few settlers. The area was virtually unchanged since the C.P.R. abandoned the Yellowhead route in 1881. From its experience with the other "railway parks," the government astutely recognized that a new railway across the Rockies offered another opportunity to turn scenery into a tourist draw, and Jasper Forest Park was established in September 1907.

Since 1930, the park's area has been 10,878 sq km. Today Jasper is the largest of the four mountain parks, and the third most visited

JASPER STREET MAP

1. PARK INFORMATION CENTRE
2. POST OFFICE
3. BUS DEPOT AND TRAIN STATION
4. HOSPITAL
5. SWIMMING POOL AND ACTIVITY CENTRE
6. MUSEUM
7. POLICE
8. LIBRARY
9. PARK ADMINISTRATION

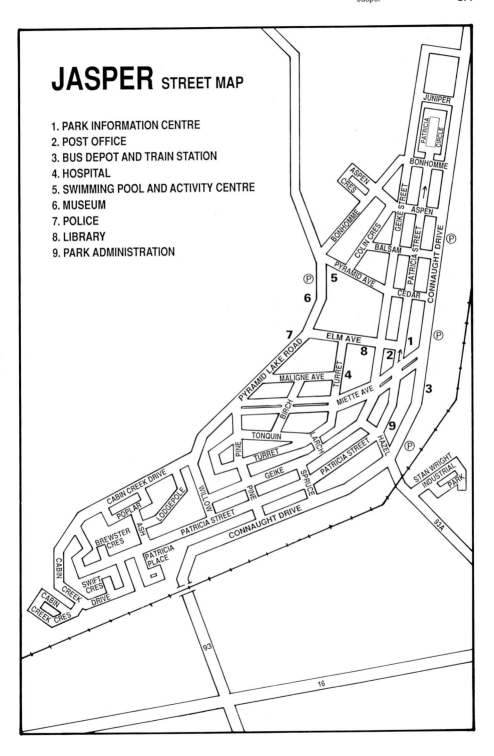

Top: This view looks south over the town of Jasper towards the Icefield Parkway.

Bottom: The town of Jasper had its humble beginnings in 1911 in the shacks and tents of a railway construction camp called "Tent City".

national park in Canada, after Banff and Kootenay.

The town of Jasper had its origins in 1911 as a railway town named Fitzhugh, for the vice-president of the Grand Trunk Pacific. The railway steel reached Fitzhugh in August that year, and crested Yellowhead Pass in November. Completion to Prince Rupert on the Pacific coast was achieved in 1914. Jasper House, a Hudson's Bay Company supply post, had been a well known feature of the lower Athabasca Valley for 70 years, and the name Jasper was in common use to describe the surrounding area. Hence "Jasper" was a logical choice for both park and town when boundaries were officially surveyed.

A second railway, the Canadian Northern, was constructed through the park and Yellowhead Pass in 1913, and carried its first traffic in October 1915. Locally, its operations were based at Lucerne, just across the Continental Divide in B.C. The lines of the two railways were only metres apart in places. The redundancy was soon obvious to all involved and, beginning in 1916, a consoli-

dation of the rails west of Edmonton took place. The new railway alignment through the park utilized the most favourable grades of both railways, and the torn up rails were shipped to Europe for use in the First World War. In 1922, the two railways came under government ownership, and were amalgamated as the Canadian National. Rail operations at Lucerne were moved to Jasper in 1924, boosting the local population considerably.

Some of the abandoned railway grades were eventually used for roadbeds. The Jasper-Edmonton Road opened in 1931 and was paved 20 years later. Although vehicles were driven over Yellowhead Pass as early as 1922, with the drivers building bridges as they went, it wasn't until 1968 that

the Yellowhead Highway was finally completed through Jasper National Park.

Jasper Park Lodge

The Grand Trunk Pacific Railway was well aware of the Canadian Pacific Railway's successful hotel business further south, and had grand plans for hotel development in Jasper. One facility was

Top: Jasper Park Lodge was constructed in 1923 by the Canadian National Railway. At the time, the main lodge building was the largest log structure in the world.

Bottom: The swimming pool at the Jasper Park Lodge.

to be built in the townsite and another was to occupy a 20 hectare lease at the mouth of the Fiddle River, near the park's present east boundary. From there, patrons would be transported to Miette Hot Springs by a 15 km monorail, and the waters of the springs would be piped to the hotel.

Financial problems plagued the young railway, and the townsite lodge never developed beyond a "Tent City" — Jasper Park Camp — on the shores of Lac Beauvert (bow-VAIR). Plans for the Chateau Miette were dropped in 1916, when the railway line at that location was moved to the opposite side of the river.

In 1922, the newly formed Canadian National Railway was in a better financial position, and began the construction of Jasper Park Lodge. A central building, claimed to be the world's largest log structure, replaced the Tent City. For $3 a day, the guests slept in log cabins, and wined, dined and socialized in the main lodge. By 1925 they could partake in golf on an 18 hole course as well. Re-

Hoary Marmot

The hoary marmot, one of the largest members of the rodent family, is a resident of boulderfields and rockslides at higher elevations, where it lives in small colonies. "Hoary" refers to its white-tipped, grayish coat, which resembles hoar frost. The feet are black. In profile the marmot looks a lot like the woodchuck, to which it is related.

Initially wary, and apparently possessing poor eyesight, the marmot can often be approached quite closely. When alarmed, it emits the shrill, piercing whistle for which The Whistlers is named. The sound carries very well, and alerts fellow marmots that danger is near. The greatest threat is the grizzly bear, which will spend considerable time and energy attempting to dig into a marmot's burrow. Eagles and lynx also hunt this apparently delicious animal.

Marmots eat grasses, roots, flowers and berries nearby their den, which is located in a natural hollow between boulders. When not eating or indolently sunning themselves on a rock, marmots sleep: they hibernate nine months of the year.

flecting Jasper's increasing popularity with visitors, expansion took place in 1927-28. The new lodge had a capacity of 425 guests. A network of walking and horse trails was developed along the east bank of the Athabasca River.

The lodge burned on July 15, 1952. It was immediately replaced by the present structure, built at a cost of $3 million. Today the Jasper Park Lodge offers accommodation for 430 guest year-rounds. When those staying in outlying buildings order room service in summer, the food is delivered by bicycle. Renovations to the main lodge were completed in 1990.

Lac Beauvert, Edith Lake, Lake Annette

There are over 800 lakes and ponds in Jasper National park. Many of the small lakes near the townsite were created by melting blocks of glacial ice at the end of the Wisconsin Glaciation. Lac Beauvert, Edith Lake and Lake Annette originated in this manner.

Lac Beauvert means "beautiful green lake." It is thought that part of the inflow to the lake comes from underground discharges of the Maligne drainage system. Silty glacial meltwaters from the peaks at the head of Maligne Lake disappear underground at Medicine Lake, and may emerge here.

The townsite lakes are popular for picnicking, swimming and bird-watching. Rainbow and brook trout await the angler. Lake Edith was named for the wife of a railway superintendent, and Lake Annette for the wife of a park superintendent. The area around the lakes is a fire succession forest of lodgepole pine, a product of the forest fires that consumed much of the forest in the Athabasca Valley in 1889.

Moss Campion

Moss campion is one of the most easily recognized alpine plants. A dense mat of bright green, needle-like leaves is formed into a dome-shaped cushion dotted with tiny pink flowers. The cushion holds water, which allows the plant to grow in barren locations. Even with this advantage, moss campion grows incredibly slowly. It may take twenty years to fully develop blooms.

One of the pioneer plants in windswept, exposed places, moss campion helps break down rocks and create soil. Other plants will take root within it, thereby beginning the process of succession, whereby desolate rock is turned into alpine meadow.

The Jasper Tramway offers quick access to the alpine ecoregion. The Tramway climbs almost 1000 m to the mountain crest, affording spectacular views of the Athabasca Valley, and the lakes and mountains in the vicinity of Jasper.

The Whistlers
2464 m/8084 ft

The Jasper Tramway provides the visitor with a unique opportunity to explore the alpine ecoregion, without having to toil up a mountainside. The aerial tramway has a vertical rise of 937 m, and spans the three ecoregions of the Rockies: montane, subalpine and alpine. For purists, an eight kilometre trail leads to the same destination, and gives a close-up view of the ecological transitions en route.

The upper terminal of the tramway provides an overview of the Athabasca and Miette River Valleys, the townsite of Jasper, a multitude of lakes, and several mountain ranges. On a clear day, the view will include the lofty, glaciated summit of Mt. Robson, over 80 km to the northwest. With

an elevation of 3954 m/12,972 ft, Robson is easily the highest mountain in the Canadian Rocky Mountains.

A rough trail from the upper terminal leads to the summit of The Whistlers, where you may sign the register. Along the way, keep an eye out for pika, golden mantled ground squirrels, ravens, white-tailed ptarmigan and the hoary marmot — whose sharp whistle gave the mountain its name.

Visitors to The Whistlers should be prepared for cold temperatures, high winds, harsh sunlight and snow underfoot. Please keep to the marked trail, in order to prevent damage to this ancient and very fragile landscape.

Old Fort Point

While fur trader David Thompson made his successful crossing of Athabasca Pass in the winter of 1810-11, an associate, William Henry, remained near the present site of Jasper to construct an outpost for the North West Company. Old Fort Point commemorates a possible location for this post. Named Henry House, it was the first permanent European habitation in the Rockies.

In 1813 the North West Company built another outpost, Jasper House, on the shore of Brûlé (broo-LAY) Lake just beyond the east boundary of the present day park. Together, these two outposts helped supply the voyageurs of the fur trade in their annual journey over Athabasca Pass.

Annette Lake at sunrise.

Top: Pyramid Lake is one of more than 40 lakes in the vicinity of Jasper townsite.

Bottom: Cottonwood Slough is a wetland created by beaver dams. The slough is one of the best bird-watching areas in Jasper, and features stands of black spruce, a relatively rare tree in the Rockies.

view of this reach of the Athabasca River, and pleasant, half-day walks can be made using several loop trails in the area. One of these connects the point with Lac Beauvert — the "beautiful green" lake next to Jasper Park Lodge.

Pyramid Lake Road

As anyone who has been to the top of The Whistlers will attest, the vicinity of Jasper townsite is a land of lakes. Some of these are remnants of the lake that once filled the Athabasca valley. Others are ponds created by beavers. A majority are lakes of glacial origin.

Jasper House was moved to a site near Jasper Lake in 1829, after the North West Company and rival Hudson's Bay Company merged. It is possible Henry House fell into disuse from that time onwards. Alternate locations suggested for Henry House include the grounds of the present day Jasper Park Lodge, and the vicinity of the east exit from Jasper townsite.

Old Fort Point provides a good

The Pyramid Lake Road climbs onto a bench north of Jasper townsite, and gives access to two of the largest and most picturesque lakes in the region, Patricia Lake and Pyramid Lake. Along the way the road passes through a fire succession forest of lodgepole pine and trembling aspen, and contours along the edge of Cottonwood Slough, a montane wetland created by the handiwork of beaver. The slough (SLEW) contains black spruce, and is one of the park's best bird-watching locations. Moose are sometimes seen here, too.

Fishing, canoeing and trailriding are popular at both lakes, and commercial accommodation and boat rentals are available. Pyramid Lake is one of three lakes in the mountain national parks where gas-powered motor boats may be launched. A network of hiking trails criss-crosses the area. For those who don't mind a long walk to obtain a good view of the Athabasca Valley, the 11 km Palisade Lookout trail begins at the Pyramid Lake picnic area at road's end. Allow a full day for the round trip.

With a depth of 40 m, Patricia Lake is the deeper of the two lakes. It was named for Lady Patricia Ramsay, granddaughter of Queen Victoria. Pyramid Lake takes its name from 2766 m/9076 ft Pyramid Mountain, which provides the backdrop. A communications tower is visible on the mountain top.

Operation Habbakuk

Winter 1942. The enemy has sunk over 600 Allied ships. Sir Winston Churchill puts out the word ... any idea will be considered to cut the losses, no matter how far-fetched, or how expensive. One Geoffrey Pike, a resident of a mental hospital in London, England puts forward the idea of a monstrous aircraft carrier constructed of ice. It won't burn if torpedoed, or melt in the chilly waters of the North Atlantic.

Desperate, the Allied Chiefs of Staff think it over. Lord Louis Mountbatten demonstrates the merits of an ice boat to Churchill by playing with ice cubes in the bathtub at 10 Downing Street. It is decided a 1000 tonne model will be built, somewhere cold and remote ... Canada will do.

Winter 1943. The bizarre story shifts to the shores of Patricia Lake. Here Geoffrey Pike, out on a pass, will supervise the construction of the ice boat under the code name Operation Habbakuk. A substance called pikecrete is invented – ice containing wood chips. Experimentation proves that spruce chips give more flotation than pine. Still, pikecrete is not very buoyant. The planned 650 m long, 20 story high ice destroyer will certainly bob below the surface, even without the planned crew of 2000 and the 26 aircraft it is supposed to carry. Pike, true to form, suggests the ice be filled with air. It is not known if tax dollars were spent pursuing this option.

Employed as labourers in the project are Doukhobors, who are conscientious objectors and avowed pacifists. About this time they catch on to the intent of the ice boat, and peacefully sit down on the job. Thus ends the first season of work.

The following winter, $75 million is budgeted for the project and the work site moved to another of those "cold Canadian places" – Newfoundland. But no success. Pikecrete is a failure. Despite claims that a boat that can double as a refrigerator will revolutionize the fishing industry, the idea has never resurfaced.

The Athabasca Parkway

A mountaineer's view of Angel Glacier and Cavell Glacier Lake, from the summit of Mt. Edith Cavell.

The Athabasca Parkway (93A) follows the route of the original Icefields Parkway from a point seven kilometres south of Jasper to Athabasca Falls. When the Icefields Parkway was upgraded in the late 1950's, a different route for the improved road was chosen in this part of the valley, and the Athabasca Parkway became an alternate. The Athabasca Parkway can be combined with the Mt. Edith Cavell Road and the Icefields Parkway to make an interesting, leisurely loop drive from Jasper.

The Mt. Edith Cavell Road is a narrow, winding secondary road that leads to Cavell Glacier at the base of Mt. Edith Cavell. The road is not suitable for large recreational vehicles or camper trailers. A trailer drop-off is provided at the junction with the Athabasca Parkway. The Mt. Edith Cavell Road receives no winter maintenance, and is generally closed from October until late May.

Tonquin Valley

The Tonquin Valley Trail provides backpacker's access to one of the most picturesque upper subalpine environments in the Rockies. The principal attractions in the Tonquin are Amethyst Lakes,

at the base of a 1200 m high quartzite cliff known as The Ramparts. The popular trail is usually hiked as a 43 km horseshoe, beginning at Cavell Lake and ending at the Portal Creek trailhead on the Marmot Basin access road. Some of the high peaks of the Tonquin Valley may be seen from the Astoria River overlook at the prominent bend, on the Mt. Edith Cavell Road.

Astoria was a fur trade fort operated by the Pacific Fur Company at the mouth of the Columbia River in Oregon, and the Tonquin was one of the company's boats. Some of the company's traders crossed Athabasca Pass, just southwest of here, in the years following 1814.

Mt. Edith Cavell
3363 m/11,033 ft

Natives knew Mt. Edith Cavell as the "White Ghost," probably in reference to the snow-covered mountain's appearance in moonlight. The men who packed the furs and supplies for the fur trade — the voyageurs — called the mountain "La Montagne de la Grand Traverse" (the mountain of the great crossing). It is a landmark visible from a great distance to the north in the Athabasca Valley, and the French name refers to the mountain's proximity to the arduous route across the Continental Divide via the Whirlpool Valley and Athabasca Pass.

In the early 1900's the mountain was known for a short time as Mt. Fitzhugh. Then in 1915, surveyor A. O. Wheeler was asked by

Mt. Edith Cavell, one of the most popular attractions in Jasper, is reached by following the Mt. Edith Cavell Road from the Athabasca Parkway.

Above and Opposite: Less than 100 years ago, Angel Glacier cascaded to the valley floor, and merged with Cavell Glacier. The Dramatic retreat of the Angel is typical of many glaciers in the Rockies, and can be appreciated by comparing the contemporary photograph with the one taken in the 1920's. The Path of the Glacier trail offers a unique opportunity to explore a recently glaciated landscape.

the Geographic Board of Canada to recommend a mountain to commemorate nurse Edith Cavell, who was executed for assisting Allied prisoners of war to escape. Wheeler chose "the beautiful mountain facing the Athabasca Valley," and the name was officially bestowed the following year. A memorial service for Edith Cavell is held annually at the mountain, and climbers have taken a cross to the summit.

The road to the base of the mountain was one of the first constructed in Jasper, and has been in use since 1924. At no other location in the Rockies does one drive so directly towards such an impressive mountain wall. And so close too – the base of the cliffs is less than 1.5 km away from the parking area, and the summit rises an equal distance above. A tea-

house was built near the present parking lot, and operated from 1929-1972.

Mt. Edith Cavell is a popular mountaineering objective. The first ascent of the mountain was in 1915. The east ridge (left-hand skyline), first climbed in 1924, is considered one of the classic alpine rock climbs in the Rockies. The ascent of the spectacular north face in 1961 marked the beginning of extreme alpine climbing in the Rockies. If you're wondering which is the highest point, it's the central bump on the nearly horizontal summit ridge.

The Path of the Glacier Trail
A Disappearing Angel
The easy walk along The Path of the Glacier trail at Mt. Edith Cav-

ell immerses the visitor in a recently glaciated landscape. Less than 150 years ago, the entire area traversed by the trail was buried under the combined ice of the Angel and Cavell Glaciers. Today, one sees hardy vegetation in the process of recolonizing this area.

The Little Ice Age of 1200-1900 A.D. is known in the Rockies as the Cavell Advance. The terminal moraine, over which the Path of the Glacier trail initially climbs, was deposited at the peak of this glacial advance. A prominent lateral moraine is also visible, along the cliffs beneath Angel Glacier.

The Path of the Glacier trail also leads to Cavell Glacier and Cavell Glacier Lake. Essentially, the accumulation zone of this glacier is the north face of Mt. Edith Cavell. Snow does not usually bond to slopes steeper than 40°, so most of the snow that falls on the north face soon slides off in avalanches. These avalanches are funnelled down couloirs and gullies onto the valley floor. Here, in the near perpetual shade cast by the mountain, the snow accumulates and is transformed into glacial ice.

Cavell Glacier formerly extended the length of this valley. An old terminal moraine deposited by the glacier has dammed the meltwaters, creating Cavell Lake. This lake may be reached in a short walk from the Tonquin Valley trailhead.

The Path of the Glacier trail requires an hour for the round trip.

The Maligne Lake Road

The Maligne Lake Road features many interesting sights, including Maligne Lake, largest lake in the Rockies.

The river that flows from the largest lake in the Rockies was named using the French word for "wicked," maligne (muh-LEEN). The name was bestowed in 1846 by Jesuit missionary Father de Smet, in reference to the difficulty he had crossing this tributary of the Athabasca River.

Explorers, scientists and sightseers have been drawn to Maligne since the early 1900's, and a road was developed as far as Medicine Lake in the 1920's. From there, boat and horse brought the visitor to Maligne's north shore. The road was extended to the lake in 1962, and paved by 1970.

Visitors are encouraged to spend a full day in the Maligne area. If a boat tour is in your plans, it is best to make bookings before leaving Jasper. Camping is not permitted in the Maligne Valley. The Maligne Lake Road is open year-round.

Maligne Canyon

At the end of the Wisconsin Glaciation, the mouth of the Maligne Valley was left hanging above the Athabasca Valley. Initially, the Maligne River cascaded into the Athabasca as a waterfall. Over time, the river took advantage of

JOINS PAGE 269

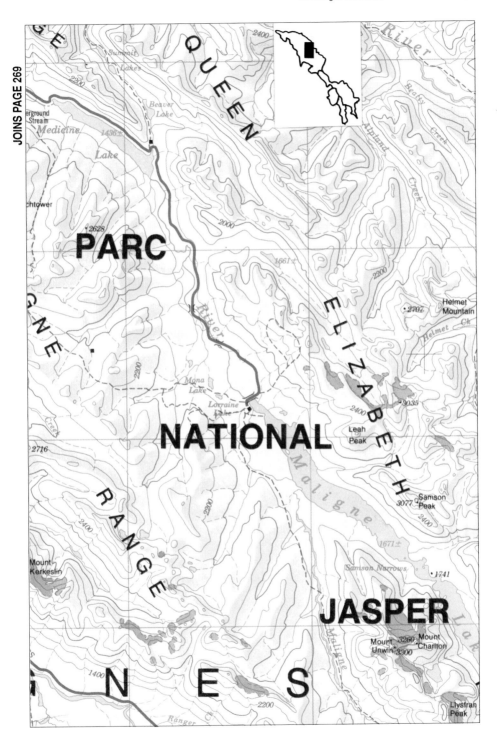

Top: Depressions in the riverbed trap boulders, which the current then swirls in place. The grinding effect drills potholes into the bedrock. Good examples of potholes can be seen in abandoned stream courses in the upper Maligne Canyon.

Bottom: Maligne Canyon is the longest and deepest limestone canyon in the Canadian Rockies. The canyon has formed where the Maligne River is eroding through a resistant rock step at the mouth of a hanging valley.

weaknesses in the rock to create Maligne Canyon — the longest, deepest and most interesting limestone canyon in the Rockies. As one early visitor commented, "any other canyon is like a crack in a teacup."

The many bends in the canyon have resulted from the river following cracks in the bedrock — the line of least resistance. Pot-holes — circular depressions drilled into the rock by pebbles carried in the water — can be seen in the upper canyon. Fossils are visible there, too. More water flows out of Maligne Canyon than appears to flow into it. (We'll discover why at Medicine Lake.) This can be verified by comparing the water volumes upstream and downstream from the Fourth Bridge.

It has taken the Maligne River 11,000 years to create this canyon, which is 55 m deep in places, yet sometimes scarcely more than a metre wide. The canyon air is cool and damp, and the adjacent slopes are shaded. An ancient canyon forest of Douglas fir and white spruce clings tenaciously to the thin, mossy soils over the precipice. Common raven, American dipper and black swift are amongst the birds that dwell here.

Maligne Canyon can be accessed from three points. The most rewarding hike is to begin from the Fifth Bridge — a four kilometre round trip that requires less than half a day. Those walking down the canyon from the tea house at the top should remember: it's all uphill on the way back!

Medicine Lake
Leaky Sinks and Hidden Plumbing

The Maligne Valley is the setting for two of the most bizarre features in the Rockies: a disappearing lake and a disappearing river. Limestone, which comprises most of the bedrock in the valley, is water soluble. Surface water is frequently able to take advantage of natural joints and cracks in irregular limestone formations to erode far into the bedrock and create underground channels. Limestone terrain characterized by such drainage is known as karst topography.

Between Maligne and Medicine lakes, the Maligne River flows on the surface. Between Medicine Lake and the Athabasca River, the course of the Maligne River reveals the karst nature of the region, for Medicine Lake has no surface outlet. Its waters drain through sink holes in the lake bottom into a cave system, and emerge near the Fourth Bridge in Maligne Canyon, 17 km distant. It is thought that some of the lakes near Jasper townsite are also fed by this water.

Not only does the river disappear, but the lake goes with it. When the volume drained by the sink holes exceeds the inflow, the lake level begins to drop. By late autumn, all that remains is a braided stream on mud flats — a good place to observe wildlife. About every other year, the capacity of the sink holes is temporarily exceeded, and Medicine Lake overflows at its north end. The overflow riverbed is visible at roadside.

The Maligne karst is the largest such system in the world, and was principal in the designation of the four mountain parks as a World Heritage Site. The underground channels carry a volume

of 57 cubic metres/second. Downstream from the lake, the Maligne River gathers surface waters from the surrounding mountainsides, so it has two streams — one visible on the surface, and one hidden in the underground cave system. In summer it takes 20 hours for the water to flow underground from Medicine Lake to Maligne Canyon.

Many unsuccessful attempts have been made to explore the cave system in the Maligne Valley. It may be the longest in Canada.

The waters of Medicine Lake drain through the lake bottom into a cave system that empties into Maligne Canyon, 17 km downstream. In summer, the lake fills with glacial runoff. By autumn, all that remains is a braided stream on mud flats.

When the Walls Come Tumbling Down

The Maligne is a valley of rock-slides. The sedimentary formations in slopes on the east side of the valley are tilted at angles up to 70°. When the Maligne Glacier retreated from this valley, it undercut the bases of these slopes. Cataclysmic rockslides have occured when the weakened formations tumbled to the valley floor.

The result is a series of overlapping slabs on the mountain sides, and boulder gardens in the valley below. Two of these rockslides, the largest measured in the Rockies, have created Maligne and Medicine Lakes, by acting as dams. The rockslide that dams Medicine Lake is plainly visible from the lake's south end.

Rockslides are favourite habitat for pika, hoary marmot, least chipmunk and golden mantled ground squirrel.

Front Range/Main Range

The Maligne Valley separates the front ranges to the east from the eastern main ranges to the west. The front range mountains of the Colin and Queen Elizabeth Ranges are predominantly sawtooth mountains. The sedimentary formations were tipped towards the vertical during mountain building, and the ridgecrests have since been eroded to create the sawtooth form.

On the opposite side of the valley, the rounded summits of the Maligne Range are an unusual shape for eastern main range peaks. Like most other domed

With a length of 22 km, Maligne is the largest lake in the Canadian Rockies. About two-thirds of the way to the south end of the lake is Samson Narrows and Spirit Island, with the postcard view of the glaciated peaks at the head of the lake.

mountains of modest elevation in the Rockies, they were once completely covered by glacial ice, which removed the characteristic angles, towers and pinnacles.

Maligne Lake

Maligne Lake is by far the largest natural lake in the Canadian Rockies. Fed by meltwaters from the Brazeau Icefield and other glaciers at its south end, the lake occupies 22 km of valley bottom. It has an area of 2,066 hectares, an average width of about one kilometre, and a maximum depth of 96 m. Its waters are dammed by the largest measured rockslide in the Rockies.

About two-thirds of the way to the south end of the lake, a glacially fed stream descending from Maligne Mountain has built an alluvial fan — a deposit of material eroded from the mountainside. This obstruction reduces the lake's width to 200 m. The channel is called Samson Narrows, for Sampson Beaver, a Stoney chief. Spirit Island is nearby, along with the famous postcard view of the glaciated peaks at the head of the lake.

In the view from the lake's outlet, Mt. Charlton and Mt. Unwin are to the right, with Leah Peak and Samson Peak on the left. Directly down the lake are some of the peaks at the headwaters, 30 km distant. The low mountains

Mary Schäffer

The first recorded visit to Maligne Lake was in 1875 by Henry MacLeod, a surveyor for the Canadian Pacific Railway, Not impressed with the scenery, the trail from the Athabasca Valley, or the apparent dead-end, he named it Sorefoot Lake.

It is likely settlers from the Athabasca Valley frequented the lake in the late 1800's. However, the next recorded visit was in 1908. Using a map drawn by Sampson Beaver, a Stoney Native chief, and with information garnered from explorer A. P. Coleman, Mary Schäffer and party came in search of the lake known to Natives as Chaba Imne – great beaver lake. They reached the lake from the south, and built a log raft, the "Chaba." Several days were spent exploring, during which many of the summits were named for party members and friends. Schäffer returned again in 1911 to carry out another survey, this time from the lake's northern end.

A Quaker hailing from Philadelphia, Schäffer was a talented writer and photographer who gained fame with the account of her travels: *Old Indian Trails of the Canadian Rockies.* Out of print for six decades, this enjoyable book was republished in 1980 as *A Hunter of Peace.* Schäffer befriended Stoney Natives during her journeys, and was known to them as Yahe-Weha, "Mountain Woman." In her other Rocky Mountain travels she made one of the first visits to the headwaters of the Athabasca River.

flanking the lake's outlet on the east side are the Opal Hills and, on the west side, the Bald Hills. Those with the better part of a day to spend on hikes into either of these hills will enjoy a pleasant visit to the upper subalpine and alpine ecoregions, and an unequaled panorama of Maligne Lake and valley.

The Skyline Trail, a spectacular 44 km backpacking route along the crest of the Maligne Range towards Jasper, departs from Maligne Lake. A small lake adjacent to this trail commemorates Mona Matheson, one of the first female trail guides in Jasper.

The only way to reach the far end of the lake is by boat or foot. The Maligne Lake Boat Tours, which commenced in 1928, operate from a dock nearby, making the excursion to the Samson Narrows. the floating boat house was built by guide Curly Phillips in 1928. Brook trout and rainbow trout are the two most common fish species in the lake.

Limited services and emergency assistance are available at Maligne Lake. In addition, there is a gift shop and a restaurant. Moose are frequently seen in the area.

Mary Schäffer launched the first boat on Maligne Lake in 1908. Commercial boat tours on the lake today take visitors to Samson Narrows and Spirit Island.

The Yellowhead Highway East

Roche Miette is a prominent landmark in the Athabasca Valley near the east boundary of Jasper National Park. There are conflicting stories as to how the mountain came by its name. It is thought "Miette" may be a corruption of a Native word for "mountain sheep."

The Yellowhead Highway is the only east/west road through Jasper National Park. As with the Trans-Canada Highway, it follows the line of a trans-continental railway. Originally, two railways competed for business through the region, the Grand Trunk Pacific and the Canadian Northern. When these two lines merged in 1916, some of the railway grades were abandoned. These were later used for the highway, completed in 1968.

The highway takes its name from Yellowhead Pass on the Continental Divide. Yellowhead was probably Pierre Bostonais, a blond-haired Iroquois guide who worked with the Hudson's Bay Company in the 1820's. In French, Yellowhead is "Tete Jaune," and Bostonais is further commemorated in the town of Tete Jaune Cache, 100 km west of Jasper.

Athabasca Valley

The Athabasca Valley is the largest of the major valleys in the mountain national parks, both in breadth and length, a fact that can be fully appreciated from the viewpoint on the Yellowhead Highway near Jasper. Many landmarks are visible, including Mt. Edith Cavell. The men who

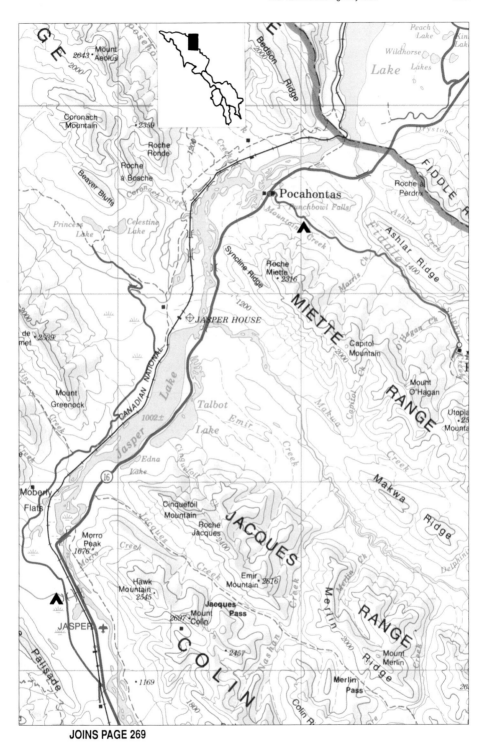

Mount Aeolus 2643

Coronach Mountain

Roche Ronde

Roche à Bosche

Beaver Bluffs

Princess Lake

Celestine Lake

Coronach Creek

Pocahontas

Punchbowl Falls

Mountain Creek

Roche Miette 2316

Syncline Ridge

Roche à Perdrix

Ashlar Ridge

Fiddle Ridge

Peach Lake

Wildhorse Lakes

Lake

Drystone

FIDDLE R.

JASPER HOUSE

Mount Greenock

Talbot Lake

Emir Lake

Edna Lake

de met 2539

CANADIAN NATIONAL

Jasper Lake

1002±

MIETTE

Capitol Mountain

Mount O'Hagan

RANGE

Utopia Mountain

Moberly Flats

Morro Peak 1876

Cinquefoil Mountain

Roche Jacques

Hawk Mountain 2545

JACQUES

Emir Mountain 2616

Jacques Pass

Mount Colin 2697

JASPER

Palisade

COLIN

1169

1800

2457

Makwa Ridge

Merlin Creek

RANGE

Mount Merlin

Merlin Ridge

Merlin Pass

Colin R.

American Lewis Swift became one of the first settlers in the Athabasca Valley when he built this homestead near The Palisade in 1895.

packed the furs and supplies for the fur trade — the voyageurs — called Mt. Edith Cavell "La Montagne de la Grand Traverse" (the mountain of the great crossing). It is a landmark visible from a great distance to the north in the Athabasca Valley, and the French name refers to the mountain's proximity to the arduous route across the Continental Divide via the Whirlpool Valley and Athabasca Pass. On sighting this mountain, the voyageurs of the fur trade knew the long approach to the Continental Divide was nearly over.

From here to the east gate of the park, the Athabasca Valley is under the influence of the drier front range climate. The gravelly soils support lodgepole pine, Douglas fir and white spruce forests. The valley bottom contains extensive montane meadows and montane wetlands. The valley is favourite and critical range for members of the deer family, and also for their predators, coyote, wolf and cougar.

"Swift's Place"

In 1895, Lewis Swift, an American expatriate, became the first settler in the area that would later become Jasper National Park. He built a cabin near The Palisade, ranched cattle and traded with the local Natives. With the establishment of the park in 1907, most settlers were bought out by the federal government. Swift, however, declined, and was granted title to his land in 1911.

Before the coming of the railways, "Swift's Place" was a well

Jasper House was a fur trade outpost operated by the Hudson's Bay Company. It occupied a site north of Jasper Lake, from 1829 to 1910. In its later years, the building served as an impromptu hotel, housing many noted travellers, including James Hector of the Palliser Expedition in 1859. "Jasper" was the fur trader originally in charge of the outpost. The name soon became descriptive of the general area, and when the new national park was created in 1907, "Jasper" was an obvious choice for its name.

known stopping place for travellers in the Athabasca Valley. Explorer A. P. Coleman called it "a delightful oasis of prairie in the heart of the mountains." Swift offered accommodation and information to travellers, and operated a cable ferry across the Athabasca River. He had a water-driven grist mill on his homestead.

The Department of the Interior hesitated at Swift's offer to sell in 1935, and so the land was sold privately. The two subsequent owners developed the leasehold as an outfitting ranch and tourist accommodation. Swift's ranch was finally sold to the park in 1962, for a quarter of a million dollars. Most of the historic buildings no longer exist. Swift's water wheel is among the

Osprey

The osprey, or "fish hawk," lives along lakes and rivers in the montane and lower subalpine ecoregions. Its plumage is dark brown, with a white head and white underside. A dark stripe encompasses the eye. Wingspan is 1.5 m. In flight, the underside reflects the colour of the water below, making the osprey less visible to prey. This bird hunts by circling over water at a considerable height, and then diving to spear fish just below the surface with its talons. Rodents and smaller birds are also eaten.

Osprey mate for life and construct prominent tree-top nests, to which they return from migration each spring. In recent years, osprey have been present here in the Athabasca Valley, and at Vermilion Lakes, Lake Louise, Emerald Lake and in the Kicking Horse Valley. The osprey is featured on the Canadian ten dollar bill.

artifacts at a site now used as a training centre and residence for park employees.

Celestine Lake Road

The Celestine Lake Road provides access to the remote North Boundary Trail and other hiking destinations at the mouth of the Snake Indian River. The Snaring campground is reached in about five kilometres. Beyond the campground the road follows the west shore of the Athabasca River for some 30 km, traversing the largest block of montane meadow and forest in the mountain national parks, before dead-ending at Celestine Lake. The montane ecoregion comprises only 5.5% of Jasper's area, and much of that is found here. This part of the Athabasca Valley is prime habitat for many species of large mammals.

Access to the upper Celestine Lake Road is controlled, with inbound and outbound traffic restricted to certain times of day. Trailers are not permitted. Check with the Park Information Centre in Jasper for details concerning access.

Jasper Lake and Talbot Lake

The level of Jasper Lake fluctuates annually. In summer, the Athabasca River floods the area to a depth of a metre. In the winter, the river level drops, the lake dries up and the sands are exposed to strong winds. The winds carry away the sand, depositing some of it against vegetation and rocks, eventually building dunes.

One series of dunes has separated Jasper and Talbot Lakes, and it is along this natural causeway that the Yellowhead Highway travels. Look for other, smaller dunes at roadside as you travel east.

As with most valley bottom lakes in the Rockies, the days of Jasper Lake are numbered. Eventually the Athabasca River will erode a deeper riverbed, and the annual flooding will cease to occur.

The sands of the arid dunes ecosite are anchored by low-growing vegetation such as creeping juniper, bearberry, and Alberta's provincial emblem, the prickly wild rose. Inactive dunes also support white spruce. Active dunes are actually advancing slowly north-eastward, covering vegetation as they go. With the dunes serving as a windbreak, montane wetlands have developed in Talbot Lake. This is a good place to look for osprey, bald eagle and waterfowl.

A trail from the Talbot Lake viewpoint leads south onto a knoll beneath Cinquefoil (SINK-foil) Mountain. The knoll is named for the five-petalled flower of the shrubby cinquefoil, and from its crest an excellent overview of this part of the valley is obtained.

The grassy rise is frequented by a herd of bighorn sheep

Disaster Point

Where the spur of Roche Miette juts into the Athabasca River, early travellers were forced to either ford the river or follow a difficult trail across the hillside above. Either way, "disasters" were common. Another more humourous anecdote tells how the point received its name – Sandford Fleming broke his brandy flask here in 1872. Presumably the flask was full.

Dynamite and heavy equipment have been used in constructing the modern roadbed, eliminating the treacherous hillside confronted by the pioneers. However, today a disaster of a different sort is unfolding here. The mixture of wild animals and fast-moving vehicles is not a good one, and road kills of sheep are common. Between 1945 and 1980, 236 sheep were killed on the Canadian National rail line, and 167 sheep died on Jasper's roads. Bighorns are particularly vulnerable to this kind of drain on their population. As their range is threatened or becomes marginal, they tend not to relocate, but persist, either until matters improve, or they become locally extinct.

Please drive with extra care near Disaster Point. Observe the posted speed limit. Park safely off the road, and do not feed or approach the sheep.

The sheep congregate here to lick the mineral lime, released into the ground water through the actions of the Fitzhugh Lime and

Stone Company, which worked a claim here just before WWI.

Pocohontas Ponds

The backwater of the Athabasca River known as Pocohontas Ponds is an excellent location for birdwatching. Many of Jasper's more than 200 reported species may be seen here, especially during spring and fall. Included are the large migratory birds, Canada goose and great blue heron. Beaver inhabit the ponds as well. Somewhat surprisingly, moose have not frequented this area in recent years.

Jasper Lake is a backwater flooded annually by the Athabasca River. In winter the lake dries up, and strong winds scour sand from the lake bed, building dunes against surrounding rocks and vegetation. The Yellowhead Highway crosses a natural dune causeway, which separates Jasper and Talbot Lakes.

Pocohontas

Named after the noted mining town in Virginia, Pocohontas celebrated the dreams of a mining company that aspired to greatness, after two prospectors discovered coal on the slopes of Roche Miette in 1908.

Jasper Park Collieries worked four coal seams in the area of its 40 sq km claim at Pocohontas, beginning in 1910. The tracks of the Grand Trunk Pacific Railway were laid along the south side of the Athabasca Valley, and a spur line to the mine was constructed the following year. Production peaked in 1912, when more than 100,000 tonnes of coal were extracted, and 120 people were employed.

The Pocohontas mine was plagued with bad management and bad luck. A series of fatal accidents took place, and mining inspectors demanded improve-

Cougar

The cougar is perhaps the most elusive animal in the Rockies. If you see this wild cat, there will be no mistaking it. The cougar is a big animal that weighs up to 70 kg, with a 1.5 m long body and a tail that's half again as long. It has a short-haired, tawny coat, with a yellowish belly and white chin and throat. Kittens are spotted. Unlike the other wild cats in the Rockies, the lynx and bobcat, the ears have no tufts.

Most frequently observed in the front range valleys of Jasper, this solitary animal ranges over a huge territory in quest of its favourite food, mule deer. The cougar hunts in the tradition of many big cats, stalking to within a few metres of its prey before lunging onto the victim's back, then biting and breaking the neck and tearing at the throat with the claws. The cougar will also hunt many of the other large and small mammals of the Rockies, and has no natural enemies.

Cougars only pair up during mating and rearing of the young. The female can bear young throughout the year, but usually times her three month gestation period so the kittens arrive in summer. In a switch, it is the female who seeks out the male in order to mate every other year. Two to four kittens are born, and they stay with the mother for at least one year, living in a sheltered den among boulders, or under a cliff.

The cougar can live up to 12 years in the wild. A major cause of premature death is injuries inflicted by its prey during the hunt. The cougar was formerly considered a pest in the Rockies, and attempts were made to eradicate it from the national parks. The population has not recovered. Outside of the parks, the animal is also suffering because of a reduction of favourable habitat. In all, it is becoming increasingly scarce.

ments from the company which were not forthcoming. When the Grand Trunk and Canadian Northern railways amalgamated in 1916, the rails were moved to the other side of the river, making access to transportation very difficult. Then at the end of the First World War the bottom fell out of the coal market, and labour disputes disrupted operations. The final straw came when the country's railways found they could obtain coal more easily and cheaply outside the parks. The Pocohontas mine closed permanently in April 1921.

Ruins of the colliery can be reached in a short walk southwest from roadside, about 150 m along the Miette Hot Springs Road. Piles of black coal tailings can still be found in the area.

Even though the Pocohontas mining claim was within the boundaries of newly created Jasper National Park, contemporary views held that resource extraction was a valid activity in national parks. This sentiment was not popular with J. B. Harkin, who was appointed first commissioner of national parks in 1911. One of his career goals was achieved in 1930 with the passing of the National Parks Act, which precluded new leases for resource extraction in the parks.

Punchbowl Falls

As with many waterfalls in the Rockies, Punchbowl Falls marks the point where a side valley stream encounters a particularly

resistant rock formation before entering into a larger valley. The resistant rock here is the natural concrete of the Cadomin Formation, which dates to 98 million years ago, making it the youngest rock visible at a roadside stop in this part of the Rockies.

The constant pounding of the water as it drops over each step of the falls has eroded several basins, called plunge pools, from which the falls get their name.

Top: The Pocohontas Ponds are typical of the many wetland areas in the Athabasca Valley. The ponds are a favourite nesting and stop-over place for many migratory birds.

Bottom: Jasper Park Collieries began working four coal seams in the vicinity of Roche Miette in 1910. The industry gave rise to a town named Pocohontas.

Picturesque
Punchbowl Falls
have been eroded
into a relatively
resistant rock
formation. An
outcrop of coal
occurs nearby the
falls.

Miette Hot Springs
The Hottest of the Hot
Of the three developed hot springs
in the Rockies, Miette Hot Springs
are by far the hottest, averaging
almost 54°C. They are also the
highest in dissolved mineral content, the most pungent in sulphur
odour, and the most prolific in
volume.

These springs were well known
to Natives, traders of the Hudson's
Bay Company and early settlers.
However it was miners from Pocohontas who began development
here. A track was roughed out to

the springs in 1910, and a bath-
house and shelter were constructed in 1913. To fill idle time
during a strike, the miners built
the first pool in 1919. The Parks
Branch completed a road in 1933,
with full development of the
springs taking place in 1937. Redevelopment was completed in
1986.

The only commercial designs
on the springs were those of the
Grand Trunk Pacific Railway. It
planned to build Chateau Miette
at the mouth of the Fiddle River,
connecting the hotel to the
springs by monorail, and the
springs to the hotel by pipeline.
Lack of finances precluded development of the plan.

The appropriately named Sulphur Skyline trail departs from
Miette Hot Springs, and is recommended to strong hikers who
have half a day to spend in obtaining a splendid view of some
remote valleys in Jasper National
Park.

A shorter walk leads to the
outlet of the springs and the 1937
facility.

Roche Miette
The prow of Roche Miette (rosh
mee-YETT) is a prominent landmark along this part of the Yellowhead Highway. There are
three stories as to how the rock
came by its name. The most popular was related by artist Paul Kane,
who stayed at Jasper House in
1846. It seems a fur trader named
Miette had made an ascent of the

mountain, and sat with his legs dangling over the abyss, contemplating life. Another version equates the crumbly nature of the limestone rock with the French word for crumb, *miette*, which is not particularly valid in this case, as the Palliser Formation comprising most of Roche Miette is one of the tougher limestones.

The story now gaining acceptance tells how the voyageurs corrupted the Cree word "myatuck", which means "mountain sheep." (Original spellings of Roche Miette are consistently "Myette.") The bighorn sheep certainly is common in the area, and was even more so in the early 1800's.

The Miette Hot Springs are the hottest in the Rockies, and the most pungent in odour. The first pool at the springs was built by striking miners from nearby Pocohontas, in 1919.

The Yellowhead Highway West

Mount Robson is the highest mountain in the Canadian Rockies. It was known to Natives as "mountain of the spiral road," and was called "Cloud Cap Mountain" by travellers in the 1860's. The tremendous vertical rise from valley bottom to summit (nearly two vertical miles), causes air to cool and clouds to form, frequently obscuring the mountain top from view.

Yellowhead Pass

Yellowhead Pass is the lowest mountain pass on the Continental Divide in the central Rockies. At first it would seem the most logical choice for a travel route, but as early as 1826 fur traders became familiar with the treacherous character of the Fraser River on the west side of the pass. At least in the longer crossing of the higher Athabasca Pass to the south, the difficulties eased once the gentle Columbia River was gained.

In 1872, Sandford Fleming, Engineer-in-Chief of the Canadian Pacific Railway, announced the country's first transcontinental railway would cross the Rockies via Yellowhead Pass. By 1877 the survey line was staked, but full political commitment to the route was lacking. When Fleming left his position with the C.P.R. in 1880, his influence quickly waned. Interest shifted to a more southerly route, to prevent loss of trade to branch lines of American railways.

In 1881, with no certainty a pass across the Selkirk Range existed, or that trains could ever descend the west side of Kicking Horse Pass, the government abandoned the Yellowhead route.

The surveyors pulled out, and Yellowhead Pass remained quiet for almost 30 years, until the coming of the Grand Trunk Pacific Railway.

The Yellowhead was originally known as Leather Pass. "Yellowhead" was probably Pierre Bostonais, a fair-haired Iroquois guide and trapper. He was based on the west side of the pass in the 1820's, near the present day community of Tete Jaune Cache (Yellowhead's Cache).

The pass marks the Continental Divide, and the boundary between Jasper National Park, Alberta and Mt. Robson Provincial Park, British Columbia. Waters flow east and north from here via the Miette, Athabasca and Mackenzie Rivers to the Arctic Ocean, and west via the Fraser River to the Pacific Ocean. The pass is also the division point between the Mountain and Pacific time zones. Westbound travellers subtract one hour.

The entire length of the Miette Valley leading to Yellowhead Pass is a mosaic of montane wetlands, and is excellent habitat for moose, beaver, osprey and waterfowl.

Mt. Robson
Provincial Park was
created in 1913, to
protect the area
around the highest
mountain in the
Canadian Rockies.

The Overlanders

In the early 1860's, reports reached eastern Canada, telling of gold discovered in the Cariboo Mountains west of Yellowhead Pass. In the spring of 1862, over 200 easterners and Red River settlers grouped together at Fort Garry in Winnipeg to begin a journey across the plains and the Rockies, seeking better fortune in the mountains of the Gold Range.

At Edmonton they traded their wagons for horses and cattle, and engaged the services of a knowledgeable Native guide. A party of 125, including one pregnant woman, eventually set out to cross the mountains. In a journey fraught with hardship and peril, The Overlanders soon ran short of food, and resorted to shooting skunk and butchering their cattle. At Tete Jaune Cache they traded with Natives, receiving salmon and berries to augment their diet.

With winter approaching, the party split. Many built rafts and ran the Fraser River to Quesnel (kwuh-NELL). At least six of their number drowned. Thirty-six others set off on foot along the Thompson River for Kamloops.

There was gold in the Cariboo Mountains. Over $10 million worth was mined in 10 years. However, the motherlode outcropped in a very small area, and the tale of many prospectors was one of hard luck. Only a few of The Overlanders became residents of the Kamloops and Quesnel areas. Most never prospected, and continued their journey to the west coast the following year.

The Overlanders are commemorated in the names of Emigrants Mountain, northeast of Yellowhead Pass, and in Overlander Falls and Overlander Mountain.

Fraser River

The 1,280 km long Fraser River, one of the major rivers of western Canada, has its sources in glaciers high on the west slopes of The Ramparts, 30 km southwest of here. These gentle beginnings are deceptive. Much further downstream is treacherous whitewater, including Hell's Gate and the Fraser Canyon. Simon Fraser, an explorer with the North West Company, first travelled the river from Prince George to its mouth in 1808. The concrete pylons visible in the river supported the tracks of one of the two rival railways that used this route before amalgamation as the Canadian National Railway in 1922.

In 1863, a year after The Overlanders made their crossing of the Rockies, the first tourists arrived — an unlikely pair named Milton and Cheadle. Viscount Milton was the sickly 23-year-old son of the 6th Earl of Fitzwilliam (for whom Mt. Fitzwilliam is named). Dr. Walter Cheadle was his 27-year-old physician. At the Earl's request, Milton was to be escorted through the wilds of the Rockies, where the clean air and hard work might restore his health. The misadventure nearly cost both of them their lives.

Before leaving Edmonton, the pair managed to pick up a pathetic companion named Mr. O'Byrne. So glad were the Hudson's Bay Company men at the fort to see him go, they took up a collection to buy him a horse! O'Byrne's fear of bears, combined with Milton's reluctance to get up before noon, stalled the expedition many times. By the time Yellowhead Pass was reached, the food supply was nearly exhausted, and marten, grouse, bear, porcupine and horse had been added to the rations.

After three months on the trail, the entourage finally staggered into Kamloops. Right away they spent $158.25 on food and clothes at the Hudson's Bay Company post. Cheadle claimed to have put on 41 lbs. during the nine day stay, before they pushed on to the coast. The pair published a popu-

lar account of this journey, *The Northwest Passage by Land*, in which the name Mt. Robson appeared for the first time. Five editions sold out in eight months.

The next celebrated journey through the Yellowhead could not have been more different in character. Railway mogul Sandford Fleming and Reverend George Munro Grant travelled the pass as part of their cross-country journey in 1872. The larder of this party was always full, and Sundays were a day off. Various food caches along the route contained brandy enough for a toast to everyone's health, and to set the weekly treat of plum pudding aflame. By contrast, this party made Kamloops in two thirds the time.

Grant published an account of this journey in *From Ocean to Ocean*. In it, many of the French names in the Athabasca Valley appeared in print for the first time.

Overlander Falls commemorates the epic journey of the Overlanders, who crossed western Canada by wagon, foot and raft in 1862-63.

The 1,280 km Fraser River has its sources along the Continental Divide southeast of Yellowhead Pass. Mt. Fitzwilliam, seen here reflected in the river, was named for the father of Viscount Milton, who travelled through Yellowhead Pass in 1863.

Mt. Robson
3954 m / 12,972 ft

Native peoples called the highest peak in the Canadian Rockies "Yuh-hai-has-hun" — the mountain of the spiral road. The huge ledges visible from the highway angle slightly upwards to the east, like spiral ramps. Unfortunately for climbers, the spiral road does not reach the summit!

Several features combine to make Mt. Robson an impressive mountain. The low elevation of the Fraser Valley at the Mt. Robson Viewpoint, and the high elevation of the summit, produce a vertical rise of over 3100 m / 10,100 ft (nearly two vertical miles) to the mountain top — a statistic no other mountain at roadside in the Rockies even closely approaches. Mt. Robson is also 200 m higher

than Mt. Columbia, the second highest in the Rockies, and 550 m higher than any other mountain in the immediate area. In a range of spectacular, high mountains, Robson is truly a giant.

Regardless of weather in the valley bottom, the summit of Robson is frequently obscured by clouds. The Overlanders referred to Robson as "Cloud Cap Mountain," and their Native guide claimed to have seen the summit only once in his first 29 visits! The clouds result from the tremendous vertical rise that the winds must achieve in order to pass over Robson's summit. The resulting drop in air pressure produces condensation.

The fact that Mt. Robson creates its own weather in this fashion is the principal reason it is so difficult to climb. The mountain is a popular objective with mountaineers from around the world, and despite numerous attempts, the summit is not reached frequently. Between 1939 and 1953, not a single party was successful. All things considered, you'll be fortunate if Robson stands unobscured before you during your visit.

Concealed from view on the mountain's north side is one of the most spectacular glacier systems in the Rockies. This area is a popular backpacking destination, reached by a 20 km hike along the Berg Lake trail.

The origin of the name Mt. Robson is disputed. Most likely it is a corruption of the last name of Colin Robertson, a Hudson's Bay Company employee who oversaw fur trapping in the area in the 1820's.

The Reverend and the Greenhorn

The first attempts to climb Mt. Robson were made by a party that included Torontonian A. P. Coleman and Reverend George Kinney in 1908. In a story typical of Robson, poor weather prevailed and only four days of 21 were conducive to climbing.

In 1909, members of the British Alpine Club, including L. S. Amery, mounted an expedition to Robson. At Jasper Lake, on their approach to the mountain, they encountered Kinney and outfitter Curly Phillips, returning from what Kinney claimed was the first ascent of Robson.

At the outset of their trip, Phillips had only once been in the mountains before, and had never seen Mt. Robson. His ignorance of the dangers of mountaineering had allowed Kinney to convince him to join the venture, when the two chanced to meet on the trail. In reality, Kinney only wanted a good horseman to get him to Robson. He was accustomed to climbing alone, having made the first solo ascent of Mt. Stephen, near Field, in 1904.

What followed was one of the most intrepid episodes in the history of Canadian mountaineering. Devoid of equipment and rations, the reverend and the greenhorn made four desperate attempts on the treacherous west face of the mountain. The last of these culminated in success, or so Kinney claimed.

Evidence, including Phillips' later testimony, indicated the pair did not quite make the summit. Still, their courage and perseverance was remarkable. The dangerous west face of Mt. Robson is avoided by contemporary mountaineers, and has likely not been attempted since.

Curly Phillips went on to become one of the most successful outfitters in Jasper. He died in an avalanche on Elysium Mountain above the Miette Valley in 1938. Amery's party continued to Mt. Robson and made several first ascents in the vicinity, but was unsuccessful on Robson itself.

In a range of impressive mountains, Mt. Robson is truly a giant. It is fully 200 metres higher than the second highest peak in the Rockies, Mt. Columbia.

The First Ascent of Mt. Robson

"Ever since I came to Canada and the Rockies, it was my wish to climb the highest peak." Austrian born mountain guide Conrad Kain arrived in the Rockies in 1909. His wish was fulfilled just four years later, when he guided two Alpine Club of Canada members, W.W. Foster and A.H. MacCarthy, to Mt. Robson's summit. This difficult and dangerous ascent was the crowning achievement of Kain's guiding career, which included 50 first ascents in Canada and 30 in New Zealand.

Kain came by his craft naturally, as a goatherd and quarryman, working in the hills of his homeland. In Canada, he developed a second craft, trapping, learned while spending winter in the wilds north of Mt. Robson with outfitter Curly Phillips. In 1917, Kain married and settled in the Columbia Valley at Wilmer, where he farmed and raised mink and marten for their furs.

During the 1911 A.C.C./Smithsonian Institute expedition to Mt. Robson, it became apparent that expedition leader A. O. Wheeler was saving the big peaks for a future A.C.C. camp. Kain stole away one afternoon on the pretence of visiting Emperor Falls. When he returned the following morning, it was after a difficult, solo first ascent of Whitehorn Mountain. Wheeler was incensed, but Kain could not bear "being among beautiful mountains and not climbing one."

It was from the 1913 A.C.C. camp in Robson Pass that Kain commenced the successful first ascent of Robson. The route, now called the Kain Face, lies out of view from the highway on the east side of the mountain. It represented a tremendous leap forward in Canadian mountaineering. The guide leading L. S. Amery's unsuccessful attempt on this route four years earlier commented: "I never before saw death so near." Kain tirelessly chopped hundreds of steps in the ice of the mountainside to achieve the summit slopes. With customary modesty, he stepped aside just before the highest point and announced "Gentlemen, that's as far as I can take you." The descent, by a different way, required another day.

James Monroe Thorington collaborated with Kain to produce the autobiography *Where the Clouds Can Go.* Kain died in 1934 from encephalitis, a year before this classic work on Canadian mountaineering was published.

A. O. Wheeler

Irish-born Arthur Oliver Wheeler is a figure so strongly connected to the history of the Canadian Rockies that his story could be told at half-a-dozen locations in Banff, Jasper and Yoho National Parks.

Wheeler was a land surveyor, trained in the use of photography in map making. As with the other topographic surveyors who preceded him in the Rockies, his work typically involved occupying survey stations on mountain tops. As a consequence he became an accomplished mountaineer.

In February 1906, Wheeler presented the seed idea for the founding of the Alpine Club of Canada (A.C.C.) to an executive meeting of the Canadian Pacific Railway. The railway immediately recognized the tourism benefits that would accrue from the association, and whole-heartedly supported the idea. This

was the beginning of a working partnership that lasted over two decades. The railway provided assistance in staging annual mountaineering camps, and the attending mountaineers published widely read accounts of their exploits, thus attracting more visitors to the Rockies. The first of these camps was at Yoho Pass in July 1906.

Wheeler organized and led a scientific expedition to Mt. Robson in 1911. One of its unofficial goals was to reconnoitre a location for an annual mountaineering camp. Most of the pioneer mountaineering in the Rockies had been accomplished by British and American climbers, frequently in the company of Swiss Guides. Wheeler was jealously determined not to let the highest peak in the Rockies fall to foreigners. From the A.C.C. camp at Robson Pass in 1913, the first ascent of Mt. Robson was made by Canadians, albeit guided by Austrian Conrad Kain. In the same year, largely as a result of the report of the 1911 expedition, Mt. Robson Provincial Park was created.

Wheeler also had a strong interest in the Mt. Assiniboine area, and was instrumental in the creation of Mt. Assiniboine Provincial Park in 1922. A few years later he oversaw the founding of Canada's first environmental group, the National Parks Association.

From 1913-25, Wheeler directed the British Columbia/Alberta Interprovincial Boundary Survey, during which he named many features. A cairn dedicated to the achievements of the survey stands on the north side of Mt. Robson, in Robson Pass. Another display detailing this survey was recently installed at The Great Divide in Kicking Horse Pass. Curiously, Wheeler's name is not commemorated in the Rockies, but in the name of Mt. Wheeler in the Selkirk Range to the west, which he also surveyed.

Waterton Lakes National Park

The Prince of Wales Hotel is at the north end of Upper Waterton Lake, the deepest lake in the Canadian Rockies. The lake extends across the U.S. border into Glacier National Park, Montana. The two parks were designated the Waterton-Glacier International Peace Park in 1932.

Waterton Lakes, Canada's fourth national park, is tucked away in the southwest corner of Alberta. Although it does not lie on a direct travel route to the better known mountain national parks, Waterton is less than a day's drive from Banff, and well worth a visit.

Upside Down Mountains

The processes that created the Rocky Mountains were identical throughout most of the range. However, in the vicinity of Waterton Lakes, a strikingly different front range landscape has resulted. The rock comprising the mountains in Waterton moved eastwards during mountain building, as a single mass known as the Lewis Thrust. This enormous thrust sheet was over six kilometres thick, and travelled as much as 70 km. Rocks one-and-a-half billion years old, from near the sedimentary basement of the Rockies, came to rest atop undisturbed 60 million year old shales. There is no transition zone between the two elements. Waterton is literally a place where peaks meet prairie. Because older rocks are consistently found over younger ones, some people refer

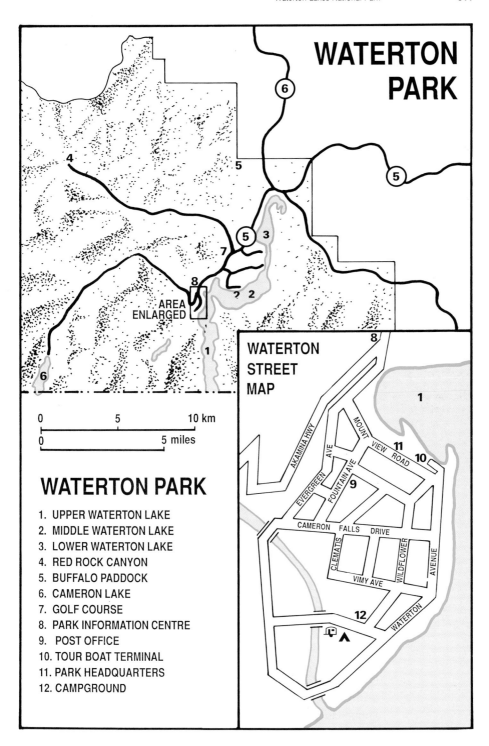

WATERTON PARK

1. UPPER WATERTON LAKE
2. MIDDLE WATERTON LAKE
3. LOWER WATERTON LAKE
4. RED ROCK CANYON
5. BUFFALO PADDOCK
6. CAMERON LAKE
7. GOLF COURSE
8. PARK INFORMATION CENTRE
9. POST OFFICE
10. TOUR BOAT TERMINAL
11. PARK HEADQUARTERS
12. CAMPGROUND

Waterton is literally a park where peaks meet prairie. Along the eastern margin of the park, the front ranges of the Rockies rise abruptly from the Interior plains. The park is known for its windy climate and the variety of its plant and animal life. More than one half of the plant species in Alberta can be found here.

to Waterton's summits as "upside down mountains."

Geologists are still entertaining theories as to why this tremendous mass of crumbly rocks held together so well during mountain building, while similar masses elsewhere in the Rockies became faulted and broken into many thrust sheets. The integrity of the rocks of the Lewis Thrust has created a topography atypical of the front ranges. The steeply tilted, sawtooth and overthrust mountains so familiar in Banff and Jasper are missing here. Instead the peaks are irregular in shape, and the sedimentary formations largely horizontal. Although these mountains are oriented along the southeast/northwest axis of the Rockies, the network of valleys is haphazard. Average elevations of mountain summits in Waterton are lower than further north in the Rockies. The highest peak in the park is 2910 m/9548 ft Mt. Blakiston, first climbed in 1942.

Some of the rocks in Waterton Lakes are the oldest visible in the Rockies. Pale limestone and dolomite of the Waterton Formation can be viewed along the Akamina Parkway. These rocks are one-and-a-half billion years old. Perhaps Waterton's most interesting rock is the red and green mudstone called argillite, in Red Rock Canyon. The red rock contains iron that has oxidized. The green rock contains iron that has not oxidized.

Although there are no glaciers in the park in the present day, the mountains and valleys of Waterton owe much of their appearance to the effects of glaciation. On several occasions in the past, a major glacier exited northwards onto the prairie through the valley now containing the Waterton Lakes. Upper Waterton Lake occupies this glacially scoured trough and, with a depth of 150 m, is the deepest lake in the Rockies. The Middle and Lower lakes resulted from the melting of a detached lobe of ice, left when the glacier last receded some 11,000 years ago. Alluvial fans have built out into these waters, dividing one lake into two.

A Forgotten Corner

As elsewhere in the Rockies, nomadic Natives were the first inhabitants in the Waterton Lakes region. In glacial times they roamed from the south along an ice-free corridor that bordered the eastern edge of the Rockies. With the retreat of glacial ice 11,000 years ago, Natives began to hunt and fish in the valleys now included in Waterton, following the seasonal migration of game between the prairie and mountainsides. The Plains bison was central to their livelihood. The meat of the animal provided sustenance, while clothing and shelter were fashioned from the hide.

The recent human history of Waterton Lakes differs markedly from the other mountain national parks. The valleys were untravelled by the voyageurs of the fur trade, and first came to the attention of Europeans as a result of the Palliser Expedition of 1857-60. This expedition was organized by the British government to explore and map its remote North American territory, with an eye to settlement, transportation and development. While James Hector travelled the divide north of Banff, and Captain Palliser the Kananaskis region, meteorologist Thomas Blakiston explored to the south, in the area including Waterton. In his report to the expedition, Blakiston commented favourably on the scenery and abundance of wildlife in the Waterton area.

Obscurity followed. In the 25 years after the Palliser Expedition, while the young country of Canada schemed and dreamed of a railway linking sea to sea, the prairies and peaks of Waterton saw neither the railway surveyor nor hotelier. They remained the

sole domain of a few intrepid travellers and settlers. It was during this time that Waterton's most famous resident, John "Kootenai" Brown, arrived on the scene.

Brown was a character who epitomized the old "wild" west. For almost 20 years he was in the thick of adventure and enterprise — serving with the British army in India, successfully prospecting in the Cariboo gold rush, surviving life and death skirmishes with Natives on the trail, and trading, trapping and hunting at various locations in British Columbia, Alberta and Montana. In 1879 he built a cabin at Waterton Lakes.

Brown supported his family by hunting, trapping and fishing, and by guiding hunters and travellers. In the early 1890's, more and more of these outsiders were arriving each season, and settlement was approaching the mountain front. Brown and local ranchers became concerned that Waterton would soon be engulfed in uncontrolled development. One of the ranch-

Waterton Lake and townsite, ca. 1935. Waterton has changed little since this photograph was taken. The Prince of Wales Hotel stands at the northern end of the lake.

ers, F.W. Godsal, contacted the Department of the Interior, and asked that a park be created at Waterton Lakes. In 1895, Kootenay Lakes Forest Park was set aside.

John Kootenai Brown continued to reside in the park, acting as its unofficial benefactor. In 1911, at age 71, he became its first superintendent, when national park status was conferred and the name changed to Waterton. Three years later, at Brown's request, the area of the park was increased thirty-fold, to 1,095 sq km. Today the park is slightly less than half that size. Kootenai Brown died in 1916. His grave may be viewed near Lower Waterton Lake.

In its relatively remote setting, and with no transportation corridor bisecting it, Waterton Lakes has escaped many of the developmental pressures to which the other mountain parks have been subjected. Plans to build a dam between the Middle and Upper Waterton Lakes in the early 1920's never came to fruition, and oil and mineral extraction in the early 1900's proved unviable, despite the fact that Canada's second oil producing well was located on Cameron Creek in the reserve, in 1901. Fortunately for the park, the technology of the day did not allow this and other wells to be drilled to the necessary depth to tap the abundance of oil underlying the area. Oil and gas production on the adjacent lands of the Waterton Gas Field are big business today.

After the establishment of the national park, the town of Waterton Lake evolved as a tourist facility. In the mid-1920's, the Great Northern Railway decided to run bus tours through the Rockies, from Glacier National Park in Montana to Jasper. Waterton was seen as an ideal place for an overnight stop. The Prince of Wales Hotel was constructed in 1926 to accommodate this enterprise, and opened the following year. The hotel was complete with a tour boat — *The International* — which plied the waters of Upper Waterton Lake.

Today, a full range of services is available at the townsite during summer. Four roads — the park entrance road, the Akamina Parkway, Red Rock Canyon Parkway and Chief Mountain International Highway — provide opportunities for auto sightseeing, and give access to the many hiking trails.

Charles Waterton

The Waterton Lakes were named by Thomas Blakiston of the Palliser Expedition for English naturalist and explorer Charles Waterton. A member of the Victorian upper class, Waterton roamed throughout South America, the Caribbean and the northwestern U.S. between 1812-29. He published several accounts of his expeditions, one of which details his riding on the back of an alligator. On return to England, he converted his estate into a bird sanctuary, the first of its kind.

Waterton never travelled in Canada. The lakes were named for him four years after his death.

Waterton's Ecology

Relative to the rest of the Rockies, Waterton's climate and ecology can be described with a single word: diversity. After your visit, you might think to add the word "windy" too. Warm chinook winds are common, moderating winters in the valley bottoms. At other times winds are created by a difference in air pressure which persists between weather systems over southern B.C. and Alberta. Since there are no major mountain ranges immediately to the west, these winds deliver more precipitation than falls in areas further north in the Rockies. Akamina (ah-kah-MEE-nuh) Pass records the highest annual snowfall in Alberta.

In common with the other mountain national parks, Waterton's mountainsides feature three ecoregions. This compliment of plants and wildlife is bolstered by those species native to the prairie, a section of which is included along the north-eastern margin of the park. As a result, over one half of Alberta's plant species can be found in Waterton. The park has a multitude of wildflowers unmatched elsewhere in the Rockies.

The common larger mammals of the Rockies all occur in Waterton: black bear, grizzly bear, elk, deer, bighorn sheep, mountain goat, cougar, coyote, beaver, porcupine and captive Plains bison. The park's lakes are in proximity to the major western migration flyways, and serve as stopping places for a variety of songbirds and waterfowl during autumn

Scenic Cameron Lake occupies a glacial cirque in the southwest corner of Waterton. The lakeshore trail makes a pleasant walk. Boating and fishing are also popular at the lake.

Waterton is noted for its red and green rock formations, which are some of the oldest exposed in the Canadian Rockies. A small creek has carved colourful Red Rock Canyon through these soft mudstones. The canyon may be explored via an easy interpretive trail.

and spring. Needless to say, Waterton is highly recommended to the nature lover, amateur botanist, birdwatcher and photographer.

Recreation

Although Waterton is a small park, it has much to offer the hiker, boater, fisherman and trailrider. Opportunities for extended backpacking are limited by the park's size, but over 160 km of trails lead through valleys and along ridge crests. Popular short hikes are: Blakiston Falls, Bison Viewpoint, Red Rock Canyon, Crandell Lake, Cameron Lakeshore, Townsite, Bear's Hump and Prince of Wales. Horses may be rented from private outfitters and taken on several park trails.

The many lakes are very popular for sport fishing, with various species of trout comprising most of the catch. Motorized boats may be launched on the Upper and Middle Waterton Lakes. Two companies operate boat tours on Upper Waterton Lake. Canoes and paddle boats may be rented at the townsite marina and Cameron Lake. Boardsailing is popular. Waters are very cold and dry suits are recommended. Tennis, bicycle rentals and public swimming round out the summer activities offered in the park. Winter access within the park is restricted by road closures. Cross-country skiing, showshoeing and waterfall ice climbing are popular activities.

There are three park-operated roadside campgrounds in Waterton: Townsite (hook-ups), Crandell and Belly River. Ten backcountry campgrounds await the backpacker. Commercial accommodation is available, and should be booked well in advance.

An International Peace Park and A Biosphere Reserve

The Canadian government was largely following the United States' lead when it granted national park status to the area around Waterton Lakes in 1911. The U.S. had created Glacier National Park in Montana the previous year, and there was an opportunity to extend protection to the adjacent area.

Because the international boundary runs through Upper Waterton Lake, the boat excursions from the Prince of Wales Hotel could have posed a problem to the governments. However, a relaxed attitude prevailed towards the multitude of tourists who regularly crossed the border on these tours.

By 1930, locals were calling for the establishment of an international park to further demonstrate the goodwill between Canada and the United States. The two governments thought this a good idea, and in 1932 created Waterton-Glacier International Peace Park — the first of its kind. Throughout the intervening decades, the administrators of the parks have embarked on a co-operative program to integrate outlooks on conservation, interpretation and resource management. Today the area is commonly referred to as the Waterton-Glacier Ecosystem.

In 1979 Waterton-Glacier and the surrounding lands were designated an international Biosphere Reserve — part of a worldwide United Nations program. This program recognizes the arbitrary nature of park boundaries, and seeks to compare the effects of resource management and industrial development on adjacent protected and unprotected lands. Local industries, farmers, ranchers and governments participate in monitoring mankinds' effects along the mountain front near Waterton. Biosphere Reserves have also been established in over 120 other countries.

Listings

Mount Robson rises majestically above Berg Lake. this spectacular view is the "back" of the mountain as seen from the highway.

GENERAL INFORMATION

Access

Calgary to Banff – 129 km/80 miles
Vancouver to Banff – 858 km/533 miles
Banff to Lake Louise – 58 km/36 miles
Lake Louise to Jasper – 237 km/148 miles
Lake Louise to Field – 27 km/17 miles
Golden to Field – 55 km/34 miles
Edmonton to Jasper – 362 km/226 miles
Prince George to Jasper – 376 km/235 miles

Most visitors to the Rockies arrive via Calgary or Edmonton in Alberta, or via Vancouver in British Columbia. Each of these cities has an international airport. Canada's main highway, the Trans-Canada (Hwy. #1) runs through Banff and Yoho parks. There is regular bus service into Banff, Jasper and Yoho from Calgary, Edmonton and Vancouver. Train service is limited. Car rental agencies have offices in the airports and in Banff, Lake Louise and Jasper. There are a number of tour companies specializing in Rockies vacations.

Travel Information

For personal travel counselling, call Travel Alberta: 1-800-661-8888 (from Canada and continental U.S.A.), 1-800-222-6501 (from within Alberta), or write:

Travel Alberta
10025 Jasper Avenue
Edmonton, Alberta T5J 3Z3
403-427-4321

ALBERTA GOVERNMENT
TOURISM OFFICES

Ontario
Suite 1110, 90 Sparks Street
Ottawa, Ontario K1P 5B4
613-237-2615

United States
#3535, 333 S. Grand Avenue
Los Angeles, CA 90071
213-625-1256

23rd Floor, 767 Fifth Avenue
New York, NY 10153
212-759-2222

1425, 5444 Westheimer Road
Houston, TX 77056
713-871-1604

United Kingdom
1 Mount Street
London, England W1Y 5AA
001-441-491-3430

Hong Kong
Room 1004B, 10th Floor
Tower 1, Admiralty Centre
18 Harcourt Rd.
Central Hong Kong
001-8-5-25-284-729

Japan
Alberta Office, 17th Floor
New Aoyama Building (West)
1–1, 1–Chome Minamiaoyama
Minato-ku, Tokyo 107
011-81-3-475-1171

Weather

The Rockies climate in a nutshell: the air is cool and dry, summers are short, and annual precipitation is moderate. However, since mountain ranges create their own minor climates and local weather in many ways, there are locations in the Rockies where the climate differs markedly from this general description. Many a day at Lake Louise or along the Icefields Parkway will bear witness to this phenomenon — local cloudiness and snow or rain showers are common when the general forecast indicates otherwise. To a traveller in the Canadian Rockies attempting to guess what weather lies ahead, the best advice is: "Be prepared for anything!" And

What to Wear and Carry in the Mountains

Activity	Summer (May-Oct)	Winter (Nov-April)
Sightseeing by car or bus	Raincoat, extra sweater, hat, gloves, sturdy shoes, sunglasses, food, water, first aid kit, walking shoes, sun hat.	Winter boots, winter coat, hat, gloves or mitts, scarf, extra sweater, sunglasses, extra food. Also carry in your vehicle: hot thermos, blankets, candle, winter tires, flashlight, booster cables, shovel, full tank of gas, map.
Day hikes	Hiking shoes or boots, full rain suit, sun hat, hat, extra sweater, gloves, sunscreen, sunglasses, day pack, food, water, first aid kit, insect repellent, map.	See cross-country skiing.
Cross-country skiing	Winter activity.	Layered clothing, gloves or mitts, hat, scarf, sunglasses, food, hot thermos, first aid and repair kits, waxes, map.

additionally: "If you don't like the weather, come back in five minutes."

What to Expect

There is no sure bet for timing a visit to the Rockies to coincide with good weather, but this summary may help.

Spring is usually underway throughout the Rockies by mid-May. Temperatures will still reach below freezing at night, and valley bottom daytime highs will be in the 12°C-20°C range. The May holiday weekend is statistically the best good weather long weekend of the year, and is quite often part of a two or three week stretch of sunshine that brings green to the trees and the brown of spring run-off to the recently thawed rivers.

June is frequently a poor month, although it may begin well. As pioneer outfitter Fred Stephens commented, it can rain "seven days out of six," and temperatures are often cooler than those typical of May. This pattern ends towards the beginning of July, when the weather improves and summer arrives. A significant snowfall often occurs around July 15. After this, summer returns in earnest, and until the first week of August, daytime highs can reach 30°C. In recent years, thunderstorms have been increasingly common during this time.

In some years a snowfall around August 10th breaks this pattern, and the remainder of the month sees a mixture of weather. In other years the hot weather continues, although frost returns at night.

The first week of September will often bring a heavy snowfall, and a chill in the air both night and day. Ten sopping centimetres of white stuff on the ground is not uncommon at Lake Louise at this time. Unsettled weather continues until the arrival (usually!) of Indian Summer. Beginning any time from mid-September to early October, this glorious stretch of weather features cloudless, warm days and cool, crisp nights, autumn colours, no bugs and uncrowded roads, townsites and viewpoints. In a good year, Indian Summer may last for six weeks.

Winter visitors to the Rockies must be prepared for harsh conditions. January daytime highs are commonly -15°C, but there might be one or two cold snaps a winter that push the mercury to -40°C or so, sometimes for a week at a time. Wind chills in townsites and at ski hills can be severe. Heavy snowfalls are no longer as common as in the past. Twenty centimetres now qualifies as a good dump. With all the lakes and rivers frozen and snow everywhere, the Rockies look very different — some say they are more beautiful in the winter than at any other time of year.

Contacts in the Parks

The Regional Office for the national parks:
Canadian Parks Service
520, 220 – 4 Ave. S.E.
P.O. Box 2989, Station M
Calgary, Alberta T2P 2M9
403-292-4401

BANFF NATIONAL PARK
Box 900
Banff, Alberta T0L 0C.
403-762-3324

In area code 403
Emergencies: 911 or 762-4506
Mineral Springs Hospital: 762-2222
Ambulance: 762-4333
Fire, Banff: 762-2000
Fire, Lake Louise: 522-2000
R.C.M. Police, Banff: 762-2226
R.C.M. Police, Lake Louise: 522-3811
Veterinarian, Canmore: 678-4425
Alberta Motor Association: 762-2266
Weather: 762-2088
Road report: 762-4733
Avalanche report: 762-3600

Park Information Centres:
Banff: 762-4256
Lake Louise: 522-3833

Park Warden Offices:
Banff (24 hrs.): 762-4506
Lake Louise: 522-3866

Banff/Lake Louise Chamber
of Commerce
Box 1298
Banff, Alberta T0L 0C0
762-3777, Fax 762-5758

JASPER NATIONAL PARK
Box 10
Jasper, Alberta T0E 1E0
403-852-6161

In area code 403
Emergencies: 852-6161 or 852-4848
Hospital: 852-3344
Ambulance and Fire: 852-3100
R.C.M. Police: 852-4848
Weather: 852-3185
Road report: 852-6161
Avalanche report: 852-6161

Park Information Centres:
Jasper: 852-6176
Columbia Icefield: 852-2241

Park Warden Offices:
Jasper: 852-6156
Sunwapta: 852-6181

Jasper Park Chamber of Commerce
Box 98
Jasper, Alberta T0E 1E0
852-3858, Fax 852-4932

YOHO NATIONAL PARK
Box 99, Field, BC V0A 1G0
604-343-6324

In area code 604
Emergencies: 343-6316 or 343-6324
Ambulance (no charge): 1-374-5937
Golden Hospital: 344-2411
R.C.M. Police: 343-6316

Park Information Centre: 343-6324

Park Warden Office: 343-6324

KOOTENAY NATIONAL PARK
Box 220
Radium Hot Springs, BC V0A 1K0
604-347-9615

In area code 604
Emergencies: 347-9393, 342-9292
Invermere Hospital: 342-9201
Ambulance (no charge): 1-374-5937
R.C.M. Police, Radium: 347-9393
R.C.M. Police, Invermere: 342-9292
Road report: 347-9551

West Gate Information Centre: 347-9505

Park Warden Office: 347-9361

B.C. Rocky Mountain Visitor Association
(for Kootenay and Yoho)
495 Wallinger Ave., Box 10
Kimberley, BC V1A 2Y5
604-427-4838

WATERTON LAKES NATIONAL PARK
Waterton Park, Alberta T0K 2M0
403-859-2445

In area code 403
Emergencies: 859-2244
Fire: 859-2222
Ambulance: 859-2636
R.C.M. Police: 859-2244

Park Information Centre: 859-2445

Park Warden Office: 859-2477/2275

Waterton Park Chamber of Commerce
Box 556
Waterton Park, Alberta T0K 2M0
859-2303

KANANASKIS COUNTRY
Suite 412, 1011 Glenmore Trail S.W.
Calgary, Alberta T2V 4R6
403-297-3362

Peter Lougheed Provincial Park:
591-7226
Bow Valley Provincial Park: 673-3663

Emergencies: R.C.M. Police: 591-7707
Kananaskis Country Emergency Services:
591-7767

Canmore, Bow Valley and Kananaskis
Chamber of Commerce
Box 1178
Canmore, Alberta T0L 0M0
678-4094, Fax 678-2086

MT. ROBSON PROVINCIAL PARK
P.O. Box 579
Valemount, BC V0E 2Z0
604-566-4325

Emergencies: R.C.M. Police: 566-4466

MT. ASSINIBOINE PROVINCIAL PARK
P.O.Box 118
Wasa, BC V0B 2K0
604-422-3212

Park Regulations and Etiquette

The following is a list of suggestions for visitor use and behavior that will make the National Parks more enjoyable for everyone.

WATCH FOR ANIMALS — DRIVE CAREFULLY

● use extra caution at dawn and dusk
● slow down when you are blinded at night by oncoming headlights
● don't feed or entice roadside animals — it is against the law, and dangerous for animals *and* humans
● use flashers to warn other drivers about wildlife
● promptly report any collisions you witness, so that an animal that has been struck won't be left to lure wolves or coyotes into danger

FIRES

● fires may only be lit in metal fireboxes provided by the park
● barbeques are allowed in campgrounds and picnic areas
● wood is scarce in many backcountry locations and fire restrictions apply on some trails — overnight hikers should carry gas stoves

WATER

● please don't rinse soap, shampoo or detergent in the lakes and streams
● avoid depositing any wastes, human or otherwise, into water
● parasites carried by humans and animals can contaminate water supplies — water from lakes and streams, plus water from taps in campgrounds or picnic areas where a warning is posted, should be boiled

RECYCLING

● there are depots for recycling cans, bottles and newspapers in Banff and Jasper townsites — make use of them!
● in Banff, take cans and bottles to the Banff Bottle Depot in the industrial compound, and take newspapers to the drop-off trailer in the parking lot behind the Credit Union
● in Jasper, take your cans and bottles to the depot in the Stan Wright Industrial Park, and leave your newspapers in the drop-off trailer in the Activity Centre parking lot.

HIKING

● if you are going into the backcountry, register with the wardens' office — if you don't return on schedule, they'll come looking for you
● be sure to read the information on bears available through the park information office before you set out

FISHING

● anglers must obtain a national parks fishing permit at information centres or sporting goods stores in the park
● please pay close attention to the summary of recently amended fishing regulations, available with your permit

BOATING

● rowboats, canoes and kayaks are allowed on most lakes and rivers, while the use of gas-powered boats is restricted — for complete information, contact a park information office

FLOWERS AND ARTIFACTS

● natural and cultural objects in the parks are protected by law from removal, defacing, damage and destruction — they should be left as they are found
● this includes flowers, antlers, rocks, fossils and feathers, as well as things like railway spikes and china dishes
● please report any exceptional discoveries you make to park staff

PETS

● pets must be kept securely leashed or confined at all times

Driving in Canada

• all distance markers and speed limit signs are in kilometres (km) and kilometres per hour (km/h), and gasoline is measured in litres
• use of seatbelts is mandatory
• all drivers must have vehicle insurance, and must carry proof of that insurance with them
• US drivers' licenses are valid in Canada for varying periods of time (depending on the province), and an International Driving Permit is also valid when accompanied by the visitor's regular driver's license

Currency and Banking

• the money system in Canada is based on dollars and cents
• due to fluctuating exchange rates, visitors are urged to convert funds to Canadian dollars at a financial institution — there are banks and currency exchange desks in Banff, Lake Louise and Jasper
• most credit cards are honoured by businesses in the parks

Liquor Laws

• the legal minimum age to purchase liquor is 18 in Alberta, 19 in BC
• there are liquor stores in Banff, Lake Louise, Jasper and Field
• alcohol carried in your car must not be open or within reach of the driver — it's best to transport it in the trunk
• it is unlawful to consume liquor in a public place or any place other than a residence, temporary residence or licensed premises

Metric Conversion Table

Metric	Imperial
1 millimetre	.0394 inches
1 centimetre	.394 inches
1 metre	3.28 feet
1 kilometre	.62 miles
1 hectare	2.47 acres
1 square kilometre	.386 square miles
1 kilogram	2.205 pounds
1 tonne	.9842 UK tons, 1.102 US tons
1 litre	.22 UK gallons, .264 US gallons
1° Celsius	33.8° Fahrenheit

Imperial	Metric
1 inch	2.54 centimetres
1 foot	.305 metres
1 yard	.92 metres
1 mile	1.61 kilometres
1 acre	.405 hectares
1 square mile	2.59 square kilometres
1 pound	.4536 kilograms
1 UK ton	1.016 tonnes
1 UK gallon	4.55 litres
1 US ton	.9072 tonnes
1 US gallon	3.78 litres
1° Fahrenheit	-17.22° Celsius

0° Celsius = 32° Fahrenheit

Tips for 35 mm Photography

● In general, early to mid-morning, and late afternoon to late evening, are the best times of day for summer photography in the Rockies, when the interplay of light and shade is usually at its best. These are also favourable times to observe most wildlife.

● If you want to photograph particular scenes, carefully consider the time of day and resulting angle of light. The chart on page 327 summarizes the optimum times (in summer) to photograph many popular destinations.

● The combination of high mountains and clouds can create spectacular lighting at any time. In fact, moody weather days are often the best for photography, producing many surprises.

● Early morning photography is particularly rewarding, as there is a lack of competition for the best viewing angles, and lake waters are often dead calm, yielding the reflections for which the Rockies are famous. If you expose for the light value of the reflection, the unreflected part of the scene will be overexposed. Gauge the number of stops between the two components of the scene, and bracket relative to the median value.

● The photographer taking sunrise and sunset photographs should be prepared to make some adjustments while in the mountains. The horizon is blocked at most locations, and the best effects are not obtained by including the sun in the photograph, but by capturing the colourful lighting opposite the sun. This light, called alpenglow, precedes sunrise and follows sunset. Underexpose slightly to saturate colours at these times of day.

● For most of the year, snow will be present in a majority of scenes. Difficult exposures incorporating opposing values of sunlit snow and shade will frequently be encountered. Bracketting of exposures is recommended. In many instances, the best results will be achieved by under-exposing slightly when taking a bright and uniformly lit landscape scene that includes snow. (Underexposing is not recommended for print film.)

● To obtain facial details on people in the foreground of bright landscapes, take a close-up light meter reading of the person's face, and use this exposure for the scene. In some instances, the extraordinary lighting situations encountered go beyond the limits of reversal film for producing a uniform exposure between foreground and background. At these times, expose for the background and try infilling the foreground with flash, or use a neutral density filter.

● Kodachrome 64 is the standard slide film for a majority of applications in Rocky Mountain photography. 64's film speed allows for considerable experimentation with depth of field on bright summer days. Any of the E-6 process films — including Fujichrome and Ektachrome — can also be used successfully. However, exaggeration of the blue/green spectrum sometimes results. Kodachrome 200 is indispensable for those seeking to photograph wildlife and birds, particularly at dawn and dusk.

● Although smog, firesmoke and haze are not common in the Rockies, exposed film will register a higher incidence of ultra-violet light because of the altitude. An ultraviolet filter will help reduce the resulting bluish cast. Compositions involving water, ice and clouds may benefit from experimentation with a polarizing filter.

● Those bringing a 35 mm S.L.R. format camera to the Rockies, and intent on photographing both landscapes and wildlife, will want to have a selection of lenses spanning the range from 24 mm-300 mm. A tripod is a must. Carry lots of film. Fingerless gloves or thin glove liners help take the chill out of early morning and late evening photography. Watch for condensation and frost on lens elements when stepping from a warm vehicle into the cold outdoors. On very cold mornings, hold your breath when releasing the shutter, so as not to get vapour in the foreground.

● If you plan to hike to many of your photography destinations, make sure your equipment is lightweight, accessible, and well organized. Keep the lens best suited to the kind of photograph you seek (i.e. telephoto for wildlife, wide angle for landscape) on your camera. There's nothing more frustrating than having a bear walk across your field of view when you have a 24 mm lens on your camera!

Optimum Photography Times

Location	Time of Day
Banff	
Tunnel Mountain Hoodoos	any
Lake Minnewanka	afternoon
Mt. Rundle	
(from Vermilion Lakes)	late afternoon and evening
Near Banff	
Sunshine Meadows	any
Johnston Canyon	afternoon
Kootenay	
Marble Canyon	morning and early afternoon
Lake Louise	
Moraine Lake	early morning
Lake Louise	sunrise and early morning
Icefield Parkway	
Crowfoot Glacier	morning
Bow Lake	morning
Peyto Lake	morning and afternoon
Snowbird Glacier	early morning
Waterfowl Lakes	morning
The Weeping Wall	afternoon
Parker Ridge crest	morning
Athabasca Glacier	morning
Sunwapta Falls	afternoon
Athabasca Falls	afternoon
Mt. Edith Cavell	early morning and late afternoon
Jasper	
The Whistlers	any
Pyramid Lake	morning
Mt. Robson	any
Maligne Lake	
Maligne Canyon	mid-afternoon
Medicine Lake	any
Maligne Lake	any, north shore at sunset
Yoho	
Natural Bridge	afternoon
Emerald Lake	morning
Takakkaw Falls	afternoon
Leanchoil Hoodoos	afternoon
Wapta Falls	afternoon

PLACES TO STAY

Hotels and Motels

Courtesy of the Chambers of Commerce in each area.

WATERTON LAKES (403)
For more information, please contact the Waterton Park Chamber of Commerce — see page 323.
Aspen-Windflower Motels
Windflower Ave., 859-2255
Bayshore Inn
111 Waterton Ave., 859-2211
Crandell Mountain Lodge
102 Mount View Rd., 859-2288
El-Cortez Motel
208 Mount View Rd. 859-2366
Kilmorey Lodge
117 Evergreen Ave., 859-2334
Northland Lodge
Evergreen Ave., 859-2353
Prince of Wales Hotel
859-2231
Stanley Hotel
112b Waterton Ave., 859-2345

CANMORE/KANANASKIS (403)
For more information, please contact the Canmore Chamber of Commerce — see page 323.
A-1 Motel
Mountain Ave., off Hwy. 1-A
Canmore, 678-5200
Akai Motel
1715 Mountain Ave., Canmore, 678-4664
B & B in the Mountains
1004 Larch Place, Canmore, 678-6777
Bow Valley Motel
610 - 8th St., Canmore, 678-5085
Canmore Hotel
836 - 8th St., Canmore, 678-5181
Cee-der Chalets
Harvie Heights, service road, 678-5251

Cougar Creek Inn
Canmore,   678-4751
Gateway Inn
Harvey Heights, service road, 678-5396
Green Acres Motel
Hwy. 1, 8 km east of Canmore, 678-5344
Green Gables Inn
1602 - 2nd Ave. (Hwy. 1-A)
Canmore, 678-5488
Haus Alpenrose Lodge
629 - 10th St., Canmore, 678-4134
Hotel Kananaskis
Kananaskis Village, 591-7711
Kananaskis Guest Ranch
Seebe, 673-3737
Lodge at Kananaskis
Kananaskis Village, 591-7711
Mount Assiniboine Lodge
(back country, B.C.)
Office in Canmore, 678-2883
Rocky Mountain Chalets
17th St. & Hwy. 1-A, Canmore, 678-5564
Rundle Mountain Motel
Box 147, Canmore, 678-5322
Rundle Ridge Chalets
Harvie Heights, service road, 678-5387
Skiland Motel
Hwy. 1-A, Canmore, 678-5445
Spring Creek B&B
1002 - 3rd Ave., Canmore, 678-6726
Stockade Motel
Harvie Heights, service road, 678-5212
Sundance Inn
1705 Mountain Ave., Canmore, 678-5528
Tatranka Lodge
909 Railway Ave., Canmore, 678-5131
Viscount Motor Inn
1721 Mountain Ave., Canmore, 678-5221

BANFF AND AREA (403)
For more information, please contact the Banff/Lake Louise Chamber of Commerce — see page 322.
Banff Alpine/Caribou Lodge
521 Banff Ave., 762-2713

Banff International Hostel
Tunnel Mt. Rd., 762-4122
Banff Park Lodge
222 Lynx St., 762-4433
Banff Rocky Mt. Resort
Banff Ave., 762-5531
Banff Springs Hotel
Spray Ave., 762-2211
Banff Voyager Inn
555 Banff Ave., 762-3301
Banffshire Inn
537 Banff Ave., 762-2201
Best Western Siding 29
453 Marten St., 762-5575
Blue Mountain Lodge
137 Muskrat St., 762-2222
Bow View Motor Lodge
228 Bow Ave., 762-2261
Buffalo Mountain Lodge
Tunnel Mt. Dr., 762-2400
Bumper's Inn
Marmot St., 762-3386
Cascade Inn
124 Banff Ave., 762-3311
Castle Mountain Village
Highways 93S & 1A, 762-3868
Charlton's Cedar Court
513 Banff Ave., 762-2575
Charlton's Evergreen Court
459 Banff Ave., 762-3307
Cowan, Mrs. J.
118 Otter St., 762-3696
Douglas Fir Resort
Tunnel Mt. Rd., 762-5591
Elkhorn Lodge
124 Spray Ave., 762-2299
Hidden Ridge Chalets
Tunnel Mt. Rd., 762-3544
High Country Inn
419 Banff Ave., 762-2236
Holiday Lodge
311 Marten St., 762-3648
Homestead Inn
218 Lynx St., 762-4471

Inns of Banff Park
600 Banff Ave., 762-4581
Irwin's Motor Inn
429 Banff Ave., 762-4566
Mount Royal Hotel
138 Banff Ave., 762-3331
Pension Tannenhof
121 Cave Ave., 762-4636
Ptarmigan Inn
337 Banff Ave., 762-2207
Red Carpet Inn
425 Banff Ave., 762-4184
Rimrock Inn
Mountain Ave., 762-3356
Riva, Philomina
345 Marten St., 762-2471
Spruce Grove Motel
545 Banff Ave., 762-2112
Storm Mountain Lodge
Highway 93S, 762-3032
Traveller's Inn
401 Banff Ave., 762-4401
Tunnel Mountain Chalets
Tunnel Mt. Rd., 762-4515
Y.W.C.A.
102 Spray Ave., 762-3560
Yarmoloy, M.
117 Spray Ave., 762-2846

LAKE LOUISE AND AREA (403)
For more information, please contact the Banff/Lake Louise Chamber of Commerce — see page 322.
Baker Creek Chalets
1A Highway near L.L., 522-3761
Chateau Lake Louise
Lake Louise, 522-3511
Deer Lodge Resort
Lake Louise, 522-3747
Johnston Canyon Resort
1A Highway, 762-2971
Lake Louise Inn
Lake Louise, 522-3791
Moraine Lake Lodge
Moraine Lake, 762-4401

Paradise Lodge & Bungalows
Lake Louise, 522-3595
Post Hotel
Lake Louise, 522-3989

JASPER AND AREA (403)
For more information, please contact the Jasper Park Chamber of Commerce — see page 322.
Alpine Village
Hwy. 93A, 852-3285
Amethyst Lodge
200 Connaught Drive, 852-3394
Astoria Hotel
404 Connaught Drive, 852-3351
Athabasca Hotel
510 Patricia Street, 852-4955
Becker's Chalets
Hwy. 93, 852-3779
Bonhomme Bungalows
100 Bonhomme Street, 852-3209
The Charlton's Chateau Jasper
96 Geikie Street, 852-5644 or 1-800-661-9323
Diamond Motel
West Connaught Drive, 852-3143
Jasper House Bungalows
Hwy. 93, 852-4535
Jasper Inn
98 Geikie Street, 852-4461
Jasper Park Lodge
Lac Beauvert, 852-3301 or 1-800-642-3817
Lobstick Lodge
Geikie at Juniper, 852-4431
Marmot Lodge
94 Connaught Drive, 852-4471
Miette Hotsprings Resort
Miette Road, 866-3750
Mount Robson Inn
902 Connaught Drive W., 852-3327
Patricia Lake Bungalows
Pyramid Lake Road, 852-3560
Pine Bungalows
On Athabasca River, 852-3491

Pyramid Lake Bungalows
5.6 km NW of Jasper, 852-3536
Sawridge Hotel, Jasper
82 Connaught Drive, 852-5111 or 1-800-661-6427
Sunwapta Falls Resort
Hwy. 93, 52 km from Jasper, 852-4852
Tekarra Lodge
Hwy. 93A, 852-3058
Tonquin Motor Inn
Corner Connaught & Juniper, 852-4987
Whistlers Motor Hotel
105 Miette, 852-3361 or 1-800-282-9919

FIELD AND AREA (604)
For more information, please contact the BC Rocky Mountain Visitor Association — see page 323.
Cathedral Mountain Chalets
Field, 343-6442
Emerald Lake Lodge
Emerald Lake, 343-6321 or 1-800-663-6336
Lake O'Hara Lodge
Lake O'Hara, 343-6418
West Louise Lodge
#1 Highway in B.C., 343-6486

RADIUM AND AREA (604)
For more information, please contact the BC Rocky Mountain Visitor Association — see page 323.
Addison's Bungalows
347-9545
Alpen Motel
347-9823
Best Western Radium Golf Resort
347-9311
Big Horn Motel
347-9522
Blakley's Bungalows
347-9918
Cedar Motel
347-9463

Columbia Motel
347-9557
Crescent Motel
347-9570
Crystal Springs Motel
347-9759
Gables Motel
347-9866
Kootenay Motel
347-9490
Lido Motel
347-9533
Motel Bavaria
347-9915
Motel Tyrol
347-9402
Mount Farnham Bungalows
347-9515
Mountain View Motel
347-9654
Park Motel
347-9582
Pinewood Motel
347-9529
Radium Hot Springs Lodge
347-9622
Radium Hot Springs Resort
347-9311 or 1-800-528-1234
Ritz Motel
347-9644
Skyview Motel & Campground
347-9698
Spur Valley Resort
347-9822
Sunset Motel
347-9863
The Chalet
347-9305
Tuk-In Motel
347-9464
Wayside Motel
347-9332

Campgrounds
see map, page 333

Park/ Campground	Type	Opening Date	Closing Date
Kananaskis			
Beaver Flats	Tents/RV's	May 16	Oct 10
Bluerock	Tents/RV's	May 16	Oct 10
Bluerock Equestrian	Tents/RV's	May 16	Nov 30
Bow River	Tents/RV's	May 11	Oct 10
Bow Valley	Tents/RV's	Year Rd	
Willow Rock	Tents/RV's	Year Rd	
Cataract Creek	Tents/RV's	May 17	Sept 5
Eau Claire	Tents/RV's	June 1	Oct 10
Etherington Creek	Tents/RV's	May 4	Nov 30
Gooseberry	Tents/RV's	May 4	Oct 10
Lac des Arcs	Tents/RV's	May 11	Oct 10
Little Elbow	Tents/RV's	May 16	Nov 30
McLean Creek	Tents/RV's	Year Rd	
Mesa Butte Equestrian	Tents/RV's	Year Rd	
Mount Kidd R.V. Park	Tents/RV's	Year Rd	
North Fork	Tents/RV's	May 4	Oct 10
Paddy's Flat	Tents/RV's	May 4	Oct 10
Boulton	Tents/RV's	Year Rd	
Canyon	Tents/RV's	May 17	Sept 5
Elkwood	Tents/RV's	June 15	Sept 5
Interlakes	Tents/RV's	May 17	Sept 11

Lower Lakes	Tents/RV's	June 22	Sept 5
Mount Sarrail	Tents/RV's	June 15	Sept 5
Sandy McNabb	Tents/RV's	Year Rd	
Sibbald Lake	Tents/RV's	May 11	Sept 5
Spray Lakes W. Shore	Tents/RV's	May 11	Nov 30
Three Sisters	Tents/RV's	May 11	Nov 30

Banff National Park

Tunnel Mtn Trailer Court	Large RV's	May 11	Oct. 1
Tunnel Mtn Village I	Tents/RV's	May 11	Oct. 1
Tunnel Mtn Village II	Tents/RV's	Year Rd	
Two Jack Main	Tents/RV's	May 17	May 21
Two Jack Lakeside	Tents/RV's	June 29	Sept. 4
Johnston Canyon	Tents/RV's	May 18	Sept. 17
Castle Mtn	Tents/RV's	June 22	Sept. 4
Protection Mtn	Tents/RV's	June 22	Sept. 4
Lake Louise Trailer	Large RV's/ winter	Year Rd	Year Rd
Lake Louise Tent	Tents/RV's	May 18	Oct. 1
Mosquito Creek	Tents/RV's/ winter	June 15	Sept. 10
Waterfowl	Tents/RV's	June 15	Sept. 11
Rampart Creek	Tents/RV's	June 22	Sept. 4
Cirrus Mtn	Tents/RV's	June 22	Sept. 4

Jasper National Park

Pocahontas	Tents/RV's	May 18	Sept. 4
Snaring River	Tents/RV's	May 18	Sept. 4
Whistlers	Tents/RV's	May 4	Oct. 9
Wapiti	Tents/RV's/ winter	May 17 June 15	May 21 Sept. 4
Wabasso	Tents/RV's	June 22	Sept. 3
Mt Kerkeslin	Tents/RV's	May 18	Sept. 4
Honeymoon Lake	Tents/RV's	June 8	Mid Oct
Jonas Creek	Tents/RV's	May 18	Mid Oct
Columbia Icefield	Tents	May 18	Mid Oct
Wilcox Creek	Tents/RV's	June 9	Sept 17

Kootenay National Park

Redstreak	Tents/RV's	May 11	Sept 10
Marble Canyon	Tents/RV's	June 22	Sept 4
McLeod Meadows	Tents/RV's	May 18	Sept 17

Yoho National Park

Chancellor Peak	Tents/RV's	May 18	Oct 9
Hoodoo Creek	Tents/RV's	June 29	Sept 4
Kicking Horse	Tents/RV's	May 18	Oct. 2

Hostels

Banff International Hostel
Alberta Hostelling Association
Box 1358, Banff Alberta T0L0C0
762-4122

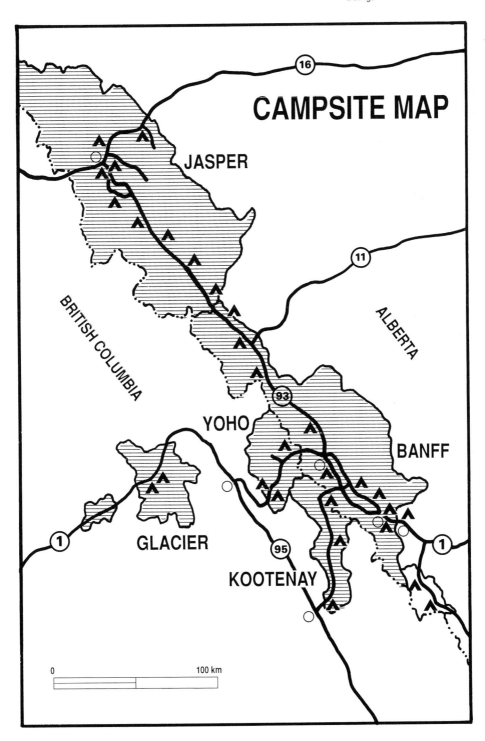

CAMPSITE MAP

JASPER

BRITISH COLUMBIA

ALBERTA

YOHO

BANFF

GLACIER

KOOTENAY

0   100 km

THINGS TO DO

Services

BANFF

● Alberta Automobile Association,
215 Bear St., 762-4506
● Banks
- Alberta Treasury Branch, Cascade Plaza,
Banff Ave., 762-5063
- Bank of Montreal, 107 Banff Ave.,
762-2275
- Canadian Imperial Bank of Commerce,
92 Banff Ave., 762-2275
- Bow Valley Credit Union, 216 Banff
Ave., 762-3368
● Churches
- Anglican/Episcopal, 762-2128
- Baptist, 762-3225
- Church of the Latter Day Saints,
762-3113
- Full Gospel, 762-2740
- Inter-Varsity Christian Fellowship,
762-5697
- Presbyterian, 762-3279
- Roman Catholic, 762-2603
- United Church of Canada, 762-2075
● Clock Tower Mall Currency Exchange
108 Banff Ave., 762-4698
Banff Springs Hotel, 762-2211
Chateau Lake Louise, 522-3511
Bank of America Canada Currency
Exchange, Cascade Inn
● Parks Information Centre, 762-4256
● Post Office, 204 Buffalo St., 762-2586

LAKE LOUISE

● Banks
- Alberta Treasury Branch Agent, Samson
Mall, 522-3870
● Currency Exchange Office, Chateau
Lake Louise, 522-3511
● Parks Information Centre, 522-3833
● Post Office, Samson Mall, 522-3870

JASPER

● Banks
- Canadian Imperial Bank of Commerce,
416 Connaught Dr., 852-3391
- Toronto Dominion Bank, 606 Patricia
St., 852-3335
● Churches
- Anglican, 852-4505
- Baptist, 852-4222
- Catholic, 852-3128
- Lutheran, 852-4518
- Pentecostal, 852-5454
- United, 852-4334
● Post Office, 502 Patricia St., 852-3041
● Parks Information Centre, 852-6176

Shopping

Although the towns in the Canadian Rockies are famous for their mountain settings, they are also home to many shops and services that cater to the international traveller. Waterton, Canmore, Banff, Lake Louise, Radium and Jasper all have grocery and convenience stores, pharmacies and gift shops. Beyond that, the towns differ markedly depending on their size. Waterton and Radium are quite small and offer a modest selection of stores. (Field, smaller still, has one small, but interesting, gift store.)

Canmore

Canmore is bigger, and growing all the time, but has a limited downtown core. There are numerous hardware stores, grocery stores and service-type businesses. Although Canmore has a more limited range of gift stores, there are a number of real gems — and be sure to search out the small craft shops for which Canmore is famous.

Lake Louise

Shopping at Lake Louise is split between two locations: at the lake itself, there are numerous excellent gift, jewelry and clothing shops in the Chateau Lake Louise. A number of the other lodges in the Lake Louise area also have gift shops. Downtown, the shops are located in Samson Mall. Here the gift and photo stores are supplemented by an excellent bookstore and an outstanding bakery.

Jasper

Jasper has a wide range of shops, including excellent craft stores, book stores, jewelry and gift shops. There are a couple of good bakeries and many service type businesses. Jasper is slowly increasing the number of retail locations and new shops open each year. The downtown shopping area stretches along Connaught Drive and Patricia Street. A few more gift stores can be found across the river in the Jasper Park Lodge.

Banff

Banff is the largest town in the Canadian Rockies and is quite a cosmopolitan shopping area. The downtown centre is a maze of shopping malls that carry a wide range of goods from the cheap to the outrageously expensive, and from the mundane to the truly bizarre. As well as gift, jewelry, clothing and book stores, there are many unique specialty shops that can provide hours of browsing pleasure. In fact, many local people from Calgary drive to Banff when looking for a special gift. There are, of course, many drugstores and other service-related businesses, as well as some outstanding bakeries. The downtown area is supplemented by the numerous shops at the Banff Springs Hotel, which also offer a wide range of high-quality goods.

Restaurants

Waterton

The restaurants in the various lodges in Waterton offer a range of culinary styles. You might try the Prince of Wales Hotel and the Kilmorey Lodge. Please ask around for further reccomendations. A few downtown locations, such as the Waterton Park Cafe, are also excellent.

Canmore

Canmore boasts many excellent restaurants, especially for Italian, Swiss and French cooking. There are also a couple of excellent "country" style restaurants that provide wonderful food, and numerous family restaurants ideal for a casual meal.

Banff

There are dozens and dozens of restaurants in Banff, catering to many different tastes and budgets. People in Banff eat out very often and are quite demanding of their local restaurants, so consequently there are a number of excellent places (you might want to ask some of the locals for their reccomendations). The food choices range from Japanese and Chinese, to Italian, French, Greek, Continental, Swiss, Mexican, "country" and so on. There is fondue, seafood, hamburgers, pizza and deli. There is also a restaurant at the top of Sulphur Mountain. And of course, many family-style restaurants throughout Banff offer good food at reasonable prices in a casual atmosphere.

Lake Louise

Most of the restaurants in the Lake Louise area are connected with the hotels. The Chateau Lake Louise offers a wide range of dining rooms which appeal to different tastes and budgets. The Post Hotel houses one of the area's best known restaurants. There is also a restaurant at Moraine Lake Lodge.

Field

There is a small sandwich shop and store in Field, but not a full-blown restaurant. Nearby, however, is Emerald Lake Lodge, which has a dining room and a coffee shop.

Radium

Like Lake Louise, most of the restaurants in Radium are connected to the hotels and motels. They offer family-style dining in a casual atmosphere.

Jasper

Like Banff (only on a smaller scale) there are plenty of restaurants to choose from in Jasper, including Greek, Japanese, Italian, French and deli. These are supplemented by a number of fine dining rooms in the Jasper Park Lodge. There is also a restaurant at the top of the Jasper Tramway.

Entertainment

● Banff has four museums: the Banff Park Museum, the Luxton Museum, The Natural History Museum and the Whyte Museum of the Canadian Rockies
● The Banff Centre offers a Festival of the Arts each summer
● The Lux in Banff contains four movie threatres
● The Chaba Theatre offers movies in Jasper
● Jasper has a small local museum on Patricia Lake Road

If You've Only Got a Day...

Here are some suggestions for those who have only limited time in the following places. Of course, each place can be used as a centre from which to explore other parts of the Rockies.

Banff
- Sulphur Mountain Gondola
- Walk the Fenland Trail
- Visit the Whyte Museum
- Visit the Hoodoos
- Drive to Vermilion Lakes
- Drive to Bankhead and Lake Minnewanka
- Visit the Cave and Basin Interpretive Centre
- Explore the Banff Park Museum in Central Park
- Drive to Johnston Canyon and walk to the Lower Falls

Lake Louise
- Stroll along the lakeshore (or go all the way to the Plain of Six Glaciers)
- Drive to Moraine Lake
- Hike to Lake Agnes teahouse
- Visit the Interpretive Centre near Samson Mall

Yoho
- Stop at the Spiral Tunnel viewpoint and watch a train go through the tunnels
- Drive to Takakkaw Falls (a good picnic spot)
- Drive to the Natural Bridge on the road to Emerald Lake
- Drive to Emerald Lake and walk around the lake
- Visit the Interpretive Centre at Field
- Walk to Wapta Falls

The Icefields Parkway
Don't miss this incredible drive — the Icefields Parkway is without doubt one of the world's most beautiful roads. Allow anywhere from one full day to a number of days if you like to get out and explore. There are roadside interpretive displays at many locations. Of course, the highlight of the Parkway is the Columbia Icefield, where you have a chance to drive to the toe of Athabasca Glacier. Also, don't miss the Information Centre and the Snocoach ride onto Athabasca Glacier.

Jasper
- Ride the Jasper Tramway to the top of the Whistlers
- Drive to Jasper Park Lodge and walk along the shore of Lac Beauvert
- Explore Maligne Canyon
- Drive to Maligne Lake and take the tour boat to Spirit Island (allow half a day, reserve ahead)
- Drive to Pyramid Lake
- Drive to Mt. Edith Cavell and walk the Path of the Glacier trail
- For longer trips (allow half a day) drive east to the Miette Hot Springs or west from Jasper to Mt. Robson

Kootenay
- Walk the interpretive trail at Marble Canyon
- Bathe in Radium Hot Springs
- Visit the Paint Pots
- Walk the Fireweed Trail

POLICY, PRAISE AND SUGGESTIONS

The Canadian Parks Service welcomes comments on your experience in the mountain national parks. Superintendents of the individual parks may be contacted using the addresses provided on pages 322-323. You may also comment on matters pertaining to the national parks by contacting the following:

National parks planning, mailing list for public input:

Public Consultation Co-ordinator
Canadian Parks Service
520, 220 – 4 Ave. S.E.
P.O. Box 2989, Station M
Calgary, Alberta
T2P 2M9

Overall policies affecting national parks:

The Hon. Minister of the Environment
House of Commons,
Parliament Buildings
Ottawa, Ontario
K1A 0A6

and your federal Member of Parliament.

ENVIRONMENTAL ORGANIZATIONS
(a selected few of the many)

These organizations are actively participating in environmental issues relating to, or affecting, the mountain national parks.

The Canadian Parks and
Wilderness Society
Suite 1150, 160 Bloor St. E.
Toronto, Ontario
M4W 1B9

The World Wildlife Fund
Suite 201, 60 St. Clair Ave. E.
Toronto, Ontario
M5T 1N5

Alberta Wilderness Association
P.O. Box 6398, Station D
Calgary, Alberta
T2P 2E1

The publisher of the *SuperGuide* would also like to hear about your experience in the Rockies. If you have suggestions, corrections or omissions concerning the *SuperGuide*, please forward them to:

Altitude Publishing
P.O. Box 490
Banff, Alberta
T0L 0C0

Photography Credits

In the following list, photographs are indicated by page number. When there are two photographs on a page, the top or left photograph is indicated as (A) and the bottom or right photograph is indicated as (B).

Contemporary photographs:

Banff National Park: 216(A)

H.U. Green 30

Monty Greenshields 125

Carole Harmon Front cover(A), 10, 36, 46, 50, 54, 55, 59, 61, 63, 65, 66(B), 77, 78, 80, 81(A), 81(B), 86(A), 93, 97, 98, 102(A), 112(A), 119, 124, 125(A), 126, 130(A), 137, 138, 140, 142, 145(A), 147, 166, 167, 173(A), 174, 182, 187(A), 201, 207, 212(B), 216(C), 230, 237(A), 237(B), 238, 245(B), 253, 254, 258, 260(A) 267, 270, 273(A), 273(B), 283, 286(A), 286(B), 287(A)

Don Harmon 68, 76(A), 120, 133, 144, 162, 193, 198, 210(A), 211, 225, 240, 242, 260(B), 261, 281, 291, 308

Stephen Hutchings 2, 12, 53, 73, 82, 99, 100, 105, 106, 139, 143, 157, 164, 175, 189, 208, 215, 218, 220, 221(A), 221(B), 226, 232(A), 234, 246, 264, 268, 272(A), 276, 278(A), 284, 287(B), 288-9, 292, 318

Rick Kunelius 92

Keith McDougall 310, 312, 3l5

Baiba Morrow 252

Graeme Pole 14, 64, 74, 83, 90, 103, 108, 109, 110, 112(B), 114, 116, 128(A), 129, 130(B), 134(A), 136, 146, 148, 150, 153, 154, 156, 163, 165, 168, 170, 172, 176, 177, 179, 180, 184, 185, 186(A), 186(B), 188(A), 188(B), 192, 194, 200, 202, 205(A), 205(B), 209, 216(B), 217, 219, 222, 223(B), 229, 232(B), 248, 262, 263, 266, 274, 275, 277, 278(B), 280, 297, 299(A), 300, 302, 304, 305, 306

R.W. Sandford 227

Dennis Schmidt 32, 95, 96

Esther Schmidt 102(B), 117(A), 117(B), 134(B), 216(D), 295(B), 298

Alex Taylor 233, 251

Waterton National Park 316

Historical photographs:

Glenbow Archives, Calgary AB 31, 41, 42, 43, 66(A), 107, 122, 123(A), 123(B), 127(B), 135, 152, 159, 171, 173, 187(B), 195, 196, 272, 282, 295(A), 299(B), 301

Whyte Museum of the Canadian Rockies, Banff AB Front cover(B), 38, 40, 72, 75, 76, 79, 80, 84, 86, 89, 91, 104, 113, 127(A), 128(B), 145,(B), 178, 183, 206, 210(B), 212, 223, 224, 228, 230(A), 235, 250, 290, 294, 309, 313

A Note from the Publisher

This first *SuperGuide* is the result of many people's endeavors.

Almost as soon as the concept took shape four years ago, we began to think about the design of the book. We felt it was vital that material be presented in a way that was not only informative, but entertaining. For this I am indebted to Robert MacDonald, who determined exactly how to handle the many disparate ideas thrown at him, and came up with some of his own.

Elizabeth Wilson had the prodigious job of editing the book. Only she knows how she managed to do this without falling into the many pitfalls that lay in her way. Elizabeth was also responsible for much of the listings section at the back of the *SuperGuide*, as well as for the interviews with people living and working in the Rockies today.

The street maps and illustrations are the work of Robert Dill and his group at dill flagler design. They even drove the streets of Jasper, Banff and Lake Louise to ensure that the information was as accurate as possible. The topographic highway maps are used with the kind permission of the Federal Department of Energy, Mines and Resources. Banff and Jasper National Parks' Interpretive Services provided useful advice from the outset of the project, and they very kindly helped check parts of the manuscript.

Selecting the photographs has been the responsibility of two people. Graeme Pole offered the resources of his extensive collection of photographs, many of which were taken from the summits of peaks he has climbed. Graeme also selected the historical images. Carole Harmon edited Altitude Publishing's photographic collection, and the result of these two efforts is a book that is visually stunning. Please note that the individual photographers are credited at the back of the book.

I would also like to thank Alberta Culture and the Alberta Foundation for the Literary Arts for their assistance in the production of this book.

But most of all, I would like to express my gratitude to the author, Graeme Pole, who has hiked and driven through the mountains and spent more time in libraries and archives than he cares to admit, in order to come up with the very latest information about this most incredible place. Graeme Pole has worked with unstinting effort on this project for three years, and his enthusiasm has never slackened. Right up to the very last minute, Graeme provided that extra effort in order to ensure that this book would, in fact, truly be a *Super*Guide.

And it is.

Stephen Hutchings, Publisher

Index

About the Author

Graeme Pole first saw the Rockies in 1982. Like so many other visitors, the mountains won him over, and he returned the following year to stay. Since then, Pole has travelled extensively in the Rockies, and cultivated a multi-faceted knowledge of the range. A keen hiker, skier and mountaineer, Graeme has climbed more than 200 Rockies summits, always with camera at hand.

Graeme lives in Field, BC with his wife Marnie. He is a licensed interpretive guide and nordic ski instructor. When not working on books, Graeme serves with the British Columbia Ambulance Service, as an Emergency Medical Assistant and Unit Chief at Field. Graeme's knowledge of the Rockies is self-taught, and for this he is indebted to the many others before him who have explored and written about these mountains. He is also the author of *The Canadian Rockies: A History in Photographs,* and *Walks and Easy Hikes in the Canadian Rockies.*

With royalties from the sales of this book, the author supports the reforestation work of *Trees for the Future.*

The Canadian Rockies: A History in Photographs

GRAEME POLE

With over 120 archival photographs, this book illustrates the fascinating visual history of these famed mountains — from their beginnings as a wild and challenging barrier to the construction of the railway, to their emergence as one of the most popular tourist destinations on earth.
$9.95, paperback
6 x 9, 112 pages

Mountain Chronicles

JON WHYTE
Edited by Brian Patton

The Canadian Rockies were among the most cherished subjects of well-known Canadian author Jon Whyte. The writings compiled here, as Whyte himself explains, "aren't history or meditation or rhapsody. But they have become a chronicle of this place..."
$19.95, hardcover
6 x 9, 160 pages

Byron Harmon: Mountain Photographer

EDITED BY CAROLE HARMON, INTRODUCTION BY BART ROBINSON

As one of Banff's earliest mountain image makers and the first official photographer of the Alpine Club of Canada, Byron Harmon has almost single-handedly made the Canadian Rockies famous. This book is a stunning collection of 80 of his best Rocky Mountain photographs.
$14.95, paperback
8 x 10, 128 pages

A Delicate Wilderness: The Photography of Elliott Barnes (1905-1914)

EDWARD CAVELL

Elliot Barnes was an American photographer who immigrated to Canada in 1905. Through the 36 beautiful, black and white pieces in this selection, Barnes portrays a romantic image of the western Canadian wilderness during Edwardian times.
$9.95, paperback
9 x 8, 39 pages

The Canadian Alps: The History of Mountaineering in Canada
Volume I: The Early Years (1800-1906)

R.W. SANDFORD

Thrilling accounts of the first ascents and colourful profiles of the mountaineers, packers and guides who have shaped the Rockies' history await you here.
$29.95, hardcover
6 x 9, 296 pages

Jimmy Simpson: Legend of the Rockies

E.J. HART

For 80 years, Jimmy Simpson graced the Canadian Rockies as one of its most important guides, outfitters, lodge operators, hunters, naturalists and artists. Here is his fascinating life story.
$24.95 hardcover
$14.95 paperback
6 x 9, 220 pages

A Hunter of Peace: Mary T.S. Schäffer's
Old Indian Trails of the Canadian Rockies
EDITED AND INTRODUCED BY E.J. HART

This is a beautiful reproduction of 60 of Mary T.S. Schäffer's photographic masterpieces. An account of her renowned 1911 expedition to Maligne Lake is also included.
$19.95, paperback
8 x 11, 152 pages

Indians of the Rockies
JON WHYTE

Liberally illustrated with over 75 paintings and photographs, this is an engaging look at western Natives from pre-historical to contemporary times.
$18.95, hardcover
7 x 10, 128 pages

Canadian Rockies Videos
TWO TITLES:
• TIME IN YOUR HANDS
• SEA OF STONE & SNOW

Videos provide a way of looking at the mountains unlike any other. Through the extensive use of aerial photography, these videos take you into the heart of the Canadian Rockies.
Noted mountain environment expert Robert Sandford conducts these splendid visual tours.
$29.95 each
Approximately 30 minutes each
Available in European and North American video formats

Panorama Maps
TWO TITLES:
• JASPER NATIONAL PARK & MT. ROBSON PROVINCIAL PARK (Including The Icefield Parkway)
• BANFF, YOHO & KOOTENAY NATIONAL PARKS (Including Kananaskis and Mt. Assiniboine Provincial Park)

Based on aerial and satellite photographs, topographic maps and personal tours, renowned illustrator Murray Hay has created two spectacular renderings of the Canadian Rockies parks as seen from the air. All the peaks, rivers, valleys, and park and provincial boundaries are identified here to give you a view of the Rockies that has never been seen before.
$6.95 each
6 x 9 folded map or 34 x 37 rolled poster format
$9.95 both maps - in rolled poster format only